ABANDONED WESTERN NORTH CAROLINA

ECHOES IN THE ARCHITECTURE

ALEXA ATKINS

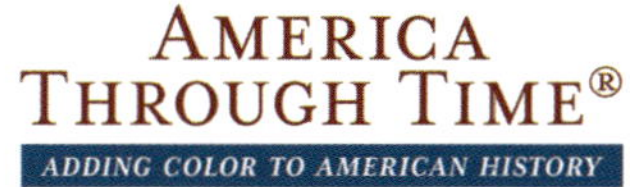

America Through Time is an imprint of Fonthill Media LLC
www.through-time.com
office@through-time.com

Published by Arcadia Publishing by arrangement with Fonthill Media LLC
For all general information, please contact Arcadia Publishing:
Telephone: 843-853-2070
Fax: 843-853-0044
E-mail: sales@arcadiapublishing.com
For customer service and orders:
Toll-Free 1-888-313-2665

www.arcadiapublishing.com

First published 2022

ISBN 978-1-63499-439-2

Typeset in Trade Gothic 10pt on 15pt
Printed and bound in England

CONTENTS

ACKNOWLEDGEMENTS

If I'm to thank anyone, I must first and foremost thank my former personal finance teacher, Don Hurley. Don, I don't know if you remember the first day in class when I answered your opener question. I can't remember the question, and I can't remember what I answered, but I remember what happened after I did. You let the room sit before looking me in the eyes and telling me, "I can't wait to read your book someday." This may not be the book you envisioned, but I hope it brings you some joy and a smug sense of satisfaction.

To Mr. Geoff Winningham: I owe you more than I can easily state. You have been an incredible inspiration to me and gifted me with skills, knowledge, and confidence that I use each day (and intend to keep using until they give out or I do). The project that led to the basis for this work bloomed under your watchful eye, and I know for a fact I wouldn't be writing this if it weren't for you—thank you, thank you, thank you.

I must thank Mr. Charles Dove for keeping a watchful eye on me during my work on this book and helping me to keep a level head both in this work and outside it. Conversely, I must also thank Mr. Brian Huberman for encouraging my habits of collecting strange materials and creating grandiose plans to continue working on until the end of time.

To my father: Don't think this gets you out of riding around with me and leaping out of the car at the next most interesting thing. I'm looking forward to mixing up our film canisters and forgetting to let someone know where we are in the midst of the next project.

To all my family and friends who have supported me in the creation of this work: know you have my eternal gratitude, and of course a favor at your disposal for the foreseeable future. I promise there's no expiration date or fine print for this one.

INTRODUCTION

Western North Carolina is not what it once was. Here lie tales of the boom and bust of industrialization—whole cities left behind in hopes of cheaper production elsewhere. Some cities are now full of boarded-up buildings that used to be large businesses, and before that a family-owned affair. Less lucky counterparts are scattered around and taken back by the earth, having been left alone for too long to be bought. Dotting the mountainside are barns without roofs and houses barely recognizable through kudzu, family homes and farms slowly growing back into the earth. I hope to give you a glimpse into the beauty I have found at sites like these, and to provide a reminder of the importance of not looking away. Rather than continue to avert the eyes in these spots, let us seek them out. These places are not devoid of life but hold it in a separate light. Western North Carolina is not what it once was, but neither are we.

In capturing the places found in the following chapters I have used a variety of methods (and cameras). Spare a few images, what you will see is a result of 35mm film photography and often my trusty Canon A-1 or AE-1. Sometimes color, sometimes black and white, and even once in infrared film I captured sites for this project. In seeking out these structures I often would pick a road I had seen promise in while traveling and set off without a direct plan. Thanks to the nature of rural roads, when I spotted a gem nested in the woods or felt a strike of intuition, I could pull off to the side and prepare to either take a shot or trek into the woods with my camera while hoping to avoid snakes and poison ivy. Other sites I had the privilege of growing up near, and the familiarity that comes with exploration of hometown offerings. I encourage you to be open to the idea of running into a place of beauty such as these the next time you find yourself on the road; it is not always necessary to seek them out for them to find you.

1

HENRY RIVER MILL VILLAGE

This defunct textile village is a well-known fixture in the county where I was born and raised. The notoriety of this development has changed significantly from when I was a child to now and has a rich history from long before I was born.

This history begins in 1902, when the land was chosen by a one David Aderholdt and the workers' homes as well as the dam (which would be used as a power source) were built.[1] The plans for these workers' homes were generally the same, with little variation, as can be seen clearly in images containing multiple of the surviving structures. One differing structure that remains is the "company store," a large two-story building where the mill workers could buy necessities such as food and clothing.

Similar to the coal mining towns in other areas of Appalachia, workers tended to live in the planned town and were provided compensation not simply monetarily, but with currency that could be used only within the mill village itself, such as at the company store. This form of currency is often referred to as "scrip." This system left workers in mining towns and textile villages at a massive disadvantage, as it made leaving the town and subsequently the job extremely difficult. This experience is described by Joseph Kovich, a son of coal miners in West Virginia, in a 1973 interview conducted by his daughter, Anna Kovich:

> All the stores were owned by companies and you had to make all your purchases by scrip. Now coal companies would issue this scrip to you as each day as you needed it and you had to spend this scrip only at their stores. It was not honored at any other store except the coal company where the scrip was made and in that way they had control over all the money that the miners made except on paydays they would be paid in cash which was a very small amount and could not provide much in clothing or groceries from any other store.[2]

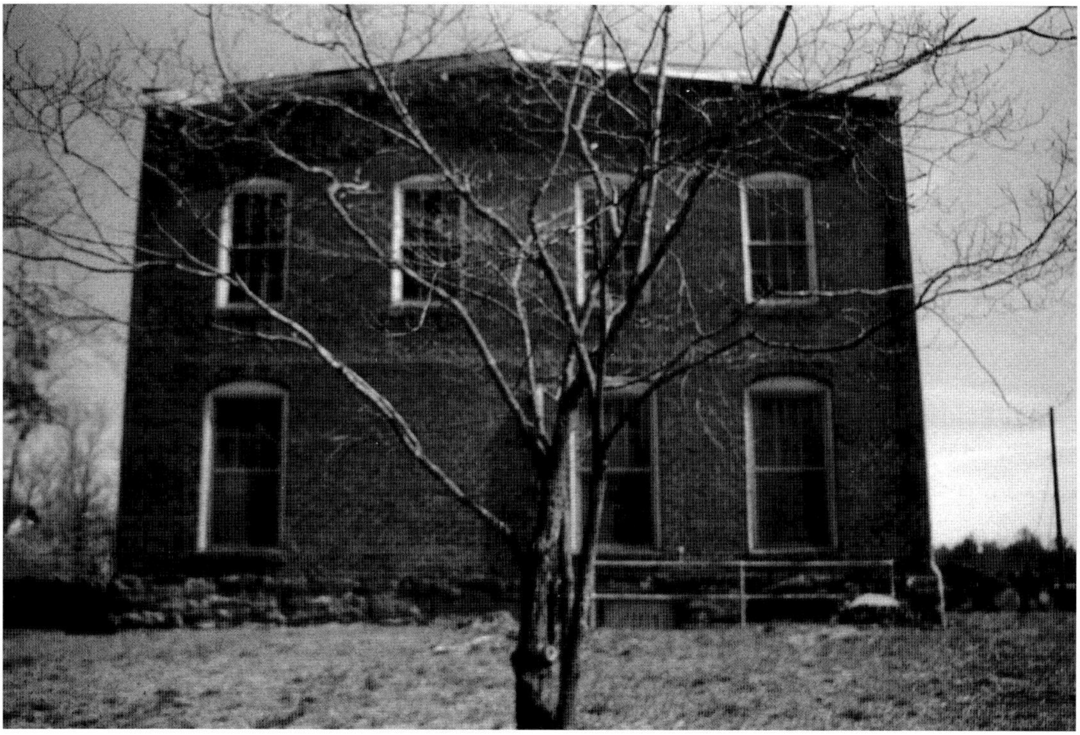

A tree splays in front of the company store, reaching past its bounds to the surrounding sky.

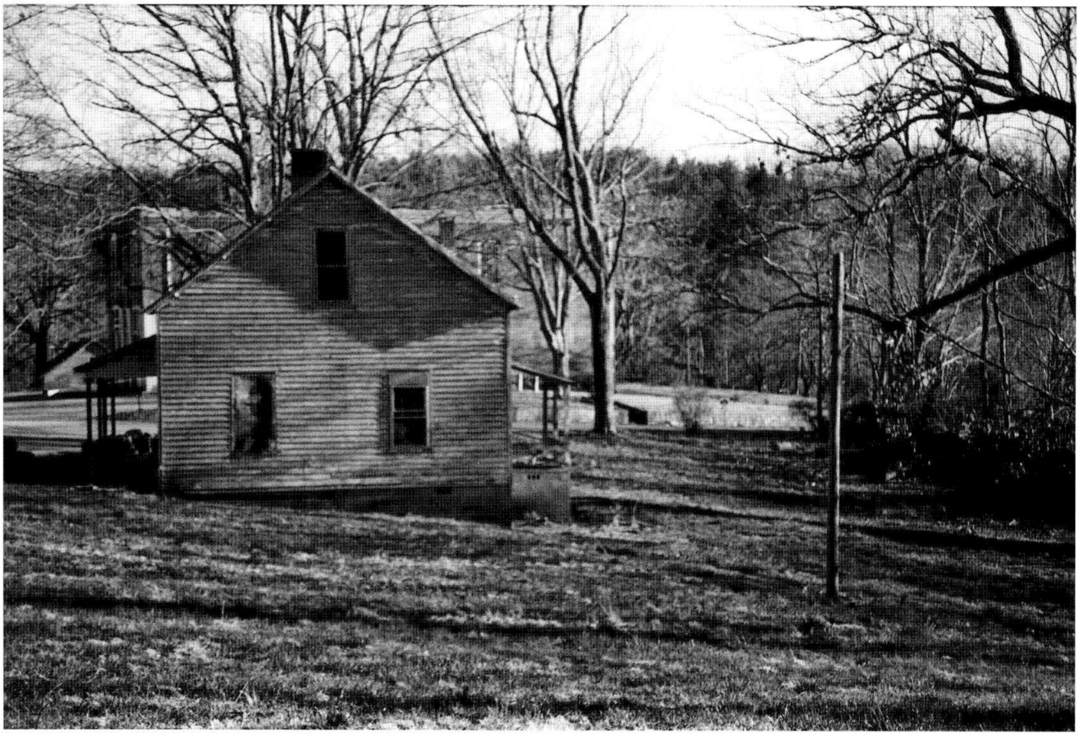

A mill house stands in front, with the company store visible behind it.

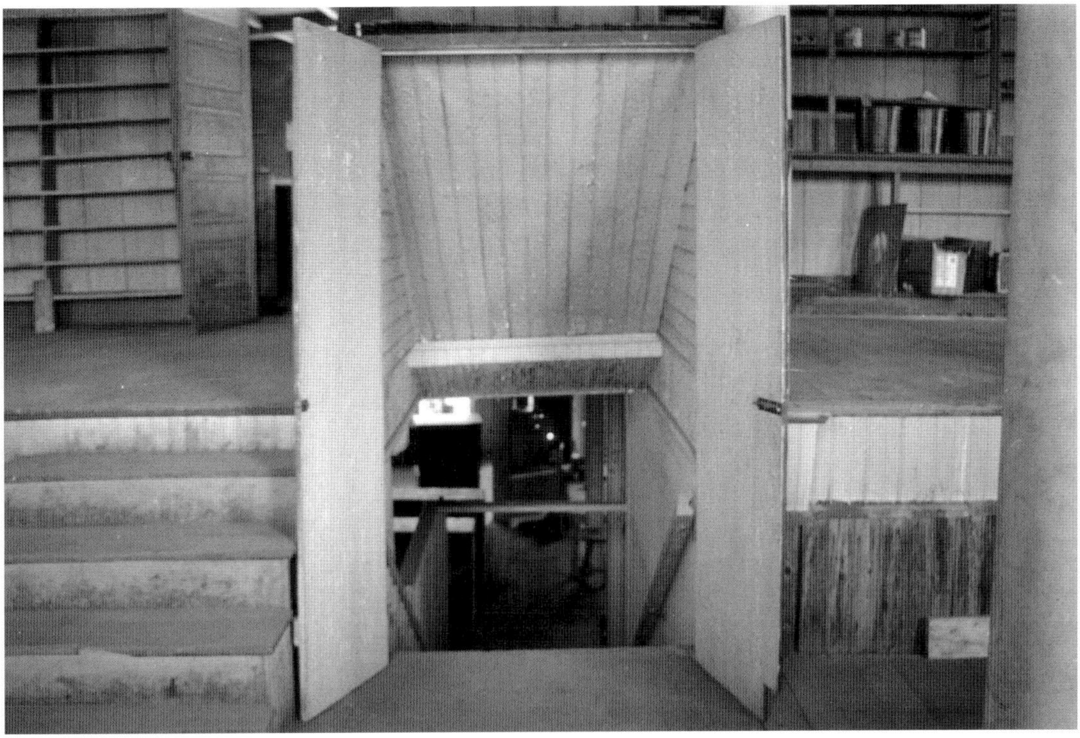

Within the company store, this open maw leads to the steps back downstairs.

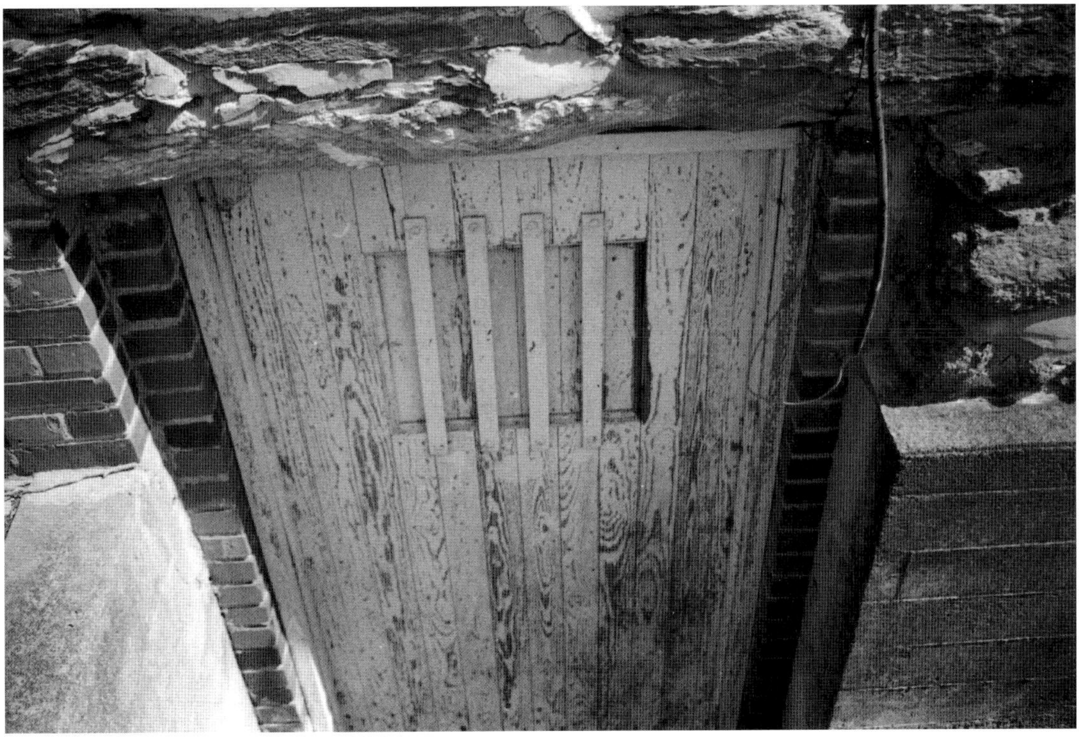

This door, possibly modified, leads below the company store.

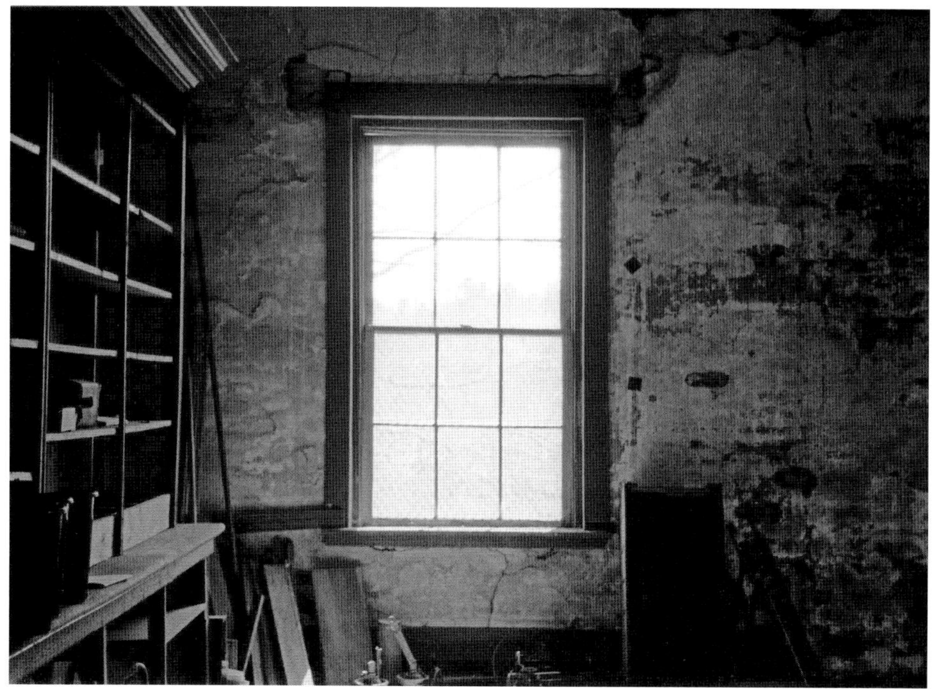

A view looking out the window of the company store's second story shows swaying branches and the distant woods.

At the Henry River Mill Village, the company currency was in token form with evidence of the tokens first being used in 1911, and evidence for the minting of more tokens in 1942 with use through the Second World War.[3] The houses, which were provided living quarters for workers and their families, remained property of the mill village and were unable to be purchased by the families that lived in them (even if they were able to secure the buying power that would have been necessary).[4] These houses did not have toilets or internal water even through the 1980s when still in use, when those who lived in remaining houses used the outhouses and spigots outside for water.[5] Again, this provides remarkable similarity to the living conditions described by Joseph Kovich in the coal mining community in which he grew up:

> Most all of the houses were owned by the coal company. They were their own houses. They were just plain inside, probably four, six, and eight rooms. They had no inside toilets, no inside water, just plain four walls in every room. All the toilets were outside, privy-type toilets and the water was from an outside pump, handle-type pump.[6]

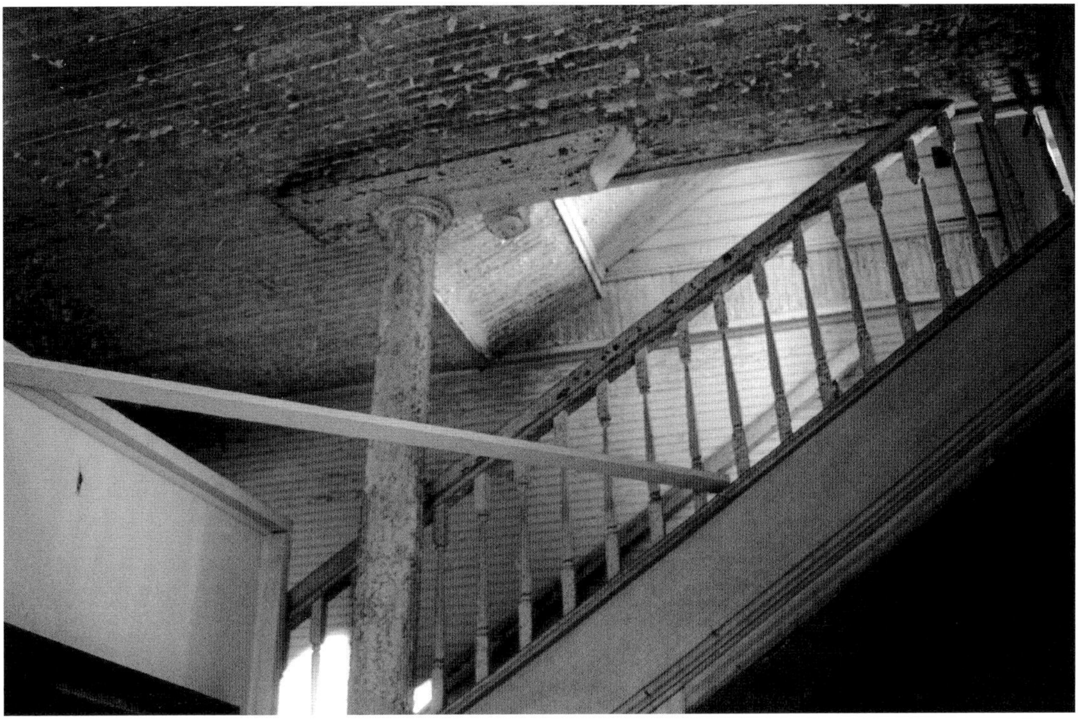

Inside the company store, great clumps of paint hang from the ceiling. A beam has fallen from above and touches the stairs.

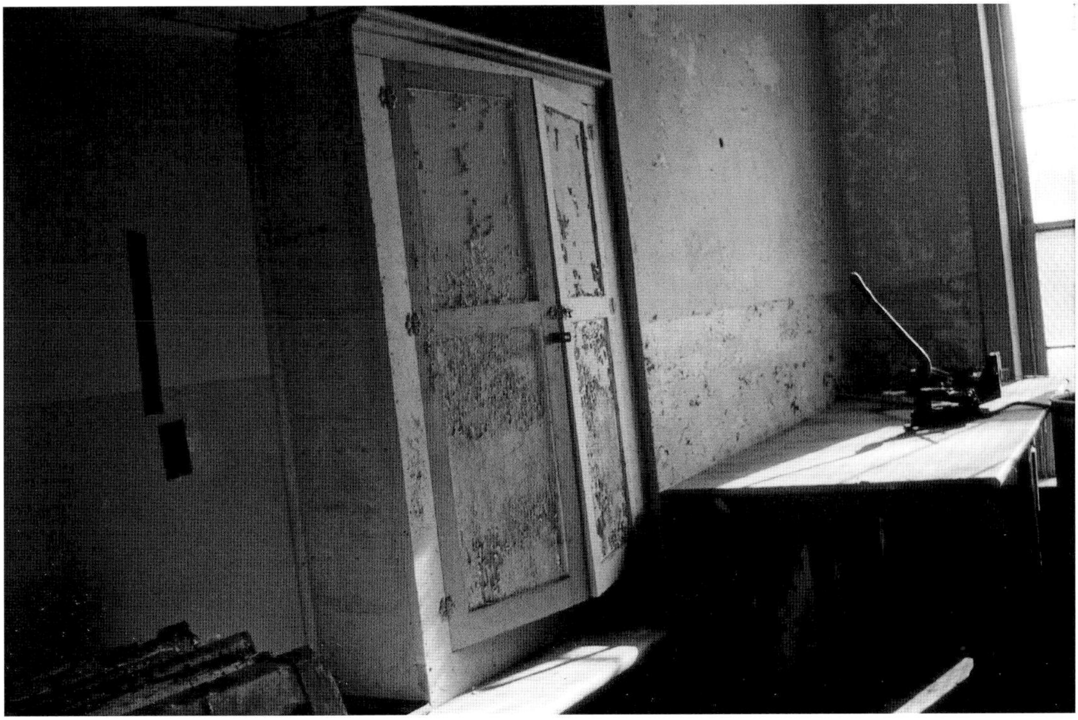

On the second floor of the company store is a cabinet with swollen doors, unclosed and with peeling paint.

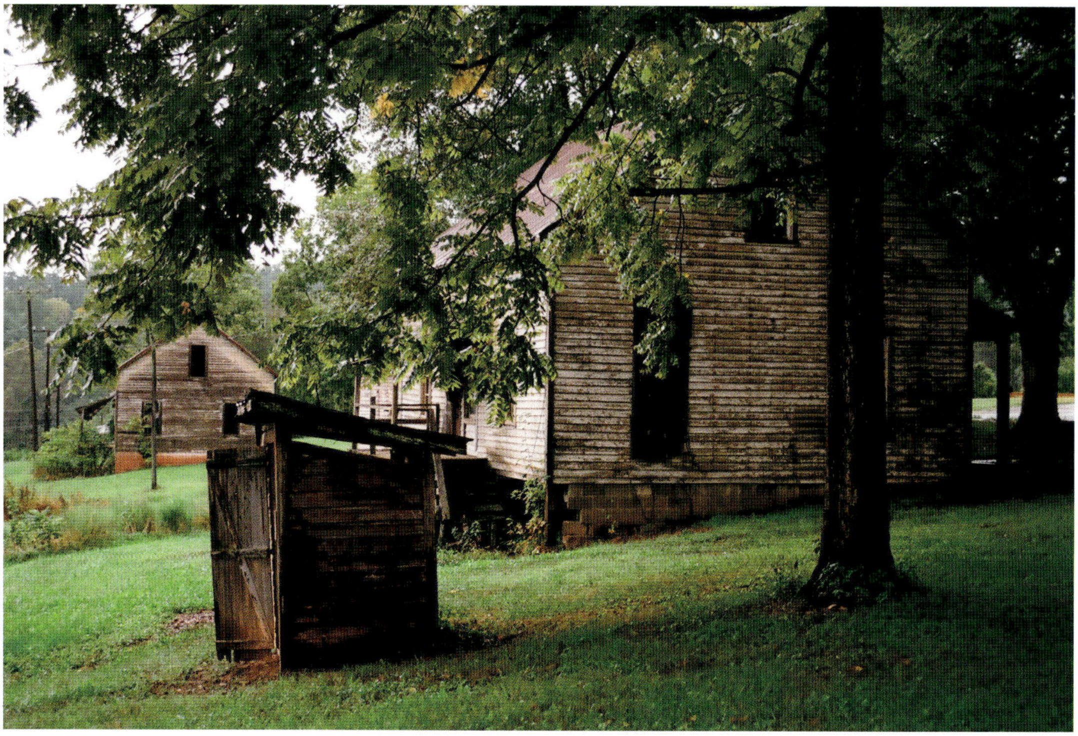

Two mill houses are visible, as well as an outhouse whose door hangs open.

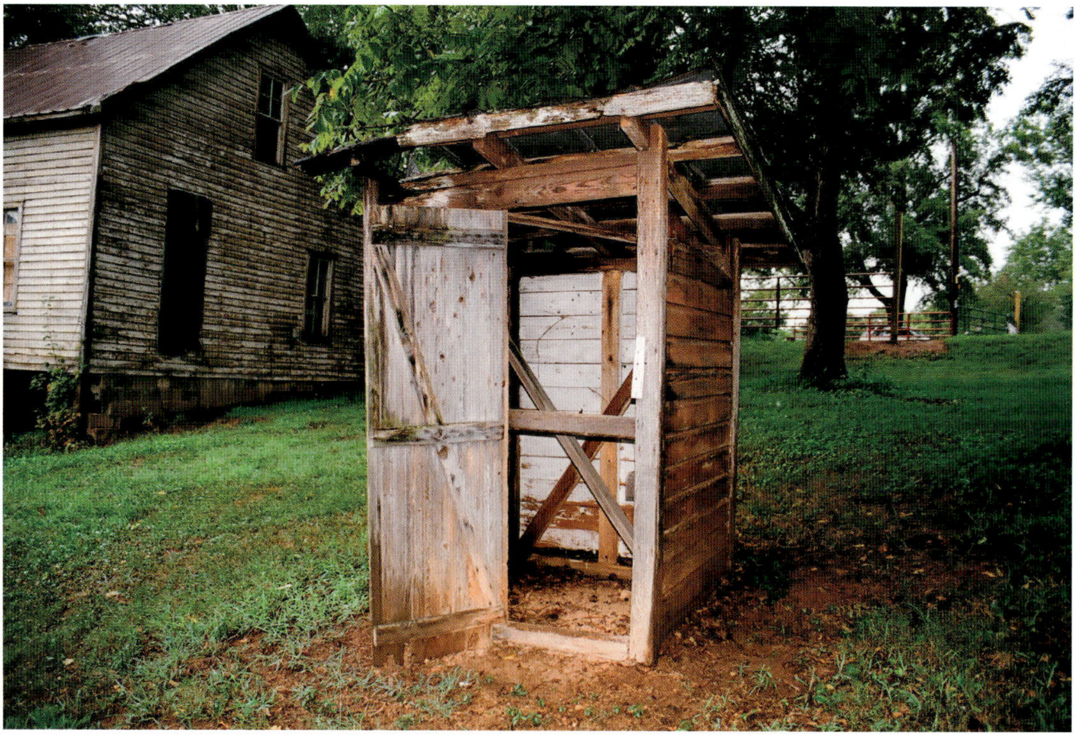

A perpetually open outhouse with a damaged roof.

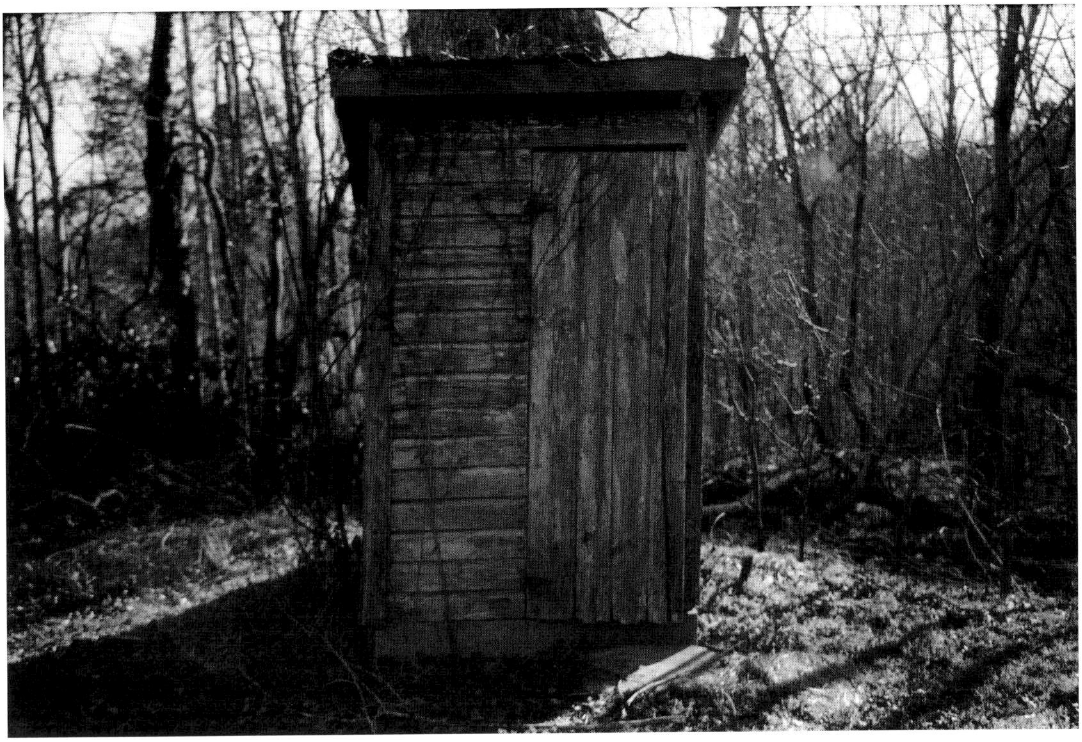

This outhouse, farther from the others, remains closed but covered in vines.

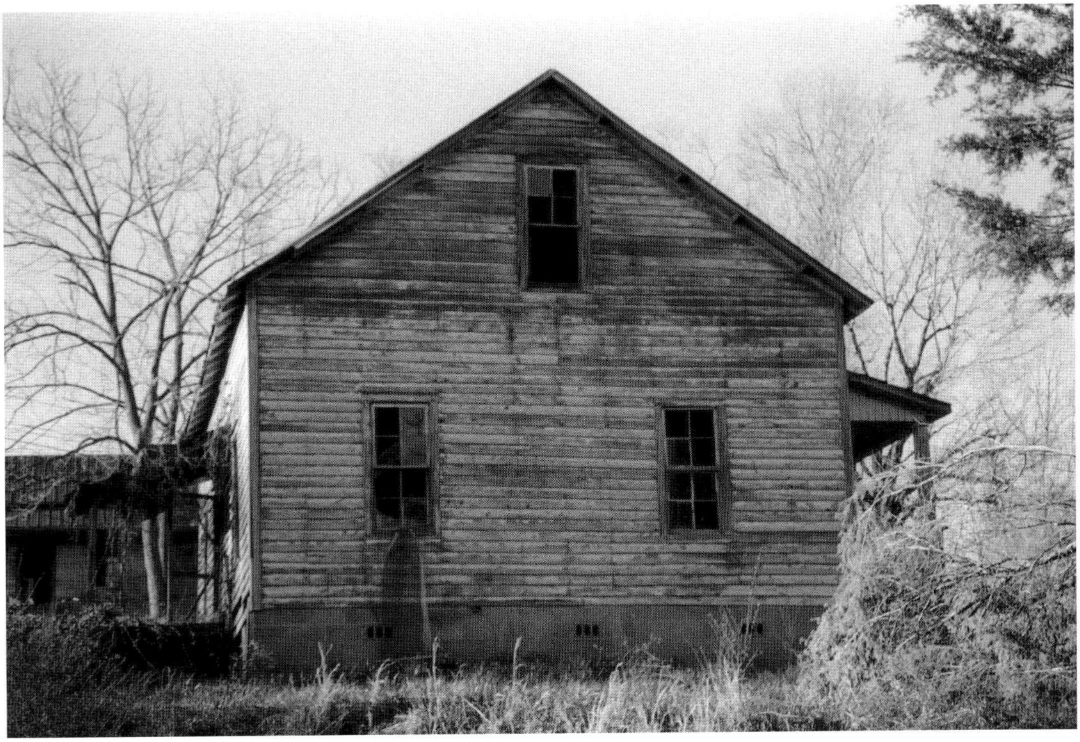

The majority of the windowpanes on this mill house are absent, but the back and front porches still stand.

These uniformly structured homes continue to dot the land of Henry River, though some have been lost to time. Differing levels of decay provide a texture to these structures that otherwise would be near impossible to tell apart. Over the years there were continual efforts to place the village under historic preservation status, which continued to fail. I remember, even as a child, having heard about some of these efforts, likely through hearing the reading of the local paper on a Sunday morning at my grandmother's house. I can also recall quite clearly the disdain for such efforts at the time, as the mill village was seen as a prime place for squatters and other "delinquent activities'" such that many didn't see why some were seeking to preserve the structures still standing. Original efforts to secure a historic landmark status, and therefore preservation of the land and structure, failed following a fire that destroyed main mill building in 1977, just on the heels of the official closing of the mill in 1970.[7,8]

After the closing of the mill in 1970, many families left the village and subsequently many of the houses began to fall into disrepair. Over time it became commonplace for squatters to use the buildings, and for others to use these buildings as a place to practice their graffiti. I recall passing through the area on the way to parks or another nearby destination and being interested in walking through, only to be told it "wasn't safe" and that the area was better off avoided entirely. This seemed to be the general consensus until around 2011, when Henry River was used as a filming site for *The Hunger Games*. Dilapidated, and decidedly unpreserved at this time, adjustments were made to the company store building to redesign it as a bakery, and one of the mill houses was even destroyed for a scene of the film.

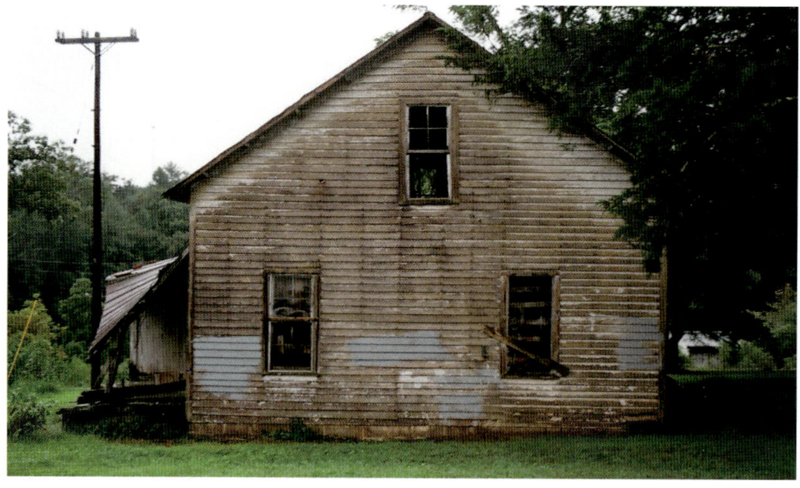

At this mill house, the back awning has fallen, and the back porch has sunken in. The top windows, *sans* glass, can be seen straight through.

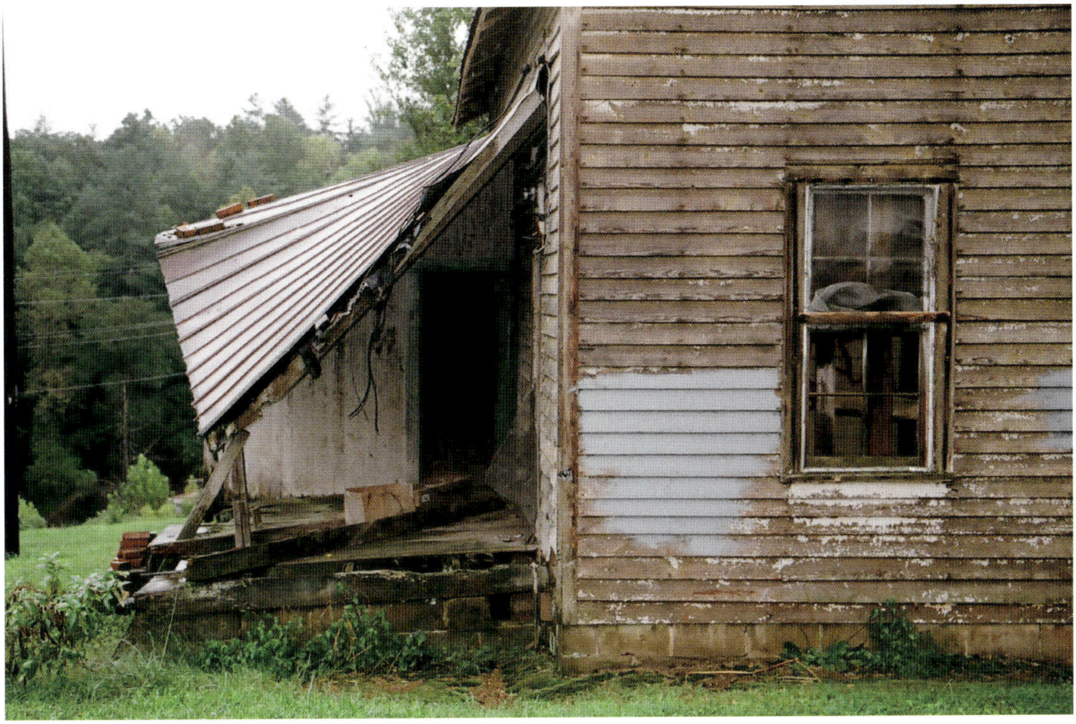

A closer look at the back porch shows missing floorboards and overturned stones. Through the window, graffiti can be seen.

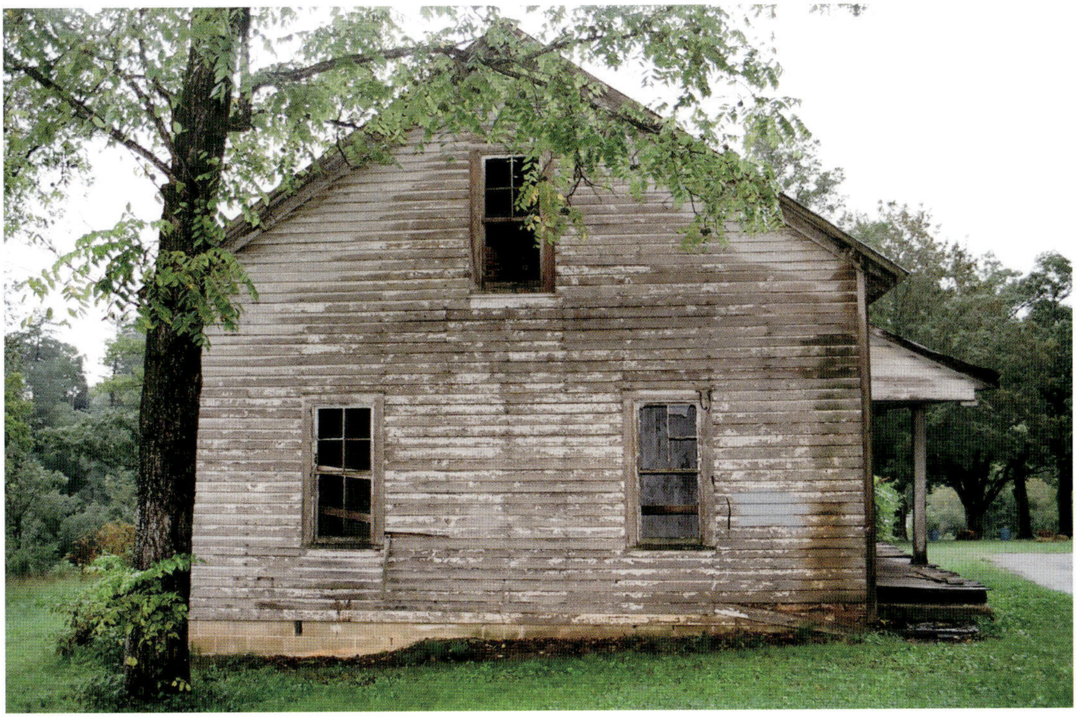

This mill house is more intact and lacks immediately obvious graffiti. One lone board is loose at the bottom right.

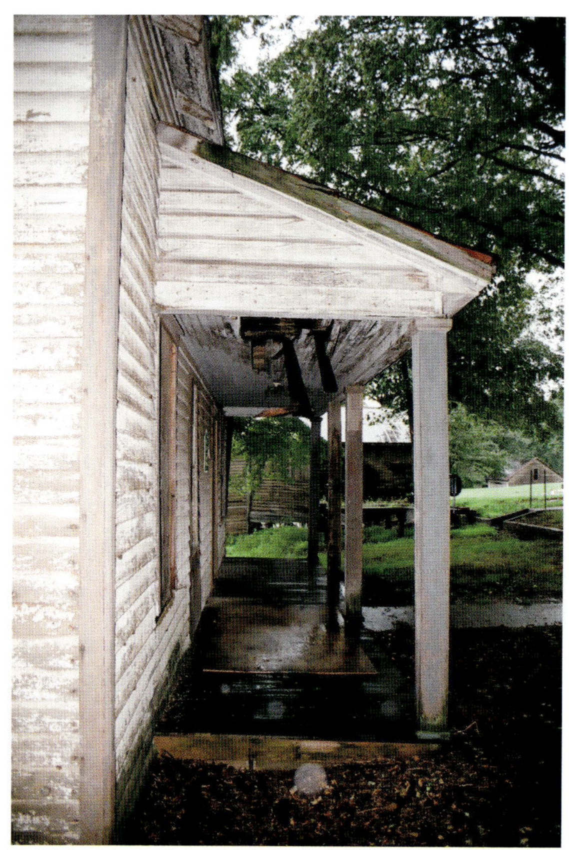

Left: At this house, plywood is placed over a weak spot in the front porch. Still, a hole and falling boards are seen above, where birds are fond of nesting.

Below: A pillar has snapped and fallen onto the porch of a mill house. Many of the floorboards of the porch are broken, and those that aren't are too soft to hold weight.

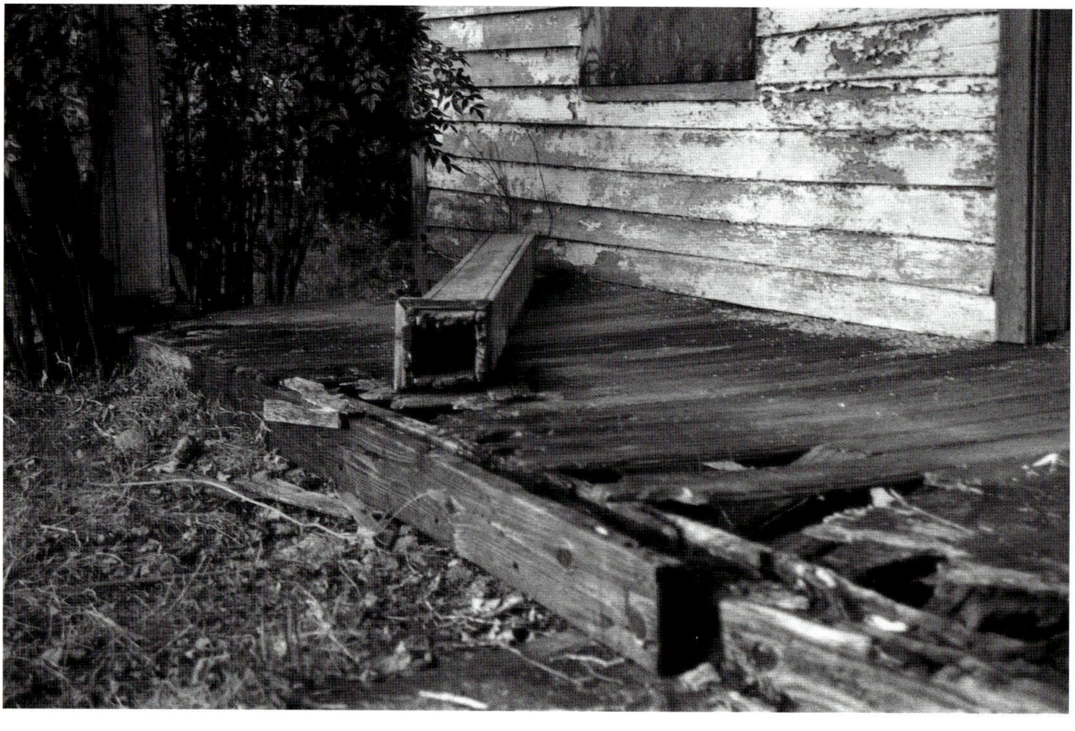

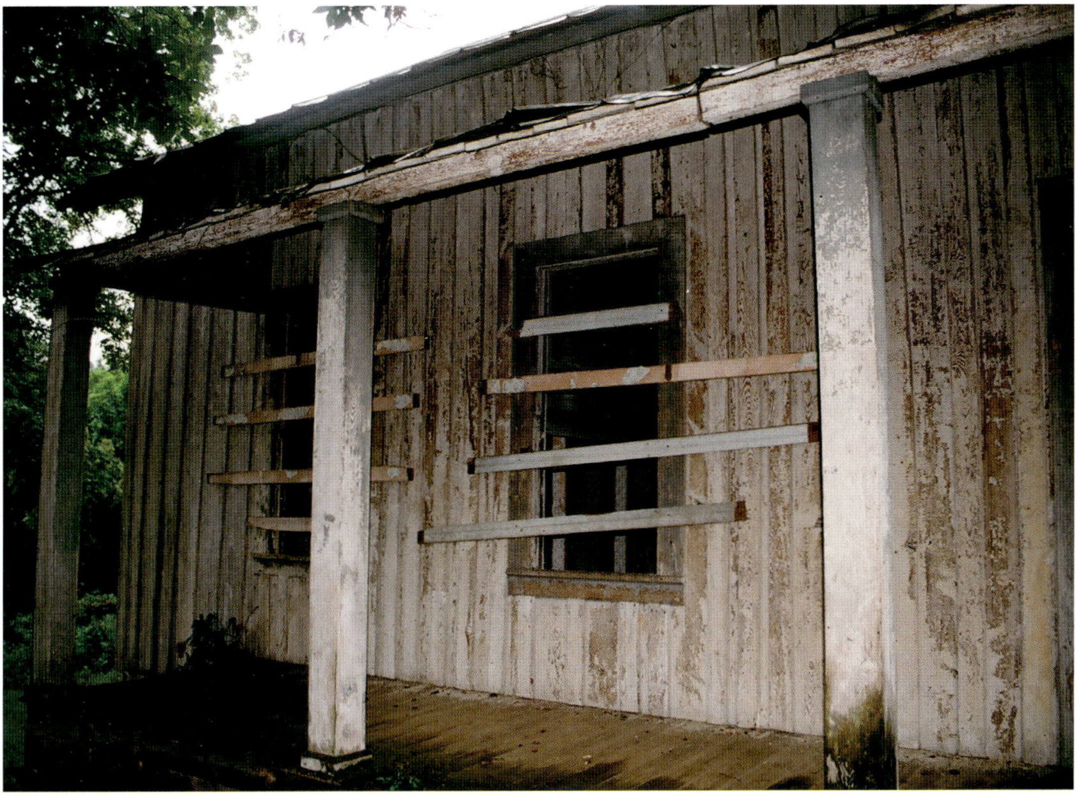

Even the boards used on the windows at this building show peeling paint.

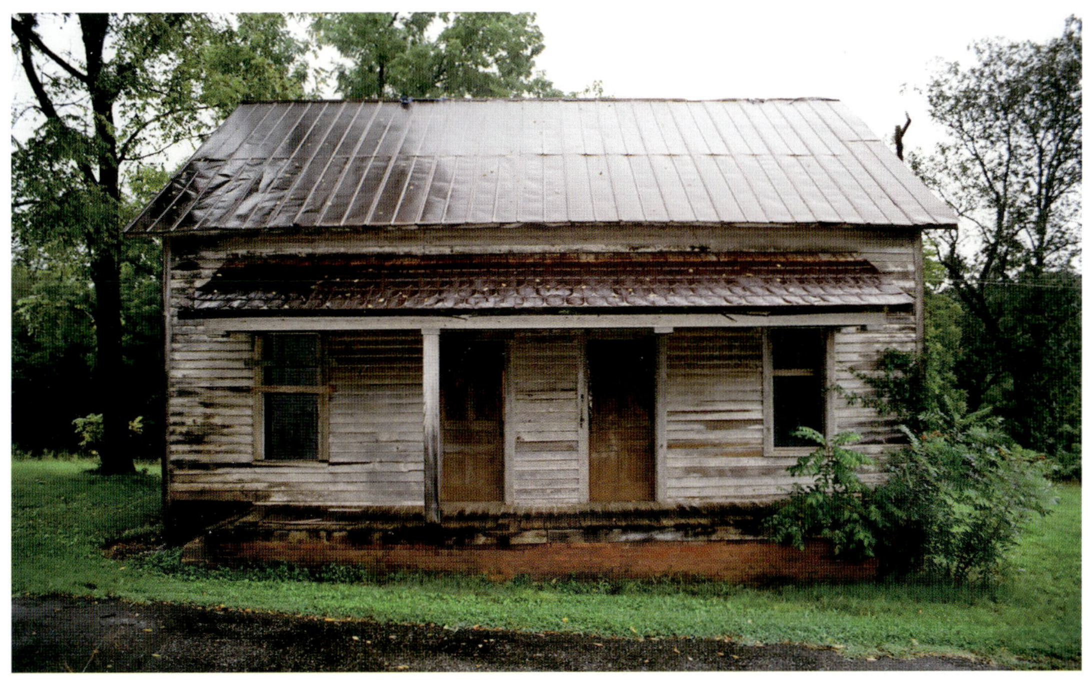

A structure with an updated roof and awning. The porch and sides of the house remain in disrepair.

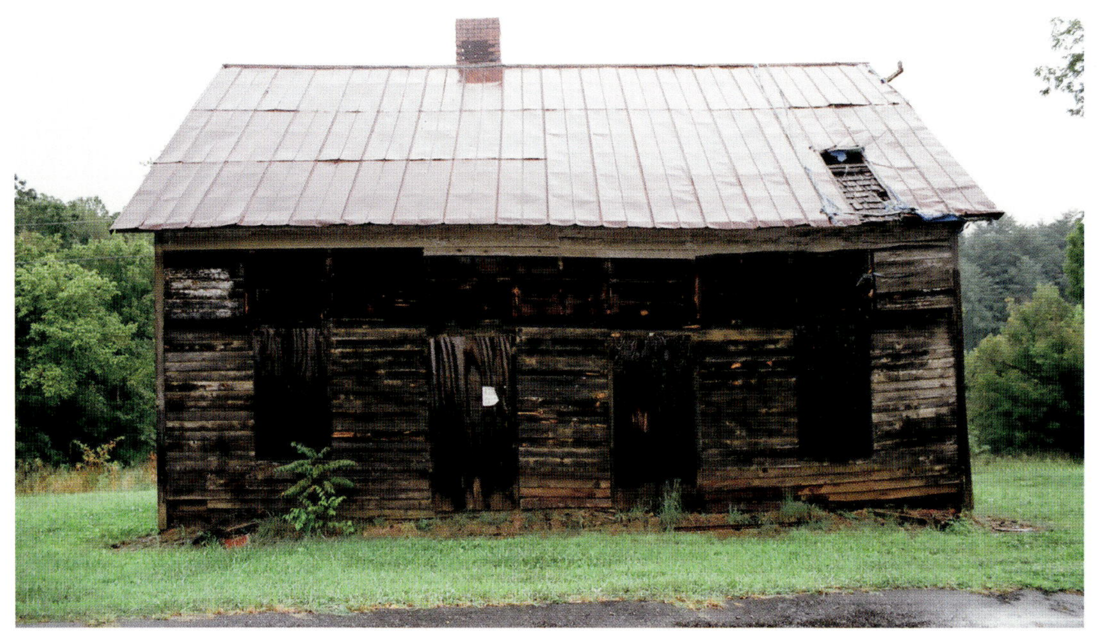

A more unusual structure at the mill town, all entrances are entirely boarded up. The roof and top of the wall contain openings to appease any animals looking for a place to rest.

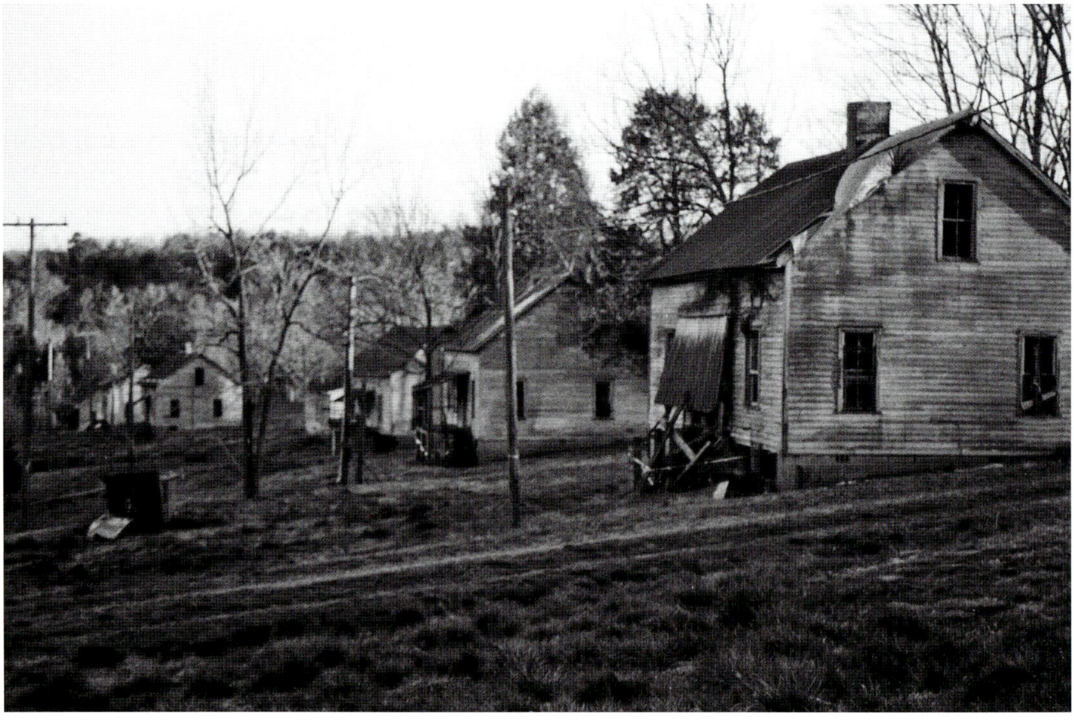

A line of mill houses, all structurally the same but with varying levels of decay.

I can recall passing through the area during this time and being confused by the traffic of people suddenly wanting to visit and go through the mill village. This was a place I had gone past many times in my life, and I had never seen so many people interested and walking on the road to take in the sight. In fact, before this point, it was more often that people would go out of their way to avoid having to walk through this area and past the homes, afraid of who may be inside or what they may be up to. This became the first point at which there began to be statements put out to avoid trespassing in the area, especially during the filming schedule. The increased attention continued for a few months to perhaps a year before it began to decrease dramatically, and then lost significant numbers of visitors. The owner of the village, post filming, was very dedicated to selling the land. Even with the notoriety gained through the film exposure, I can recall the skepticism of the locals that it would be bought. This skepticism held until the property was in fact newly purchased, with the goal of receiving historic landmark status and becoming a tourist destination.

Purchased in 2017 from Wade Sheppard by Calvin Reyes, the Henry River Mill Village did in fact receive a placement on the National Register of Historic Places in 2019.[9] I spoke with Jay Mitchell about this process in early 2019 and following its placement on the register later into the year as I came back to continue photographing the houses. After the many woes and previous attempts to receive some form of historic recognition, there was a great relief that this goal had been achieved at long last.

Another topic of discussion between us was often the issues of trespassing they had on the land, which at the time were quite frequent. Some of this trespassing must be attributed to the history of the village following the closing and destructive fire of the mill. For a long period of time, trespassing was normal and even expected at Henry River, such that "trespassing" may not even be an appropriate term for those years. Even following the on-site filming there was not a wealth of security for the land. Many visitors, fanatics of the film or otherwise, were known to take "souvenirs" or leave their mark by adding to the graffiti found within many of the buildings. Even now, with security cameras and renovations, there continue to be stories of break-ins. A news article from 2020 discusses a break-in at the village in which a door was kicked in and some items used for Halloween tours at the village were stolen.[10] A focus of the owners now is to renovate many if not all of the remaining houses to some standard of their former glory, which includes removing incidents of graffiti and other human intervention.[11]

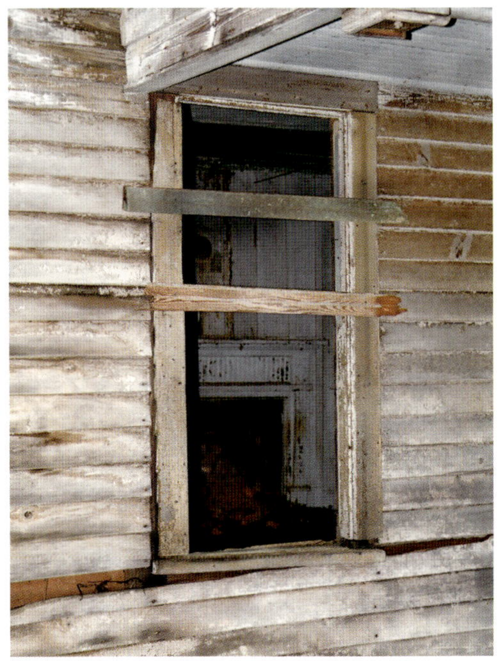

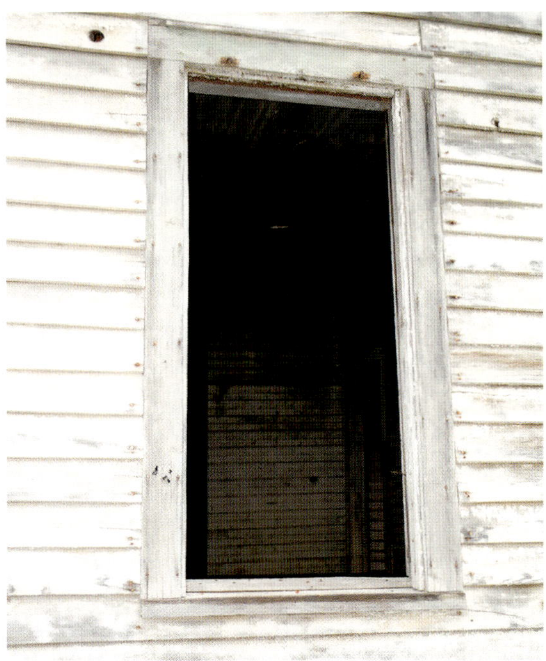

Above left: At this mill building a wood pillar is noticeably missing. Beyond that, the majority of the boards originally covering the window have been torn down, and inside, the damaged fireplace is visible.

Above right: Through this window, falling ceiling boards are visible. The boards of the back wall are partially discolored.

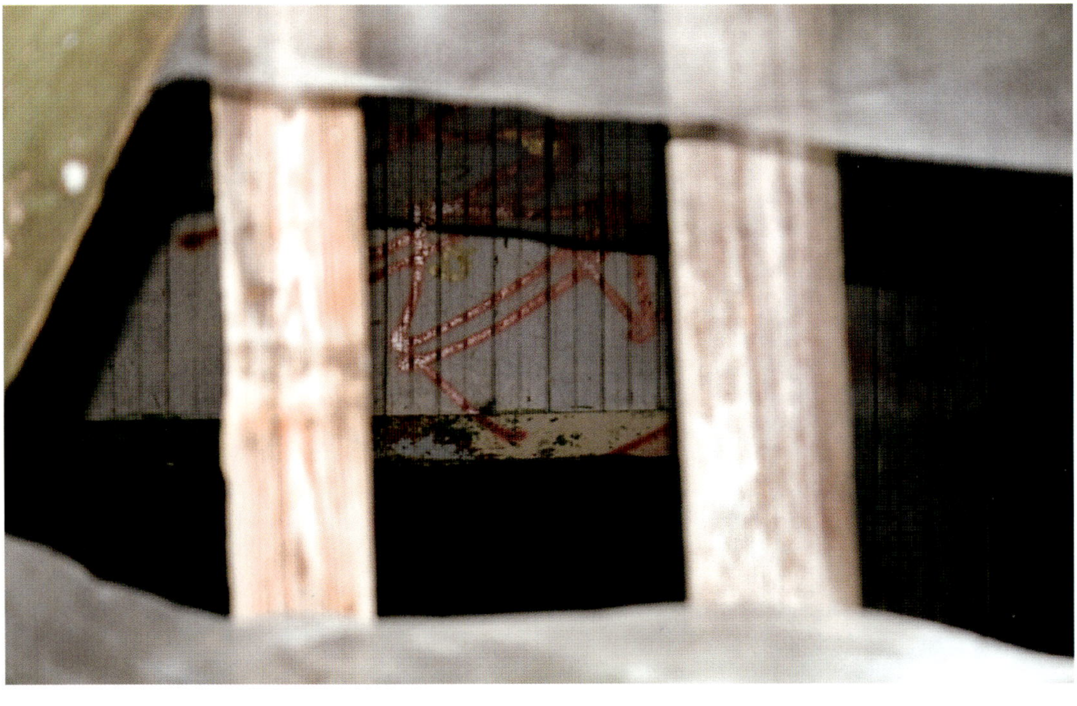

New spray paint is visible through the remains of boards and the window screen.

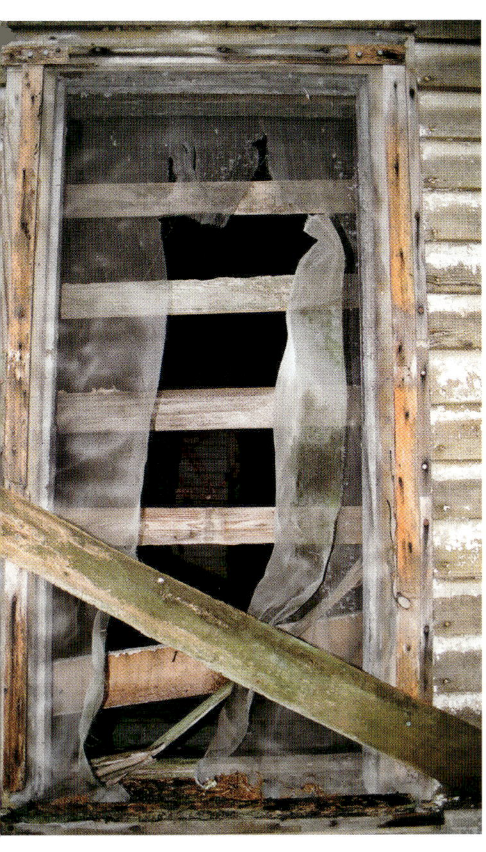

Above left: This window screen is rotten and torn, moss and mildew gathering on the screen and fallen board.

Above right: Popular graffiti tags at the mill town are visible here: smiling faces and names.

Right: In this room, a door has been torn down. "We see what we wanna see" is inscribed in weeping black spray paint alongside eyes of various colors. With careful eyes you can see through the damaged floor to the grass outside.

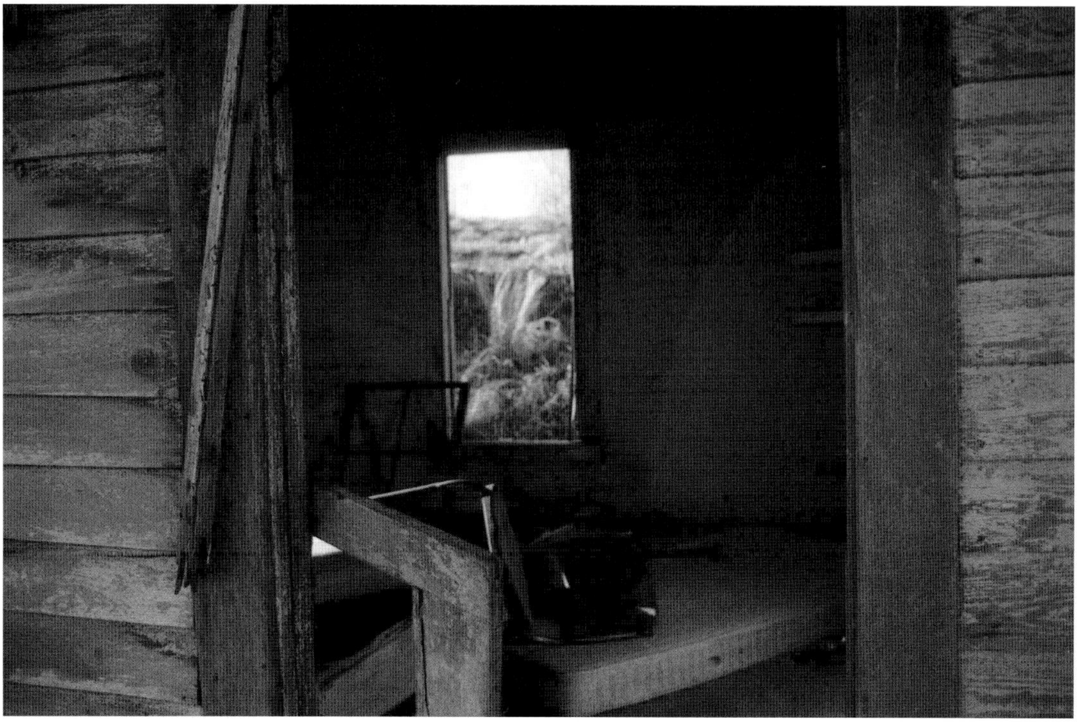

Part of the doorframe, still attached at the hinge, hangs crooked. A window frame, chair, mattress, and the remainder of the door lay haphazardly inside the mill house.

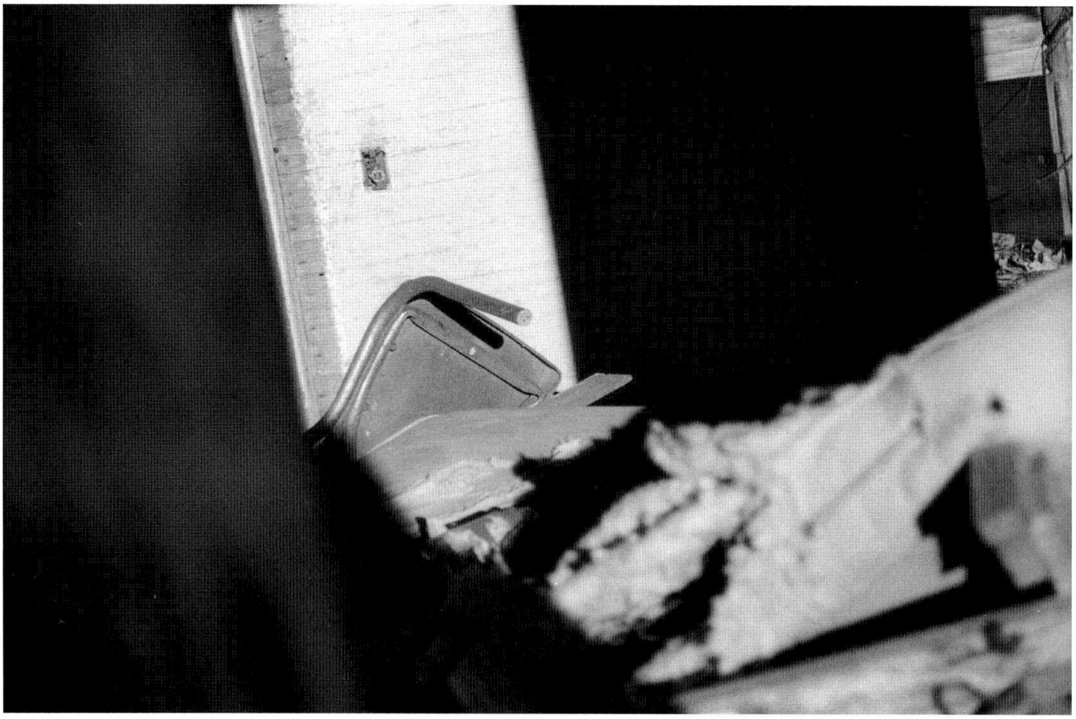

A chair lies on its side far across the room, underneath a naked outlet.

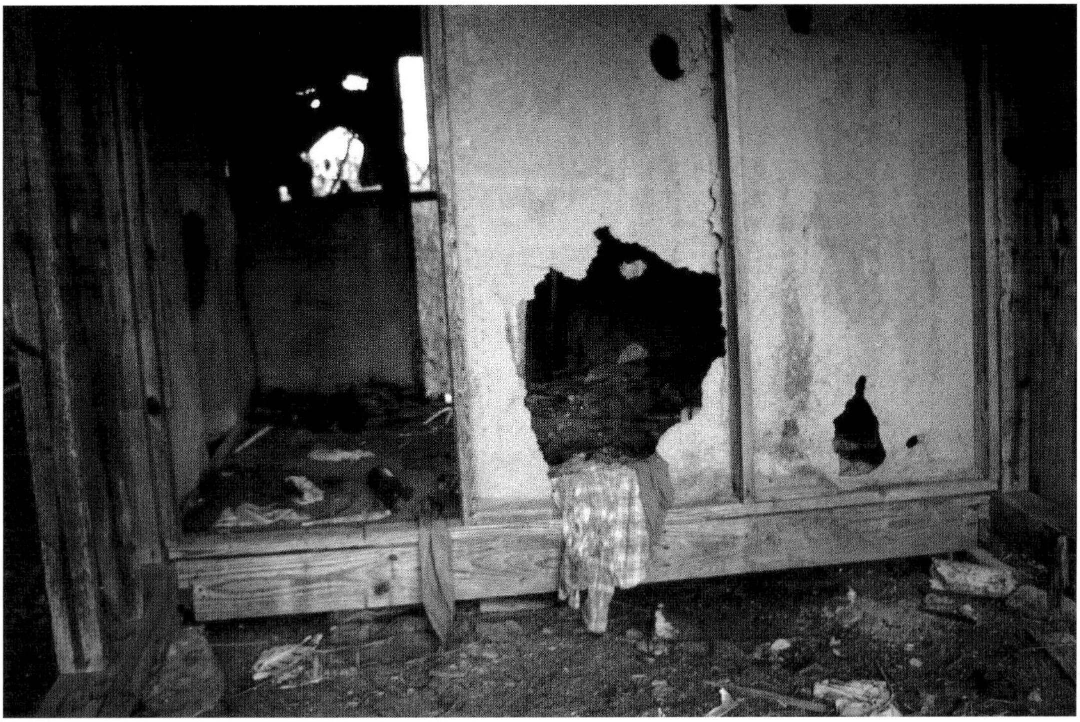

Clothes, bottles, and other evidence of human activity are concentrated in a more remote shed on the mill village property.

A pile of bricks and other debris sits in the middle of this mill house's floor.

Having grown to see the transformation of Henry River from a place "not suitable for kids" to a filming location and finally to a historic site on its way towards renovation, I am happy to have been able to capture it when I did. While there is evidence of the changes made to the company store in the photos, the mill houses remain as they were in their most affected state: changed by time and unrelenting nature, as well as many sets of unrelenting human hands. The state of the buildings captured in these photos speaks most clearly to how I have known them and understood them throughout my life. Buildings from not so long ago with less than trustworthy floors and roofs. Buildings that have held working families, people down on their luck, and many sets of bored teenagers.

I began photographing these houses before there were people interested enough to come by and see what I was doing and why I was on the land, and I recall my surprise the first time someone came up to me to ask what I was doing; it was Jay Mitchell, and we chatted for a bit before he warned me about being careful. Specifically, to be careful around the decks and trying to get inside the homes, as someone had fallen through recently and they were worried about the liability. With a bit of amusement, I remember explaining that I was no stranger to the tendency of the stairs and flooring to be less than stable. In this instance, I acquiesced and promised to remain on the exteriors on the homes and sturdy points of any decks. I had been able to shoot inside some of the sheds and homes previously, so this wasn't terribly upsetting. I did have the privilege of going inside the company store to shoot a few rolls of film later on, which I cannot thank the team at Henry River enough for considering the concerns they had at the time about the weak ceiling on the second floor. I think I gave them quite a surprise by being more excited than afraid of the prospect of heading upstairs, however briefly.

For now, it seems as though Henry River Mill Village will be around for a long time to come. It's anyone's guess as to what the future of the tours and interest in the village may be, or how extensive the renovations. If nothing else, Henry River remains a testament and visually accessible site to the history of planned developments in Appalachia at large, and carries a lasting impression on the locals. Sometimes positive, sometimes negative, it is imperative to remember all facets of this (now official) historical site.

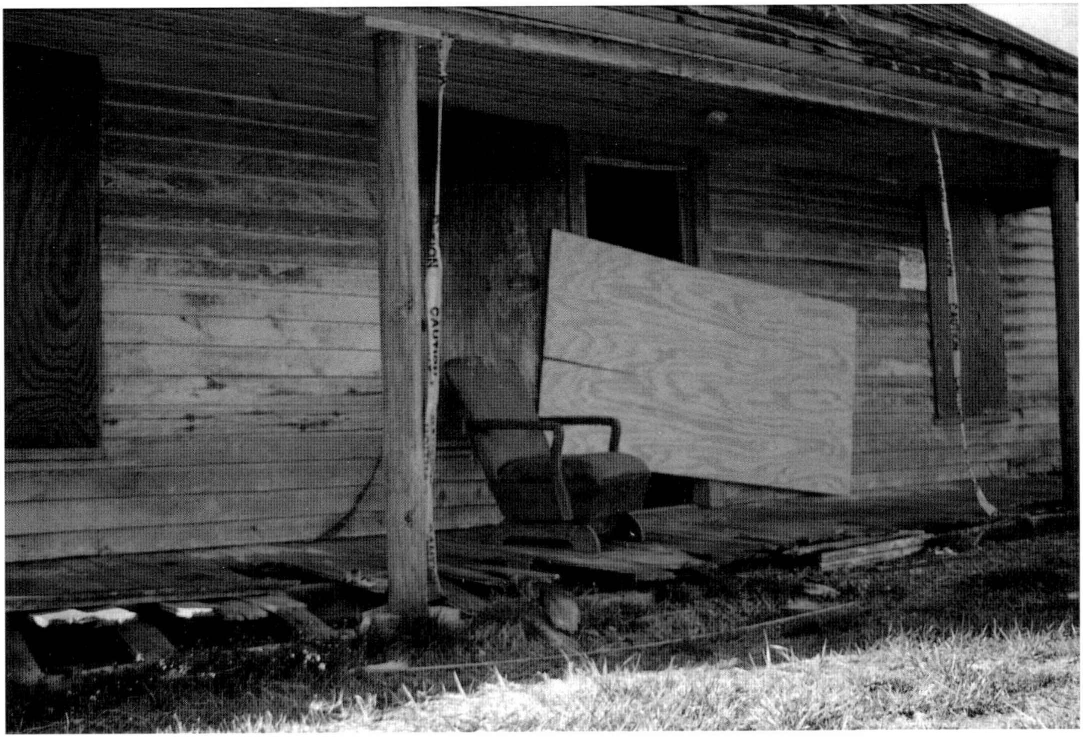

Plywood intended to block the entrance to a building has fallen. A chair sits on a few unbroken slats of the porch.

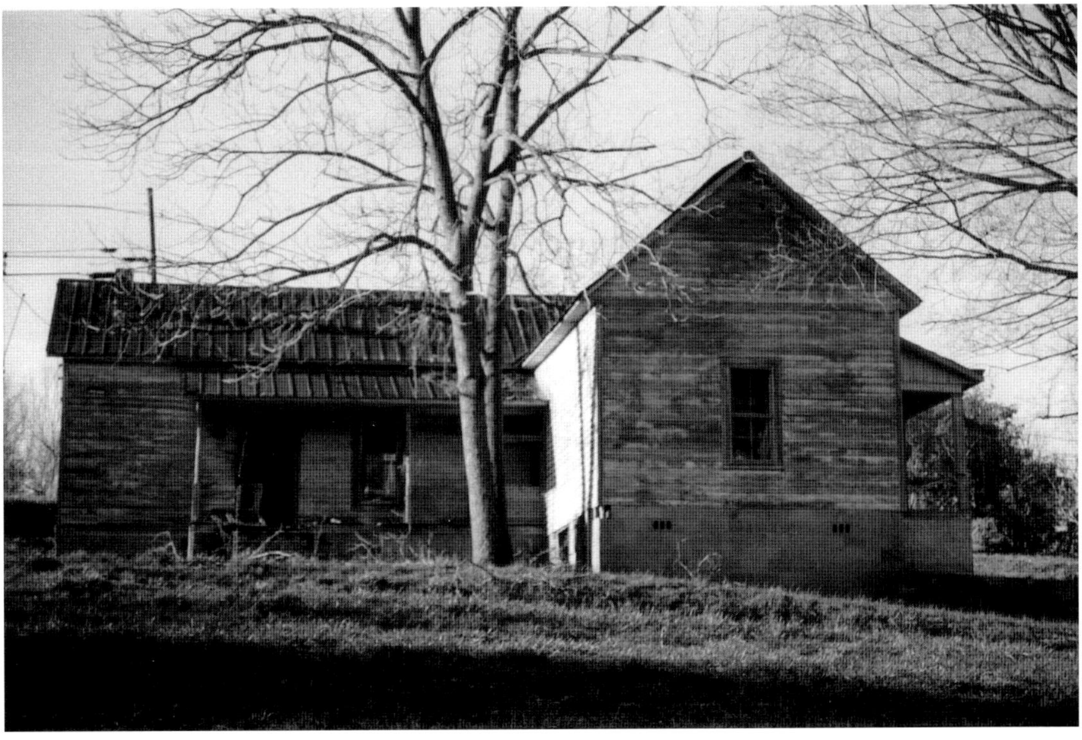

A mill house unusual in design presides over the top of a hill.

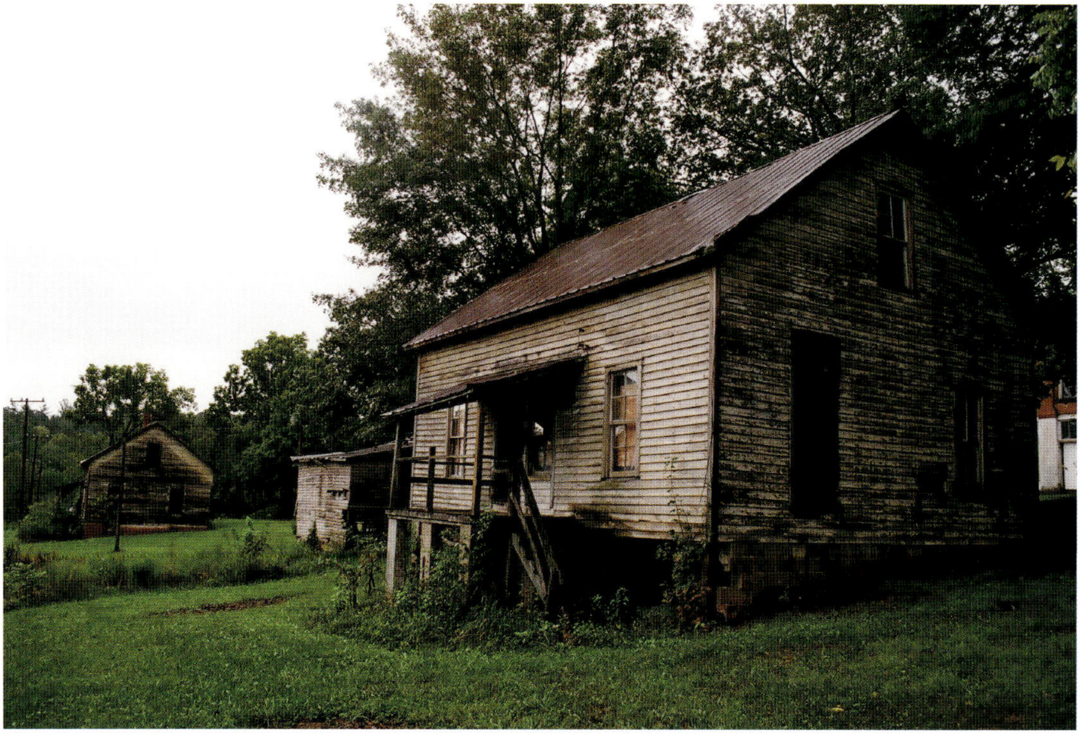

Two mill houses, identical in design, sit next to each other. The closest is missing its chimney, setting it apart.

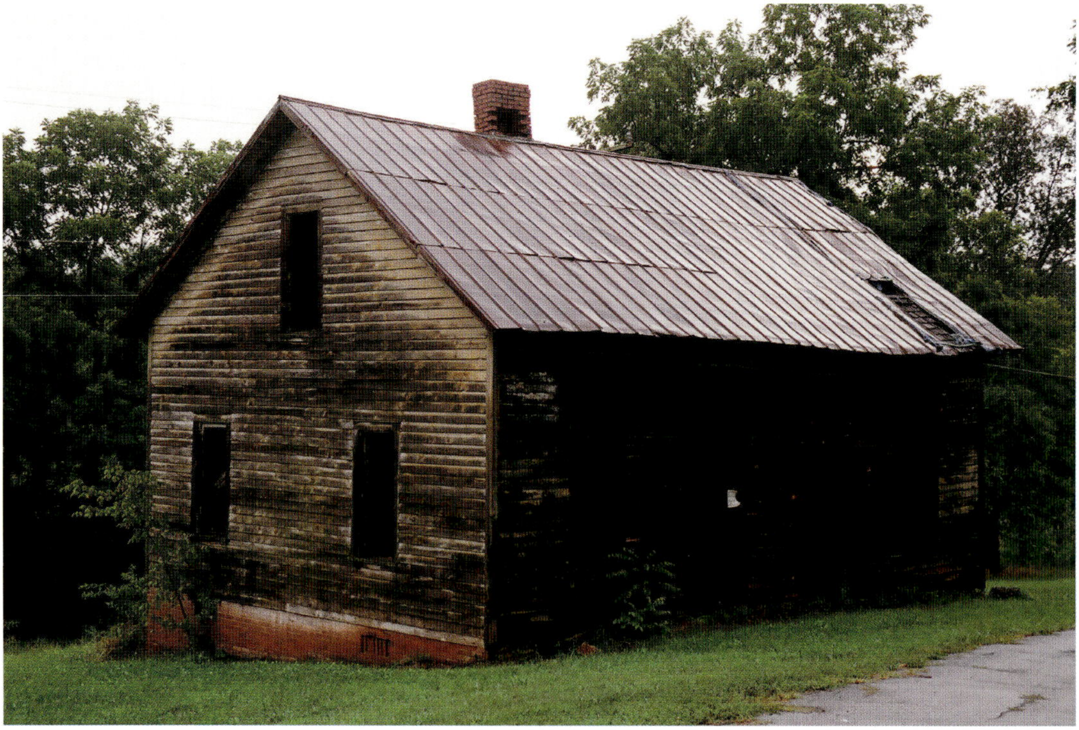

The window frames here hang empty from the side, while boarded entirely at the front.

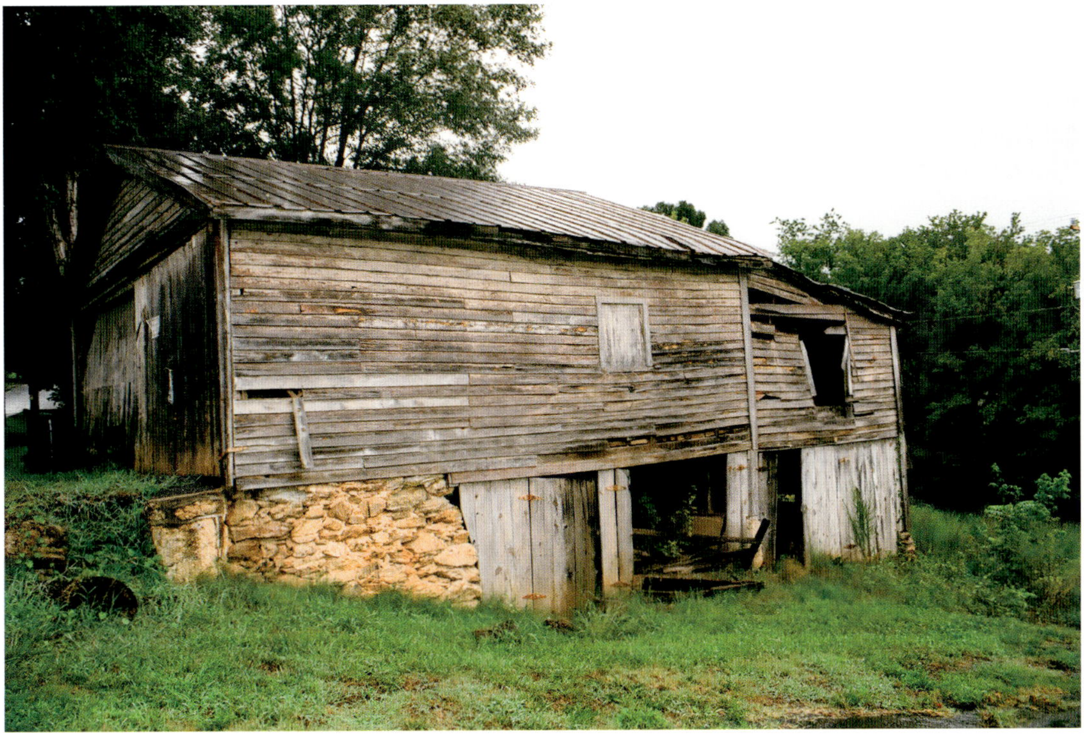

The back half and bottom of this structure are damaged but still in use for storage.

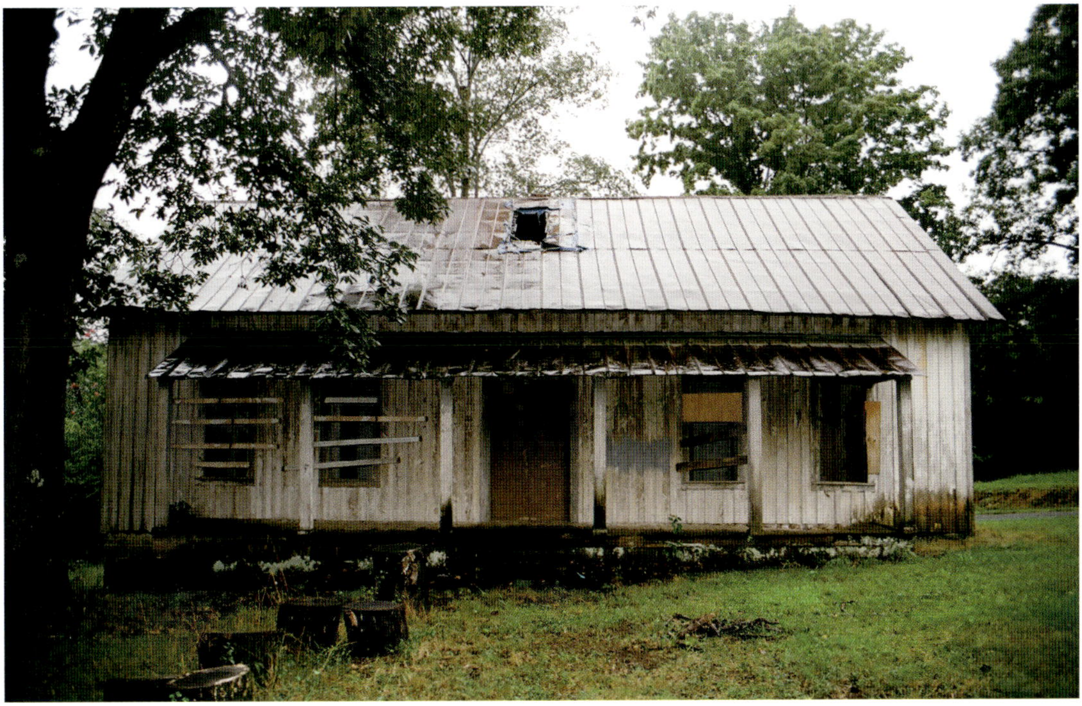

Tree stumps lead the way to this mill building. A hole, instead of a chimney, takes center stage. Unlike most buildings, many planks used to board up the windows remain.

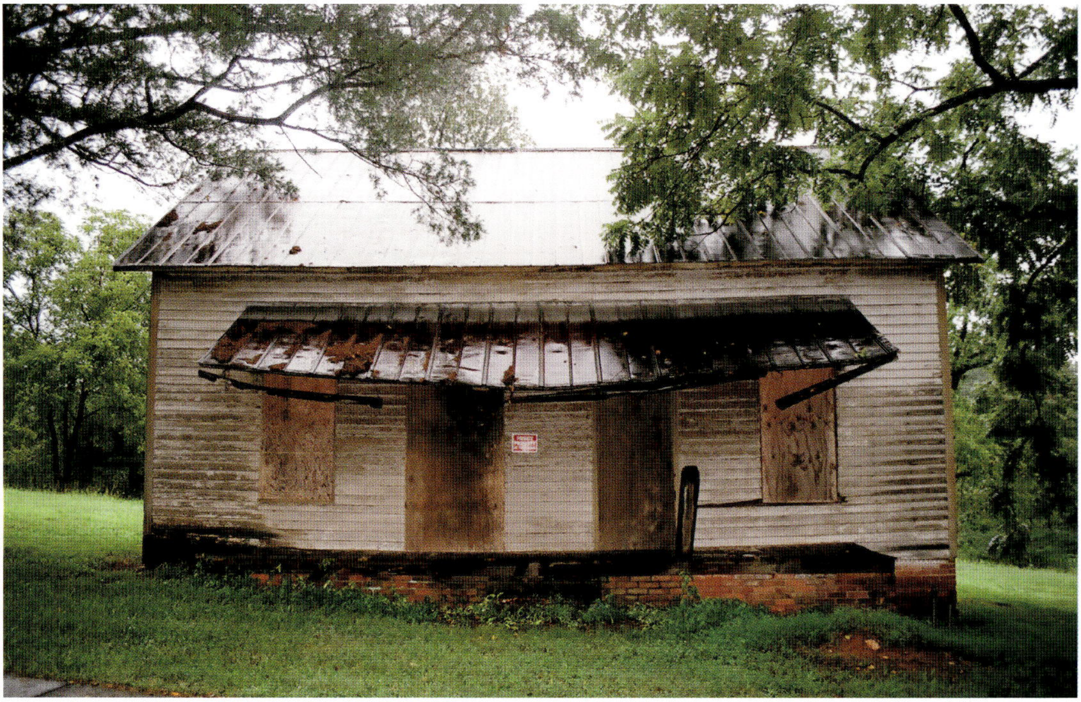

A “no trespassing” sign, new, shines on the building. The awning sways but remains steady, while the middle of the porch is entirely absent.

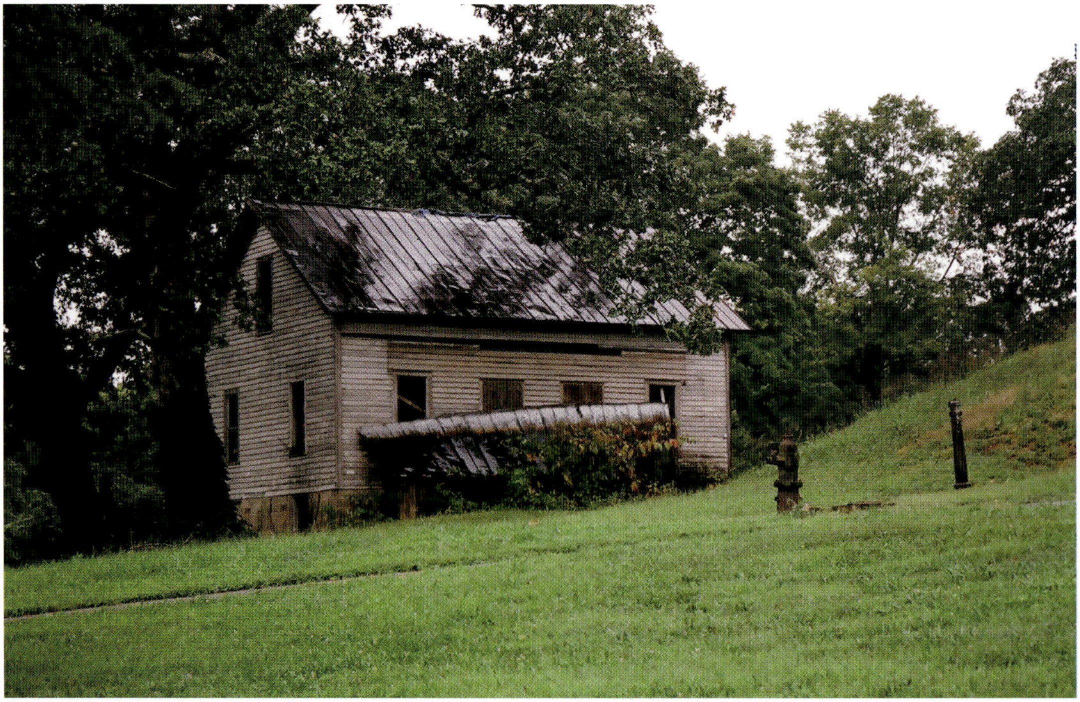

This mill house has lost its awning entirely: whole slats are missing from the front of the building, and the crawl space door is absent.

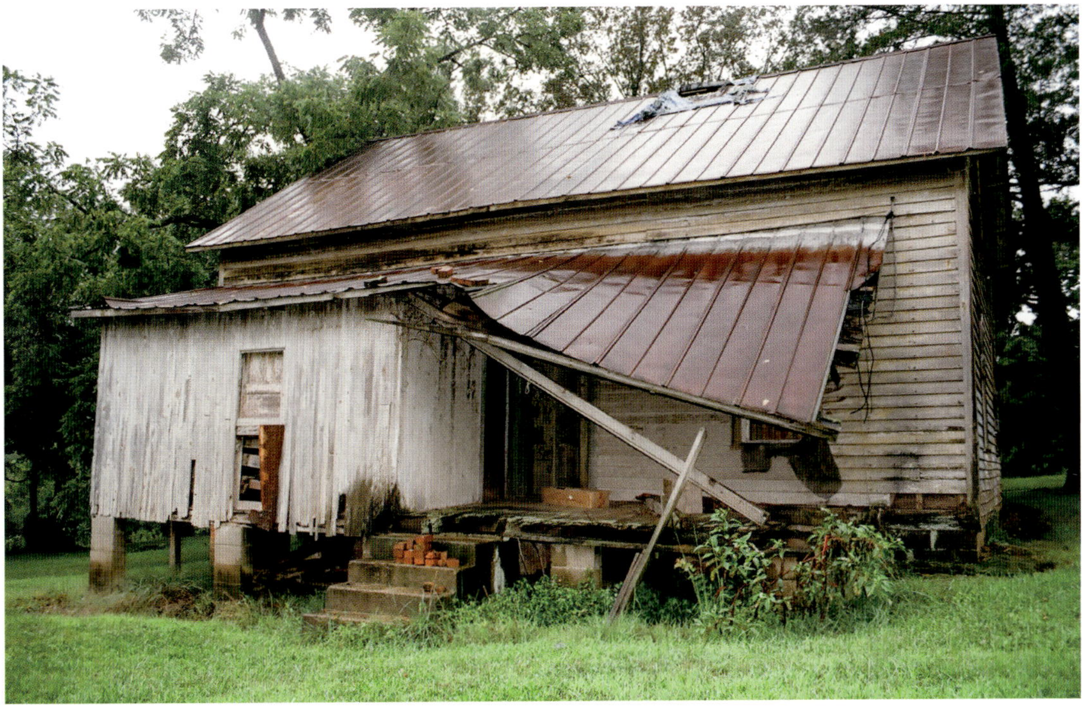

A hole has been patched with a tarp in the roof but has fallen through again. The stairs lead to holes in the porch where the floorboards have fallen through.

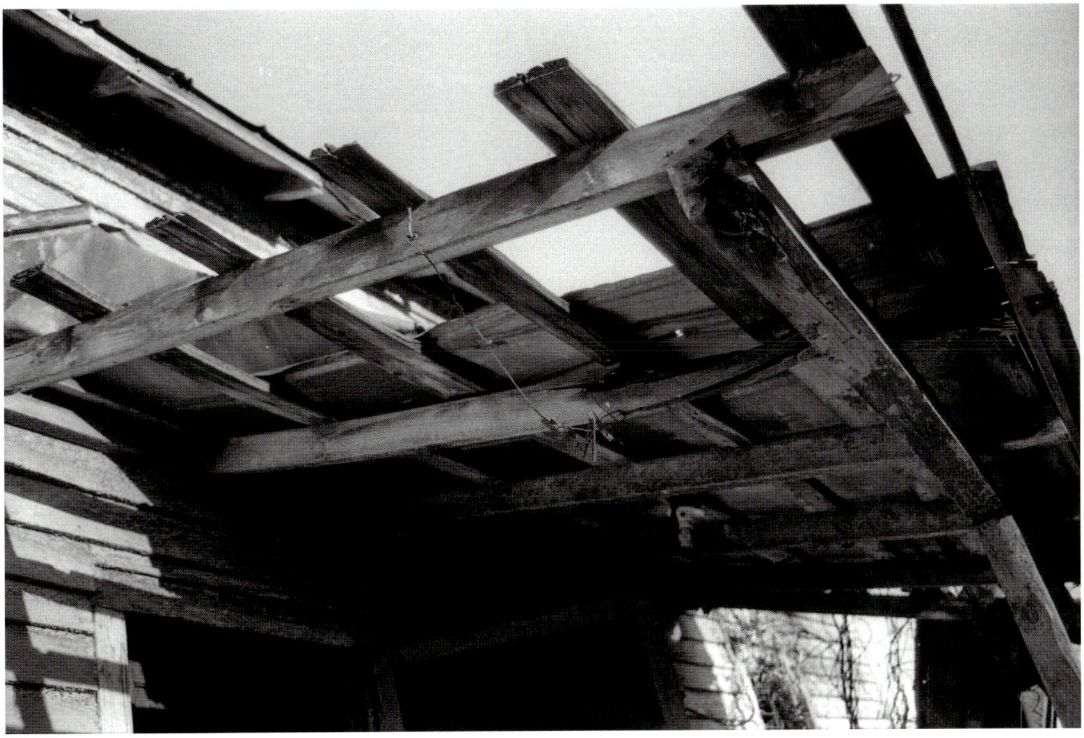

The construction of an awning is visible here, wire used to hold together beams where tin has blown away.

2

ROADSIDE GEMS

Often the most beautiful places will jump out at you as you are driving on a desolate road. To capture these, I have to be open to receiving a new place to shoot at a moment's notice. Whether on my way to a specific destination, or if I am in fact out exploring with the intention of finding something new. This results in quite a few sudden stops, turning around on a dime, or looking for the signs of something promising such as an overgrown drive or unexplainable footpath. I have a kit of tools beyond my camera for these scenarios, my camera kept securely around my neck or in close grabbing distance on the passenger seat. This "kit" often includes a grasshook (or two if I have a companion with me) for clearing debris and underbrush, a construction vest in the backseat for visibility and providing a more professional look when necessary (not to be underestimated), my tripod for shooting in low light or with sensitive film (often forgotten in the hunt and ran back towards in chagrin), a headlamp for low-light exploration, and a notebook and pen for making note of new locations and any needed reminders about when to return for the best lighting or things to be on the lookout for (such as dangerous wildlife).

The necessity of always carrying a camera can't be stressed enough. Each extended car trip provides the ability to spot out those places embedded in the side of the road, a constant temptation against punctuality. A lack of reliance on a GPS provides confidence in those sprawling areas without service and a higher likelihood of retracing your steps. Each return trip comes complete with mental markings of buildings and places of interest on the way.

Forgotten sheds, houses, and businesses that just couldn't make the cut are now seen with vines crawling deep inside of them, doors open like a gaping maw. At times they are half eaten away, obscured by the new growth reclaiming space and working to erase the evidence. While these structures are commonly left quietly to be taken back into the earth, perhaps only a single dilapidated sign entreating "no trespassing," others still hang in limbo with signs proclaiming proudly that they are for sale—seemingly unaware of the overgrown trees, crawling vines, and hungry kudzu quickly encroaching.

Kudzu, for those unfamiliar, is an invasive plant species found in the Southeastern United States. Native to China, Taiwan, Japan, and India, the vine was initially introduced as an ornamental vine as well as a possible solution to soil erosion and nitrogen loss.[1] Over time it became clear that the vine, with no natural predators, was quickly overtaking land and was extremely difficult to remove once established. Some of this difficulty for removal is attributed to its long roots, reaching depths of 3 to 16 feet, as well as its quick growth.[2] Reports indicate that these vines can grow as much as a foot a day, and up to 60 feet within a season.[3] With this growth rate, it is easy to see how these vines quickly overtake abandoned houses, sheds, and farms, and even open fields, to choke out the other plant life. It is not unusual for a home, left unattended, to become covered or near unrecognizable due to kudzu in a matter of months—if close enough to an established plant.

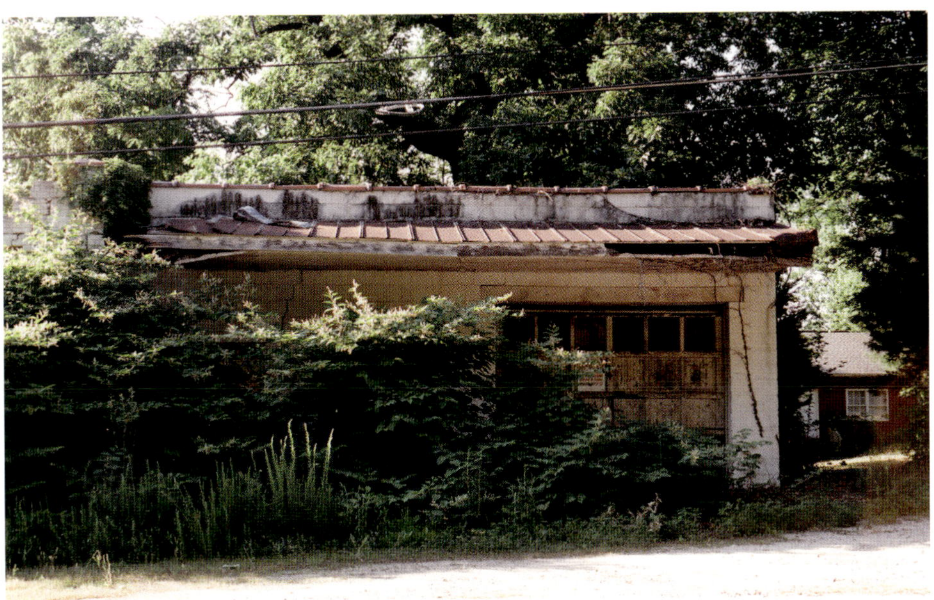

A crumbling garage, shrouded in green, can be seen from the road.

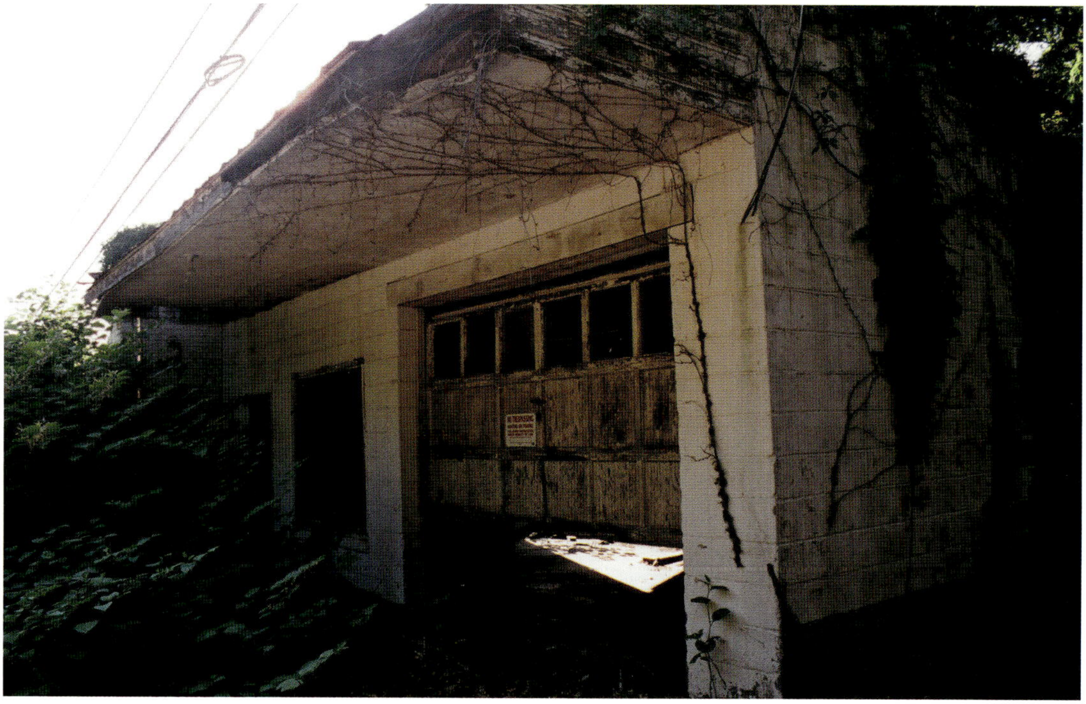

An old "no trespassing" sign adorns the front and opened garage door where light can be seen coming in from the back of the building. Vines wrap entirely around the building, leaving no spot untouched.

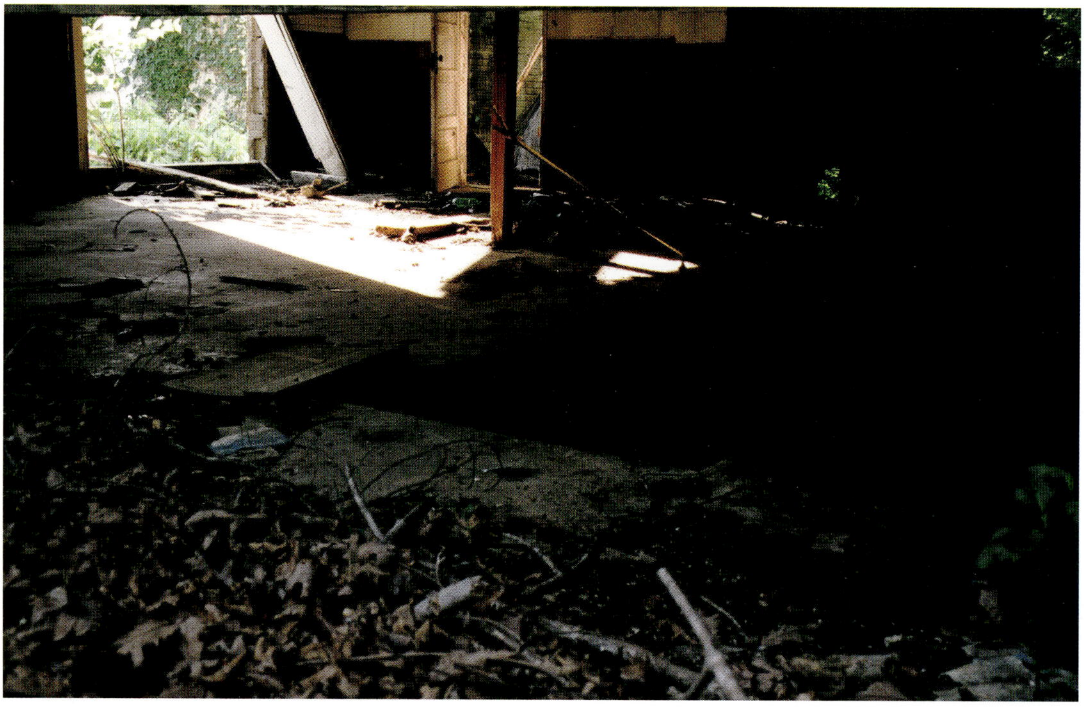

Within the garage, debris litters the ground, a back window is completely missing, and the back entrance is left open. There is evidence of people, animals, and plants all traveling through here.

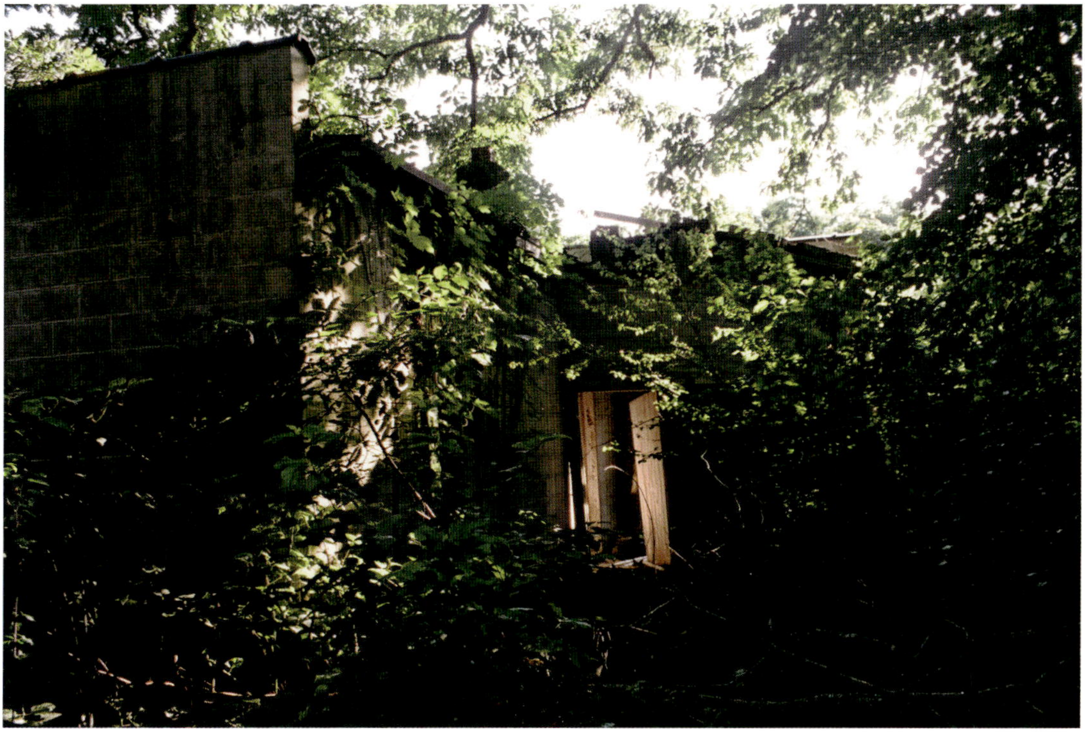

The back entrance to the garage shines with light, beckoning.

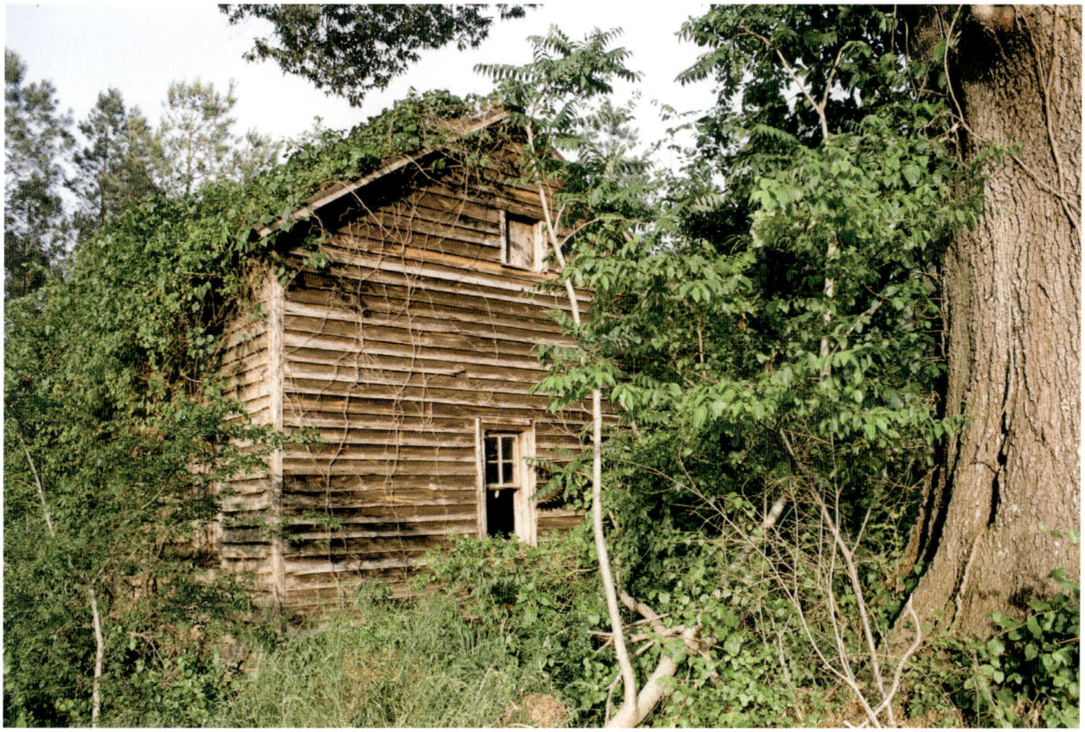

Kudzu crawls over and around this house, found down a dirt road.

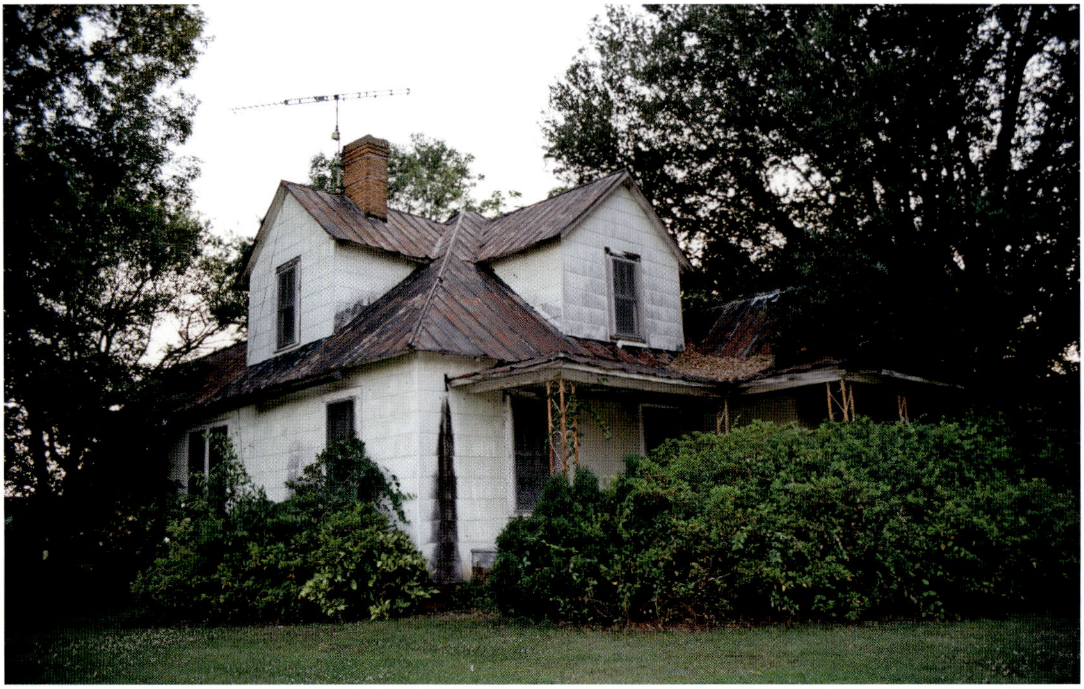

Another house for sale, this one comes with a barn. The surrounding bushes and trees are overgrown and obscure the front porch and roof. Leaves have gathered in the eaves.

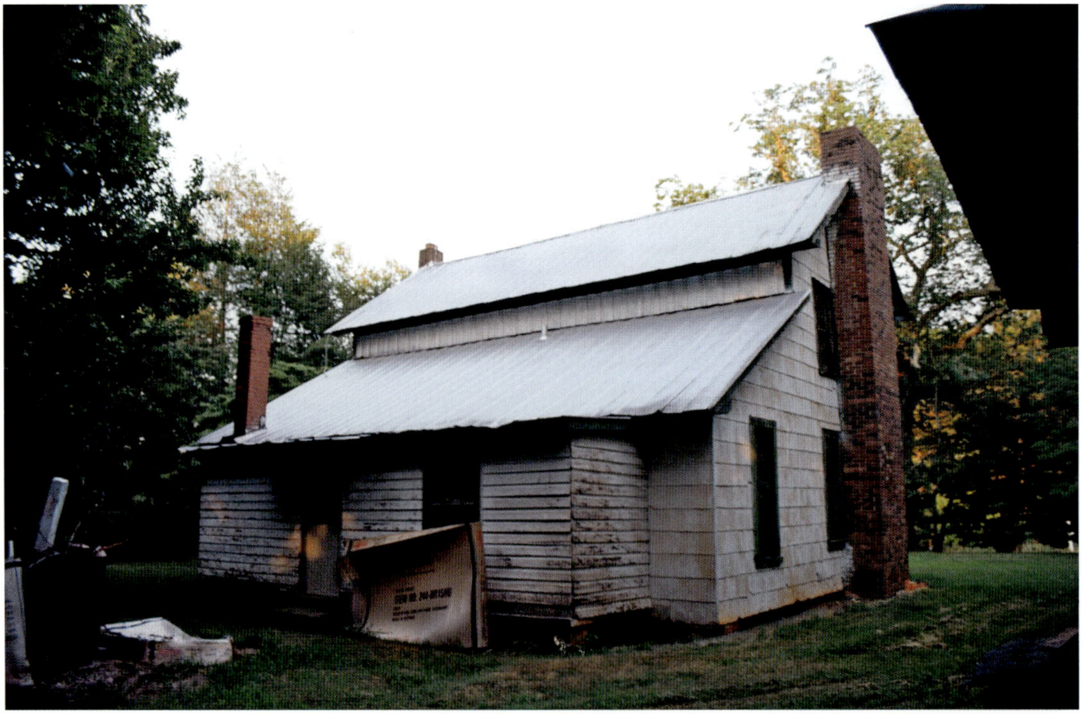

The back of the home has several piles of trash, including a few very large cardboard boxes to offset the peeling paint.

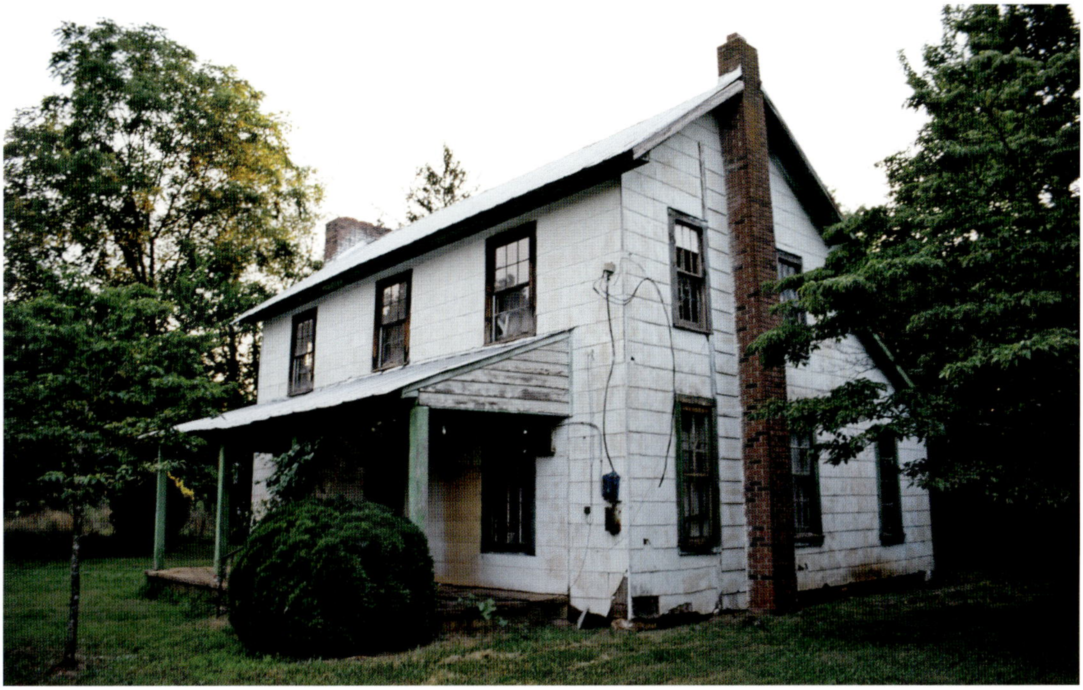

This house has a "for sale" sign and showcases stripped electrical wire and missing foundation, and some windows are cracked or missing.

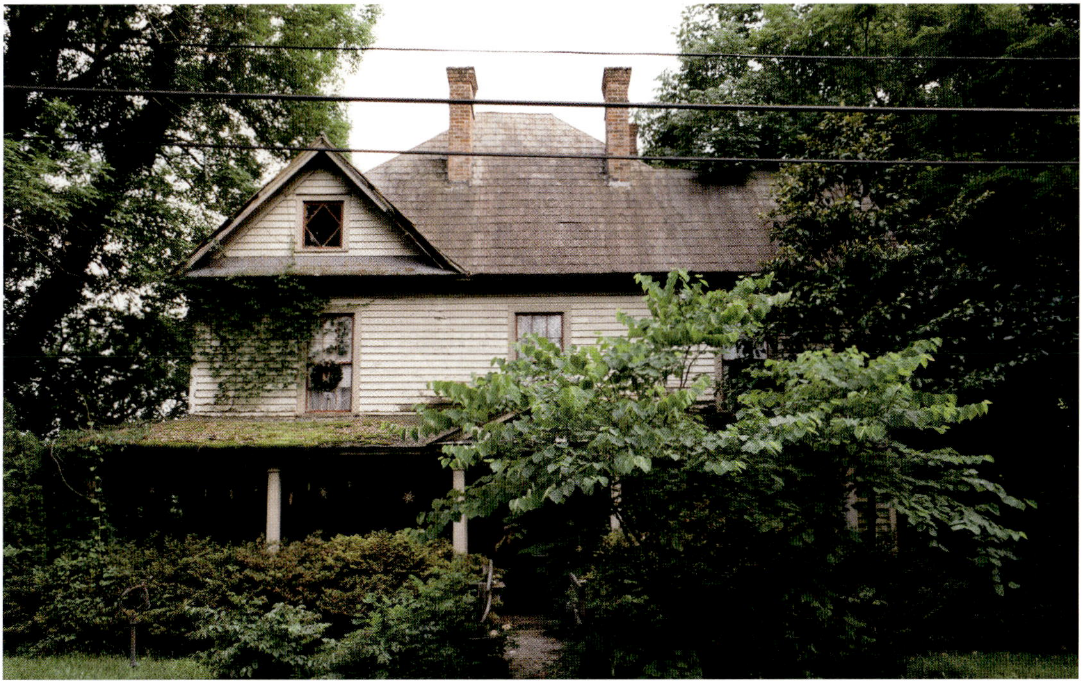

A house, complete with Christmas decorations, overgrown shrubs, lawn, and trees. From the left side of the house, vines can be seen growing into the siding, and moss is overtaking the front porch. This house was found hidden a neighborhood of upkept houses.

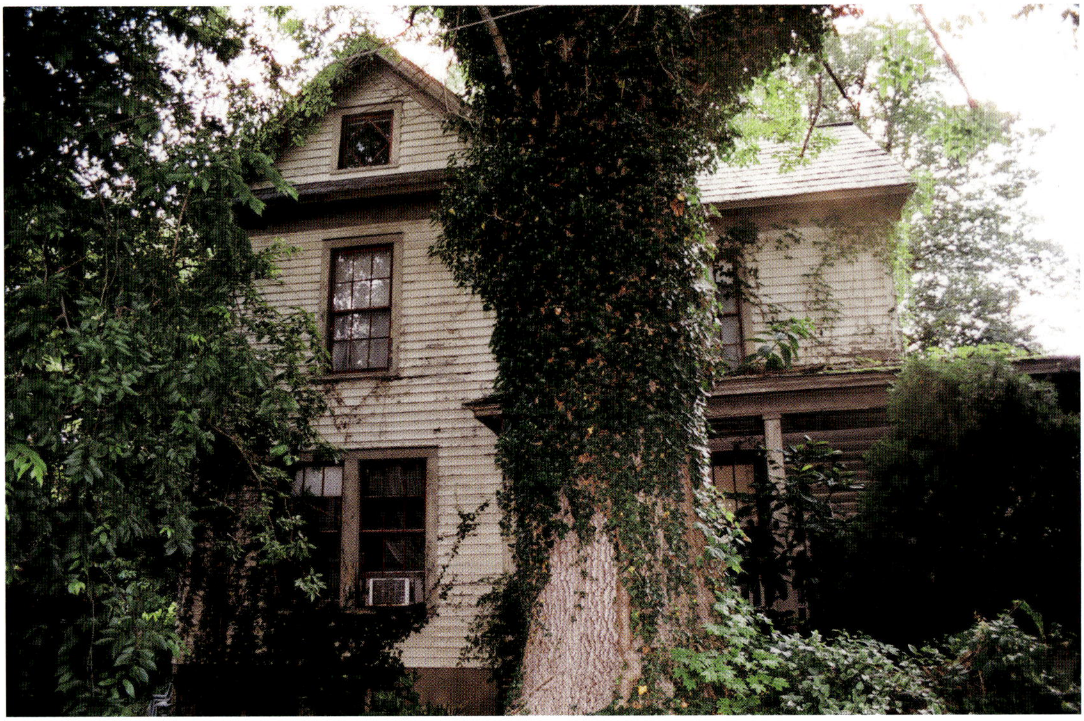

The Christmas house in side profile, with a variety of vines crawling over the outside.

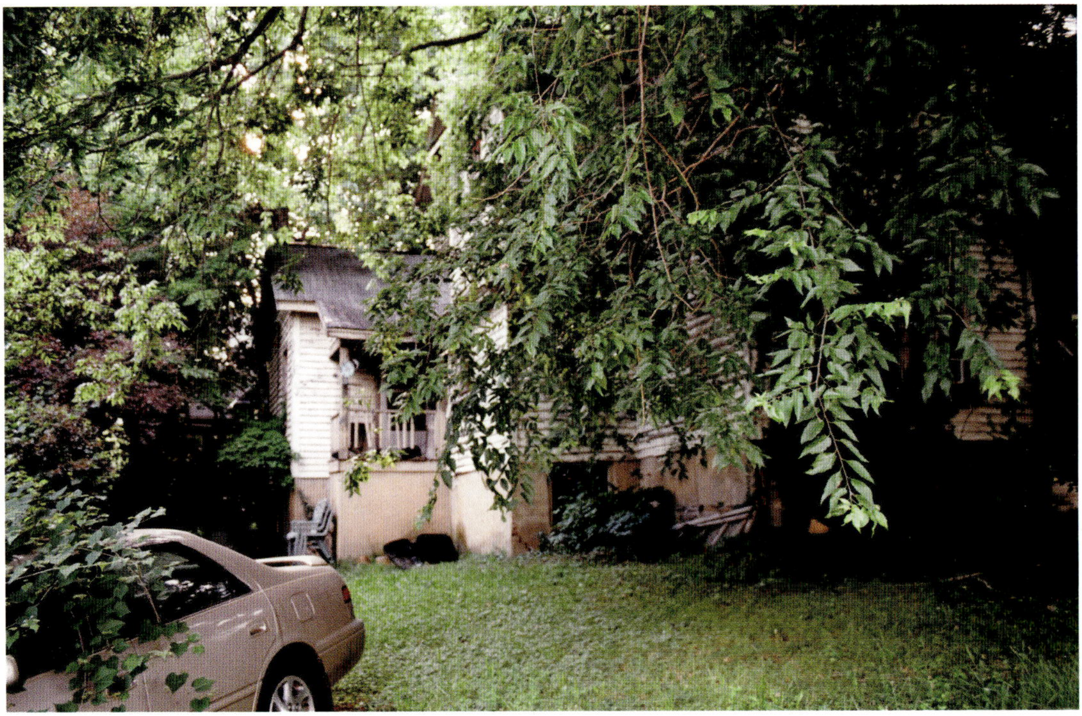

The back of the house includes an abandoned car with rotten wheels, obscured by vines covering the hood and front windows. Neighboring this car in the back lawn are chairs, window replacements, and broken trash cans.

While some structures are obscured partially or entirely by dense new growth, others still aren't quite so bad off and are easy to imagine bustling and full of life. Allowing yourself to see in double, you can place a new coat of paint on the wood, patch the roof, repair a window or two. Looking at the furniture and the design of the structure you can blinker back to a time when everything was shiny and new or in the first steps of creation. Abandoned factories are far from uncommon, those places of work with the doors left open as if they are waiting for the next shift of workers to arrive and begin their day. Some buildings remain that were once part of a strip. A lone shop is left standing in a sea of concrete and broken brick, while the separately painted sides are left open like a scar. You can see clearly that there used to be another room here, and a neighboring store there. In certain places soot marks stand out to mark long demolished chimneys. In old restaurants, there is often a duality of color. At first notice you see only the faded outside, and once closer, you can spot the bright, once matching color inside.

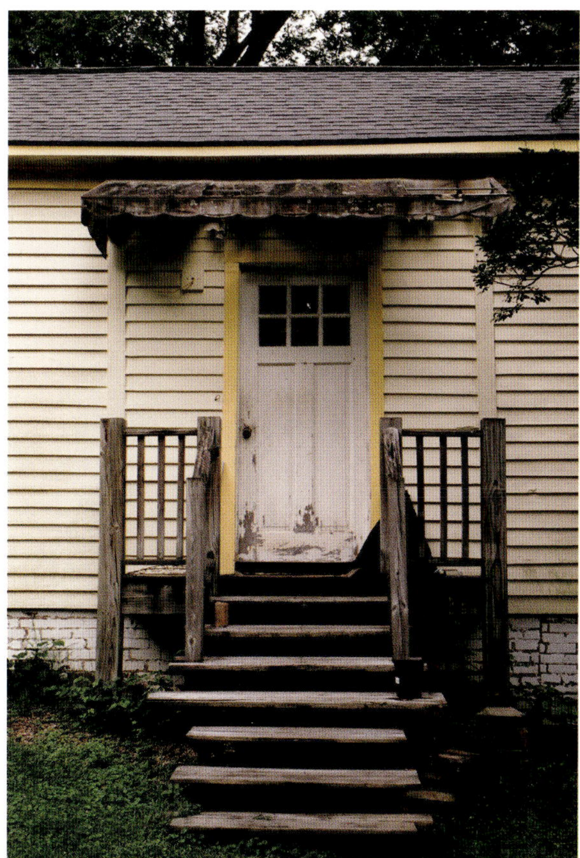

This home features a rotten awning and soft stairs. The porch light has been removed, and the wire hangs exposed.

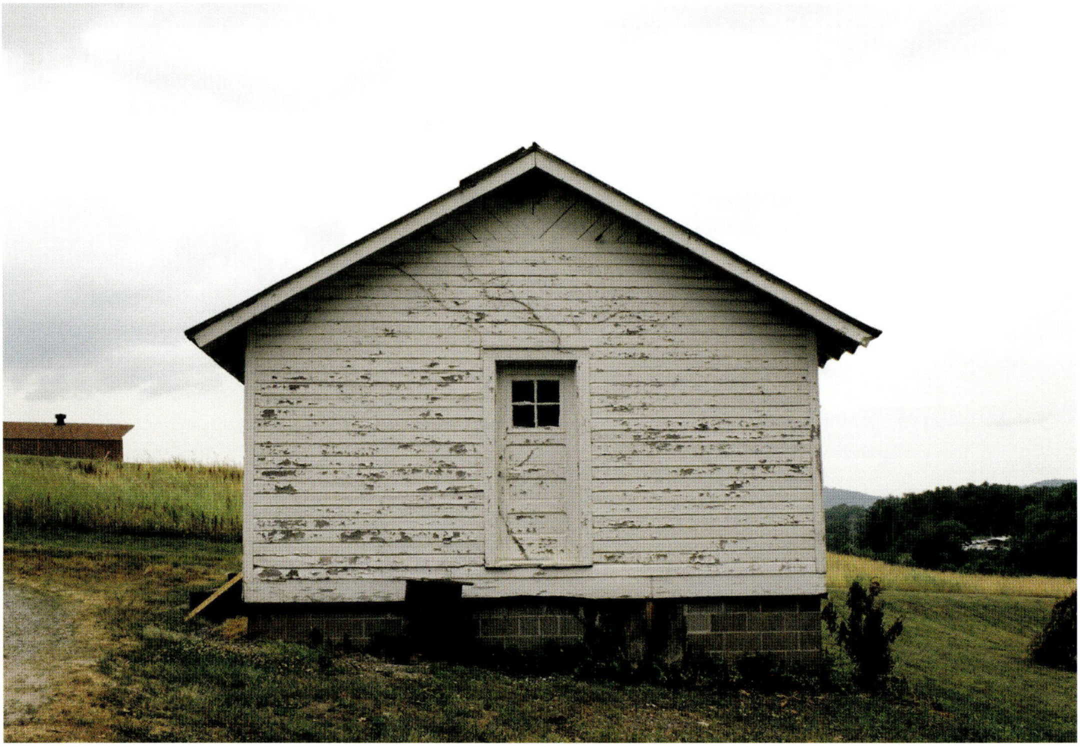

A storage shed with peeling paint and evidence of vines sits in front of a field.

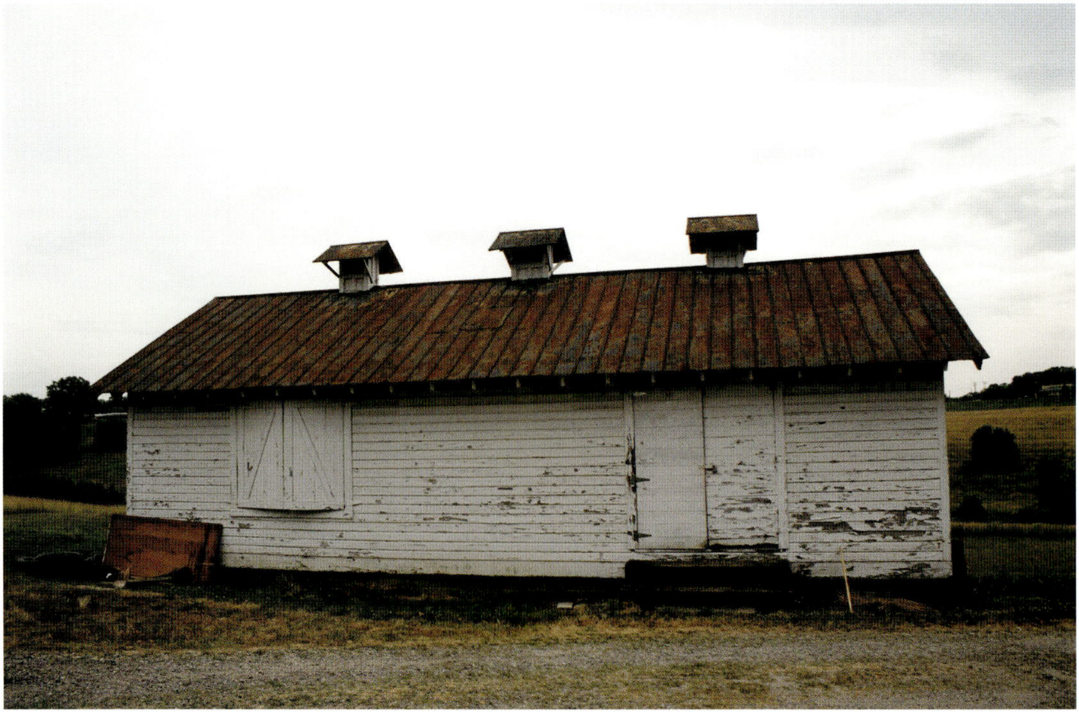

A profile of the storage shed, with its rusted tin roof and buckled shutters.

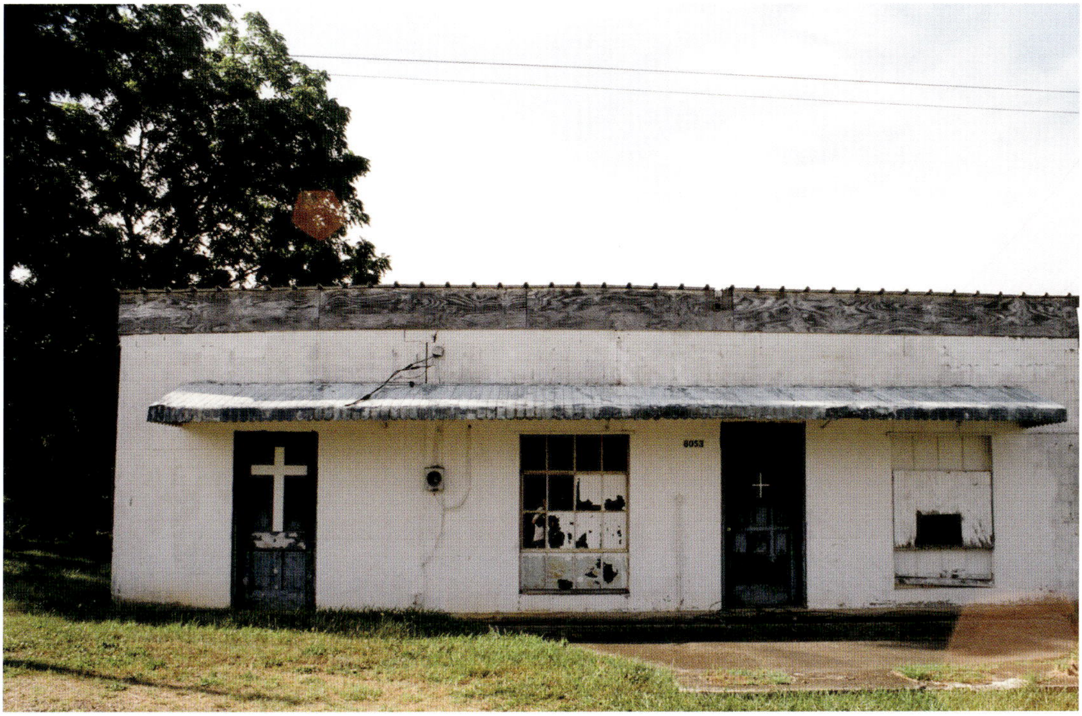

No signs remain to explain what specific denomination of Christianity this building belonged to. Parts of its windows are obscured while others are reflective.

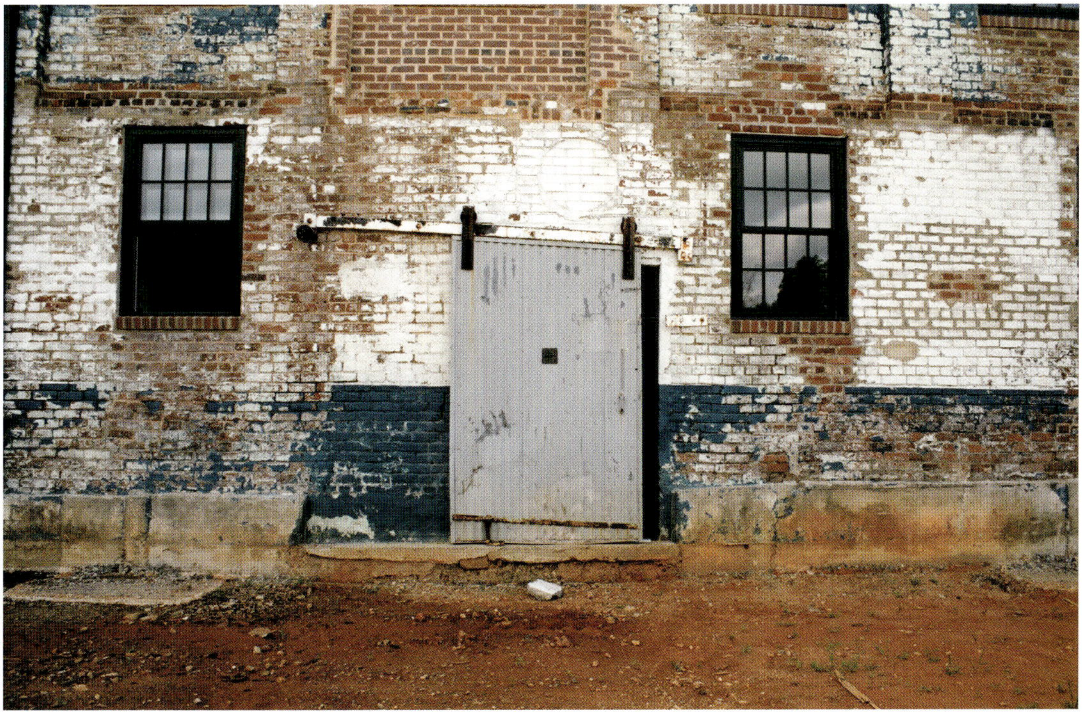

This factory sits in the middle of a town, with an open left window and gaping entrance.

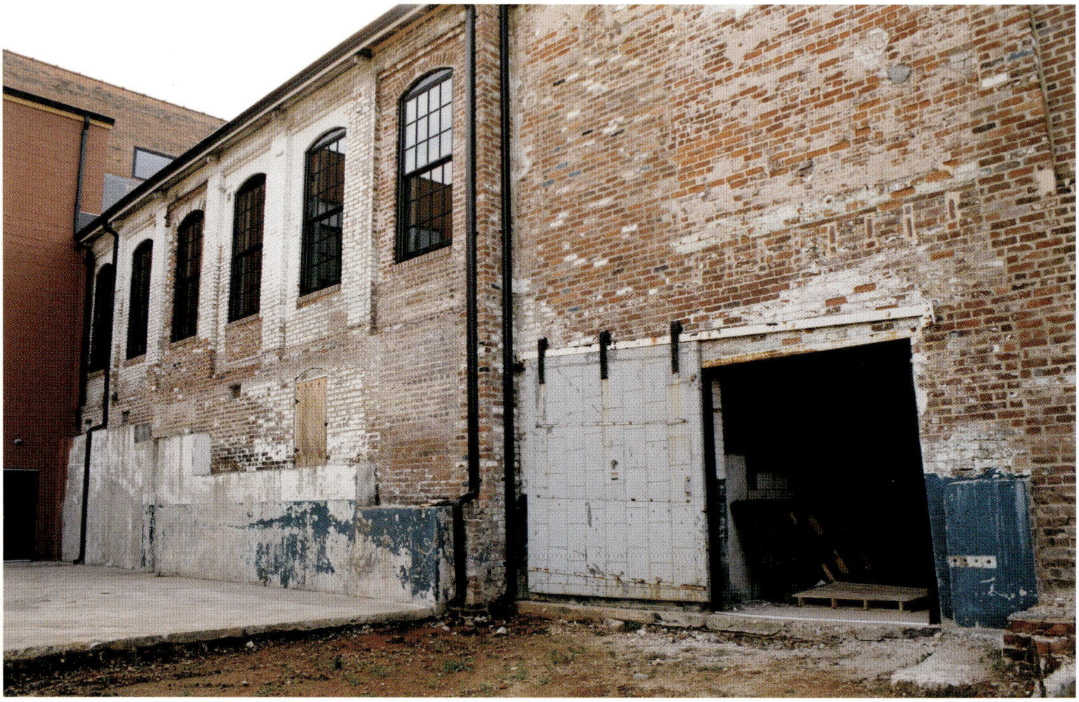

This second entrance to the factory is open and wooden crates lay inside. A boarded-up door can be seen, as well as the neighbor of the abandoned factory, a still functioning building.

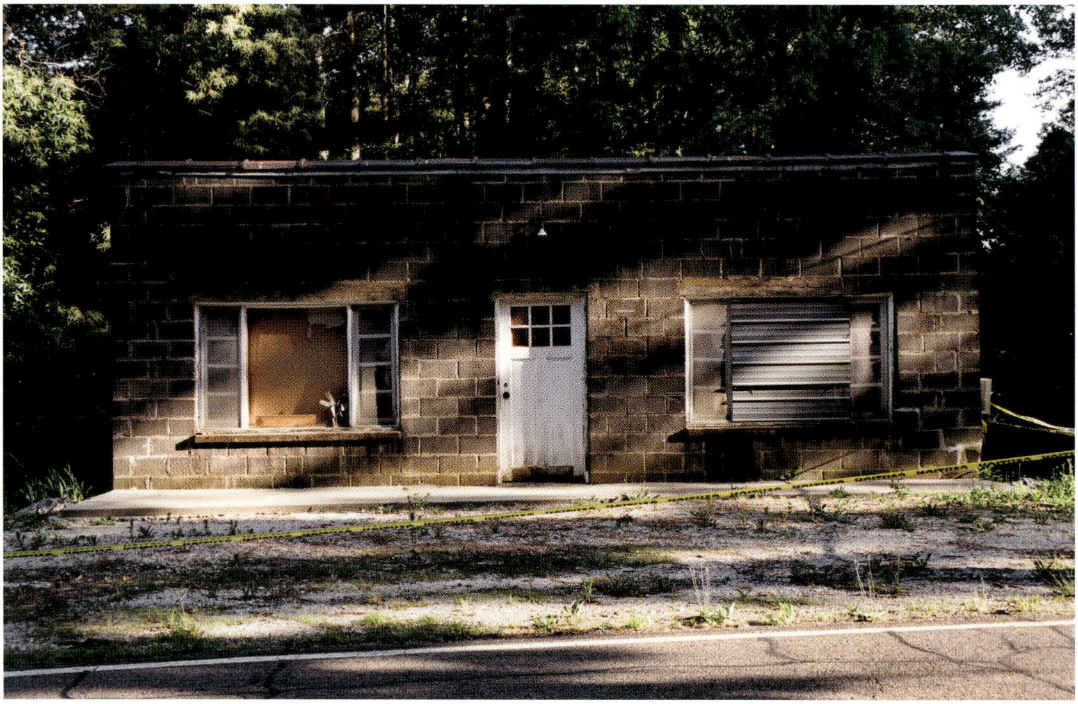

Previously an office building, this rectangular brick building is surrounded by caution tape. The backside of the building is crumbling and unstable.

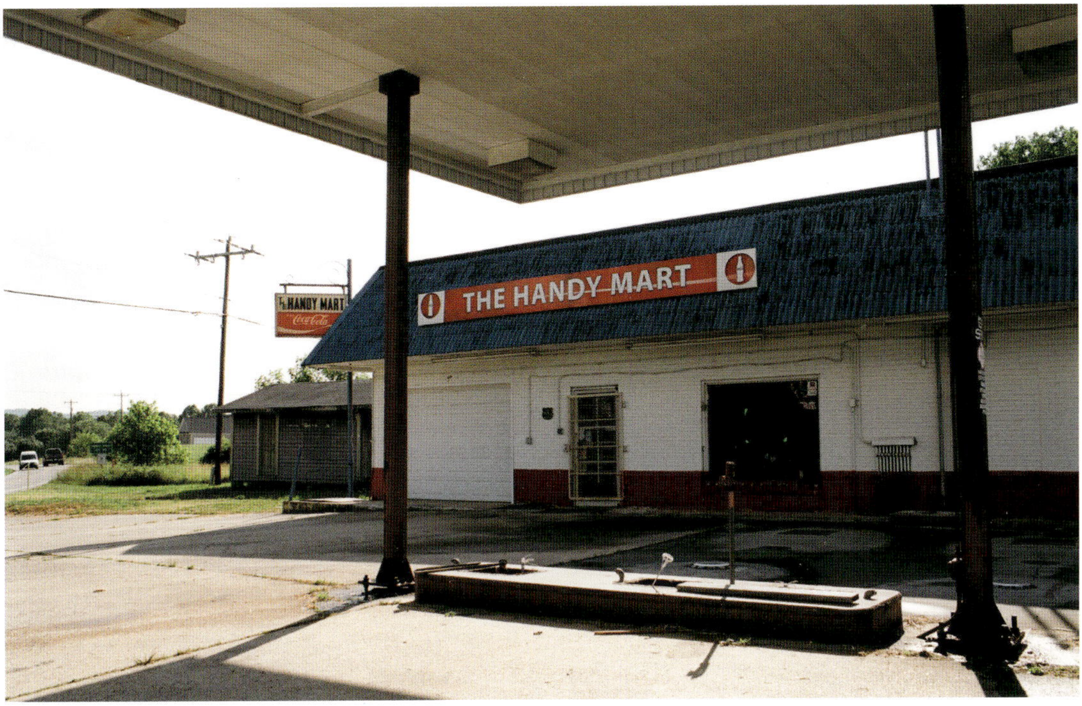

The Handy Mart changed through many hands but eventually was left empty. The gas pumps have been torn away, and remnants of window signs can be seen.

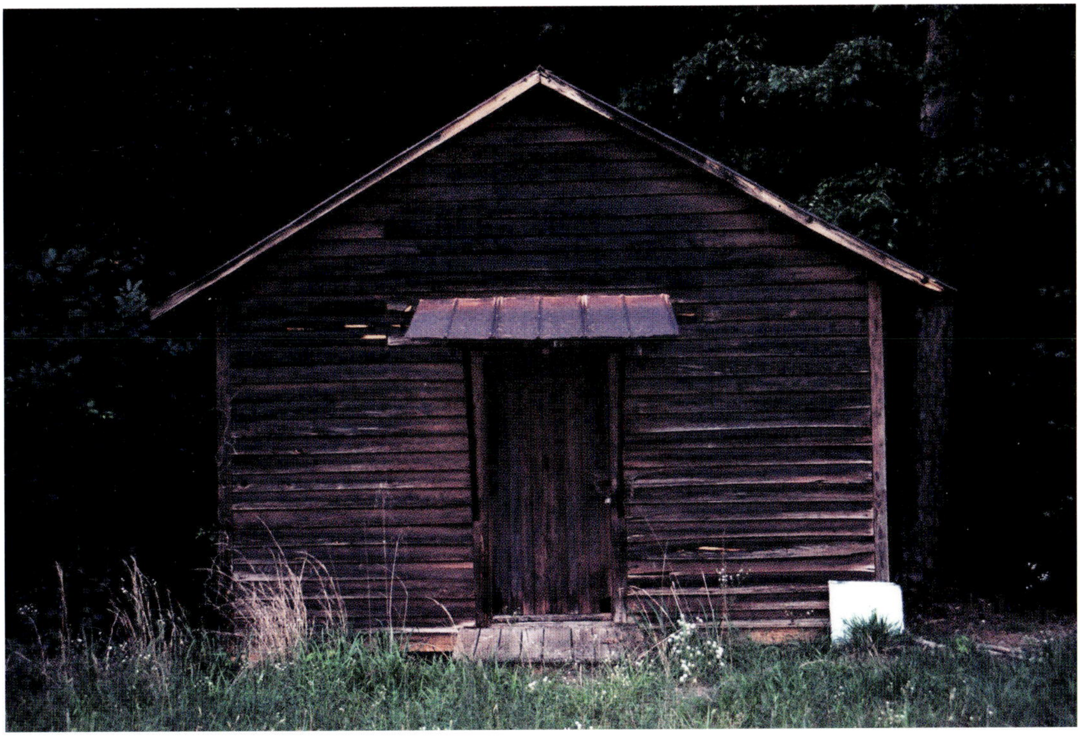

An unassuming shed found off the road with no surrounding houses.

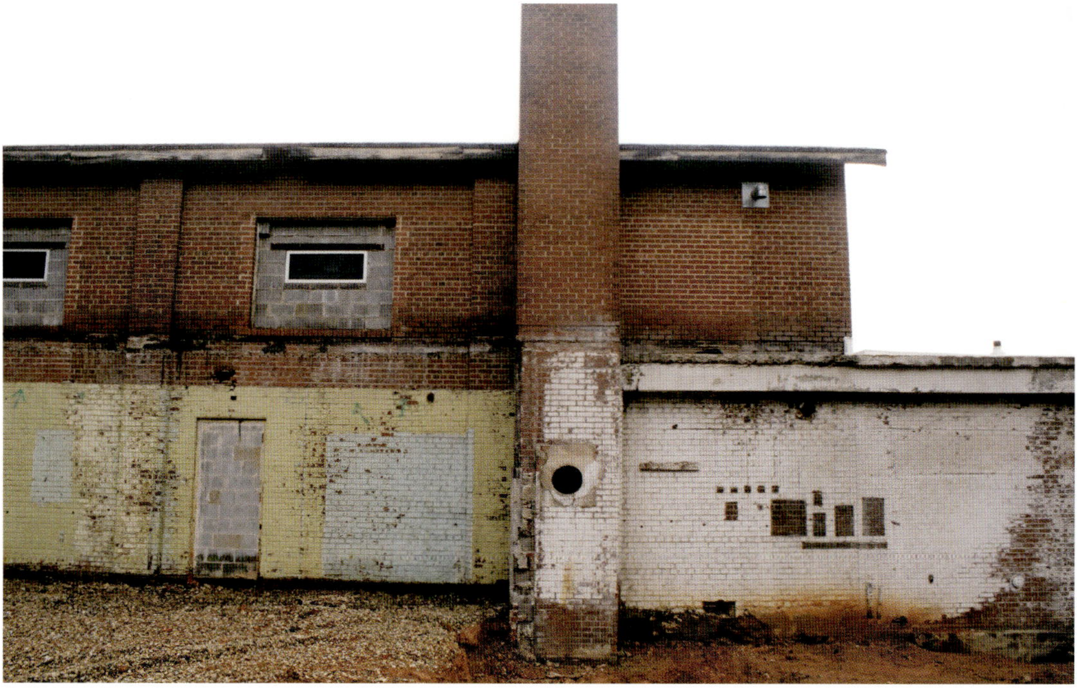

A doorway has been sealed at this part of a defunct high school, where some of the building has been torn away and previous internal paint choices can be seen.

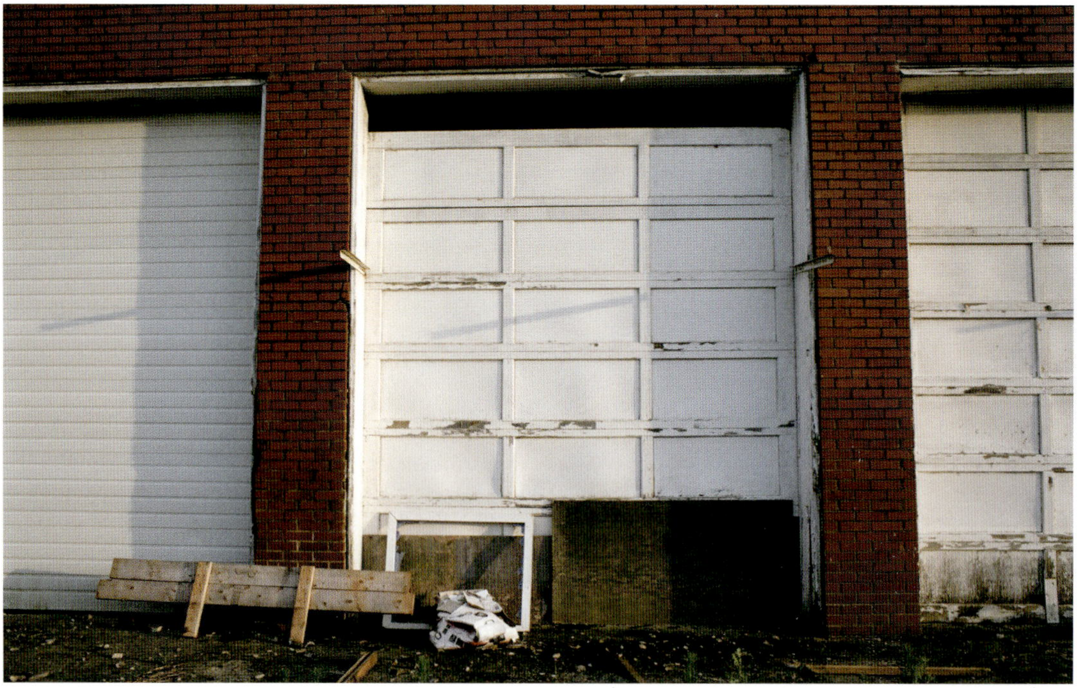

The door of this abandoned car garage is broken and remains open at the top. Pieces of wood, windows, and a cardboard box lay in front of the garage door. Some pieces of plywood have been nailed to the door to cover what holes were at the bottom.

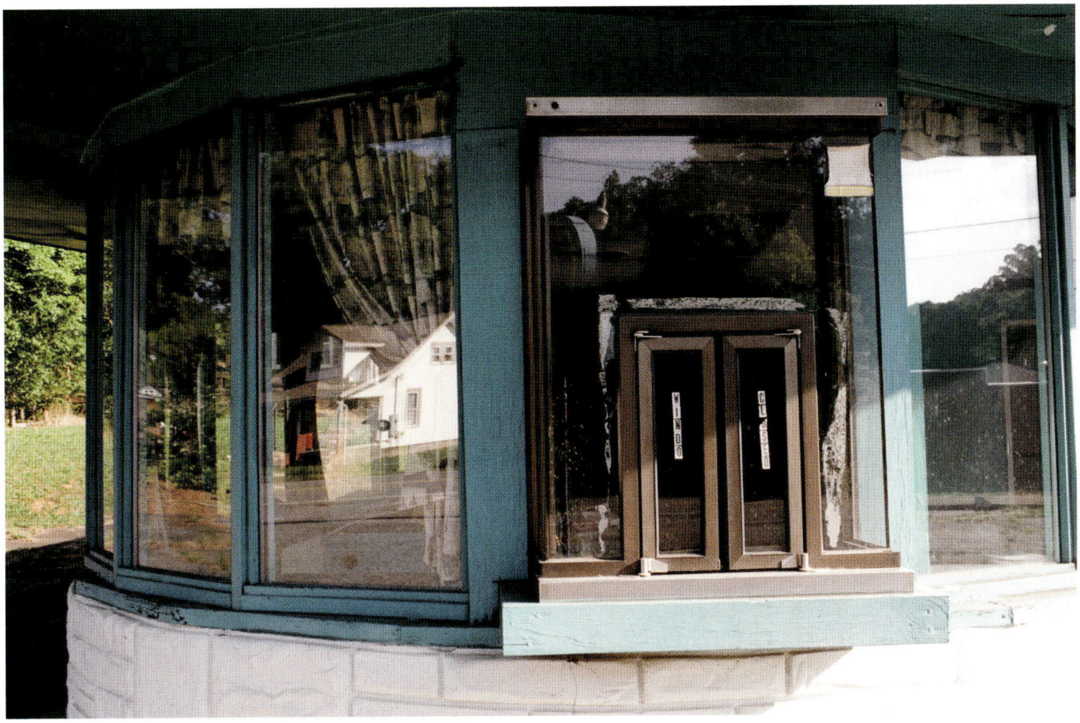

“Windo Closed” calls a bright blue facade on an abandoned modern restaurant design.

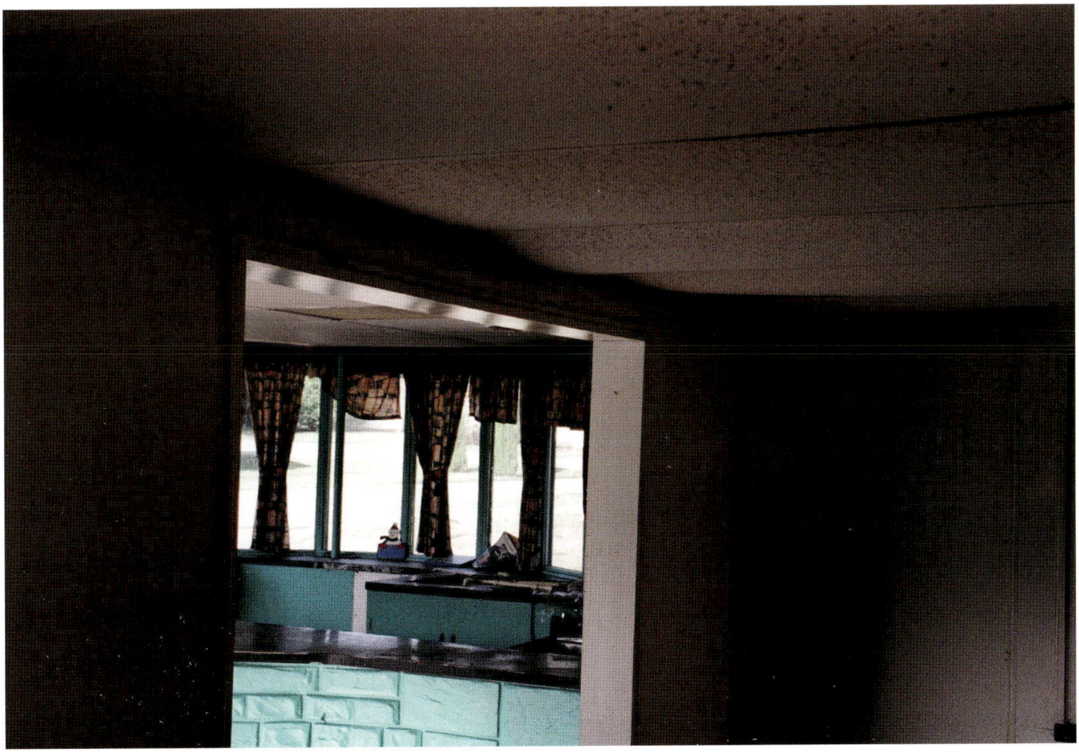

The inside of the restaurant shows long forgotten Christmas decorations and moldy, drooping ceiling tiles.

This type of thinking can be deceptive in a lot of buildings. Assuming the best, you may get closer or circle around and notice only one side is structurally solid, like you've stepped onto a movie set and forgotten only the facade was built to stand. Even more dangerous are the buildings that are too tempting to avoid entering. Rotten stairs and floorboards are generally the rule, not the exception. Edging around the more solid outer limits of a room, testing and prodding the floor, and being ready to flee or face the worst isn't unusual. Another standard in my shooting set is a first aid kit, often used and components replaced time and again.

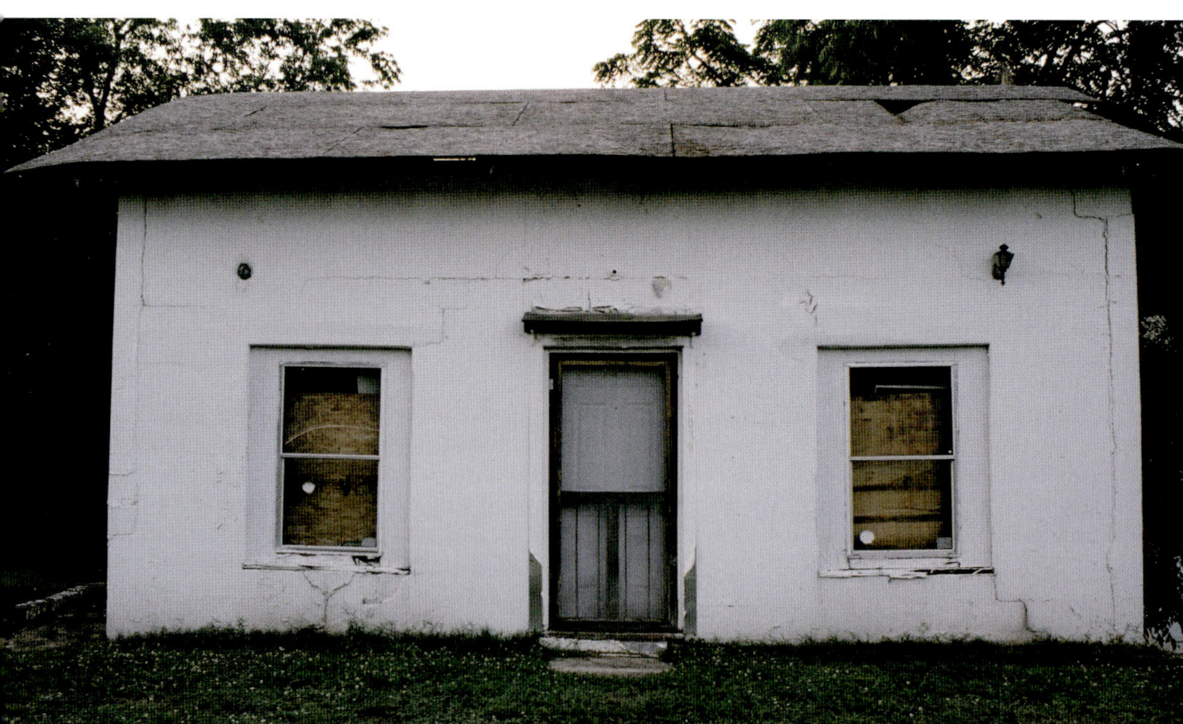

The front view of a shed or possible house addition found directly off the road.

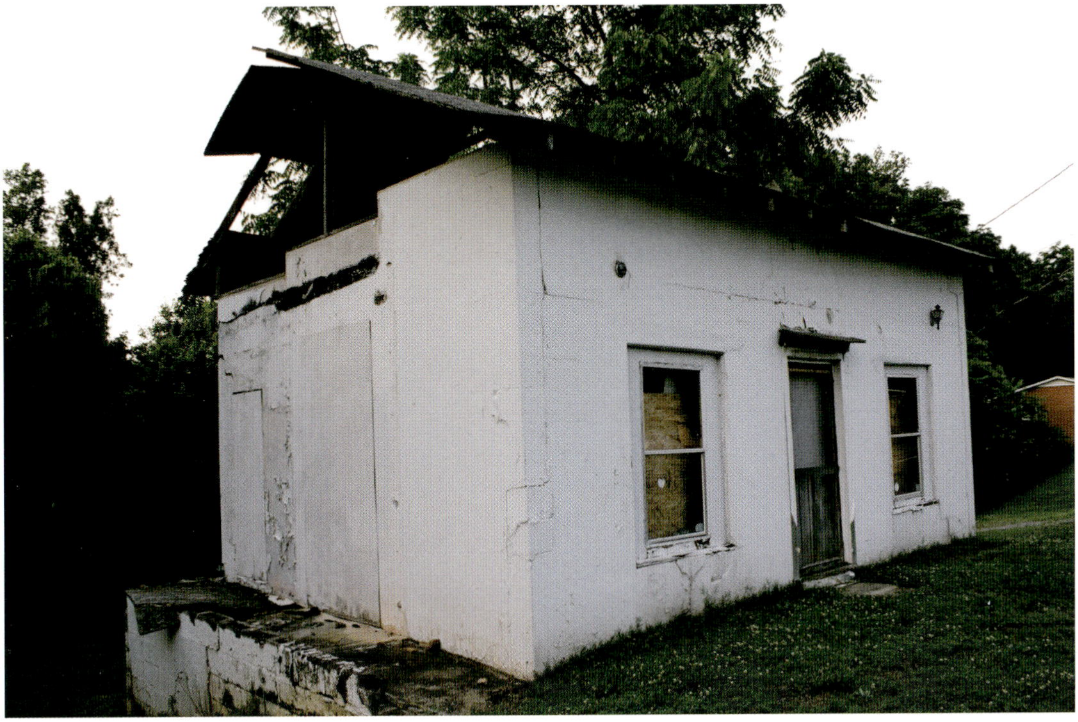

The shed viewed from the left, where it is missing sections of roof.

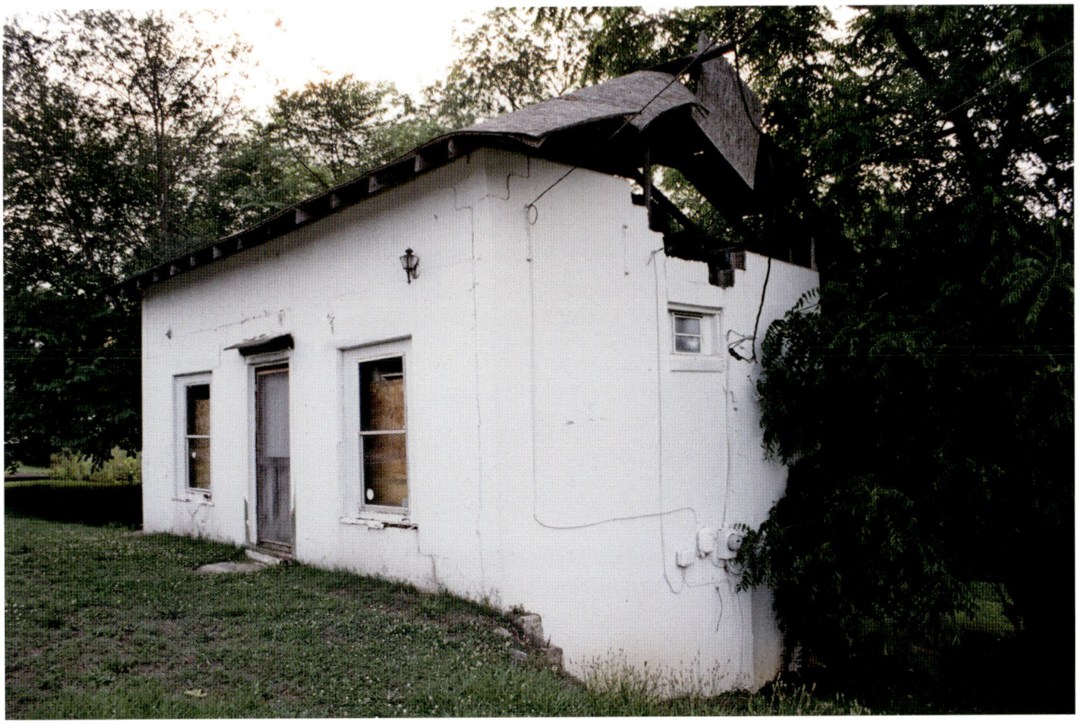

The same shed as seen from the right, where now missing components of the brick wall as well as roof are seen with plywood replacements falling.

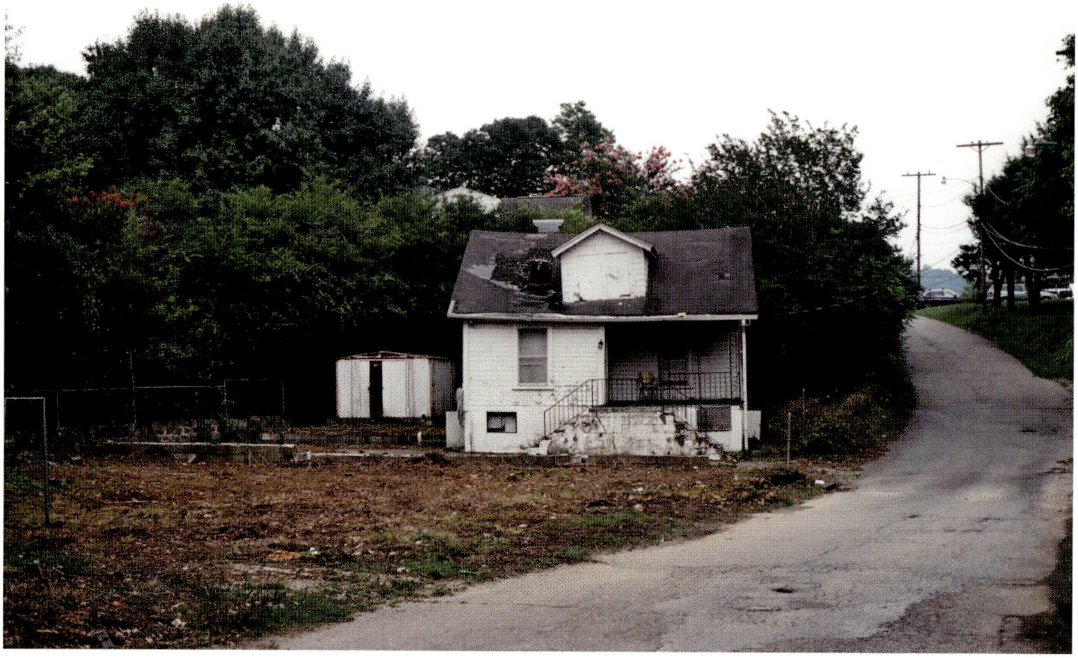

An abandoned house found near the back of a neighborhood side street, its roof partially collapsed.

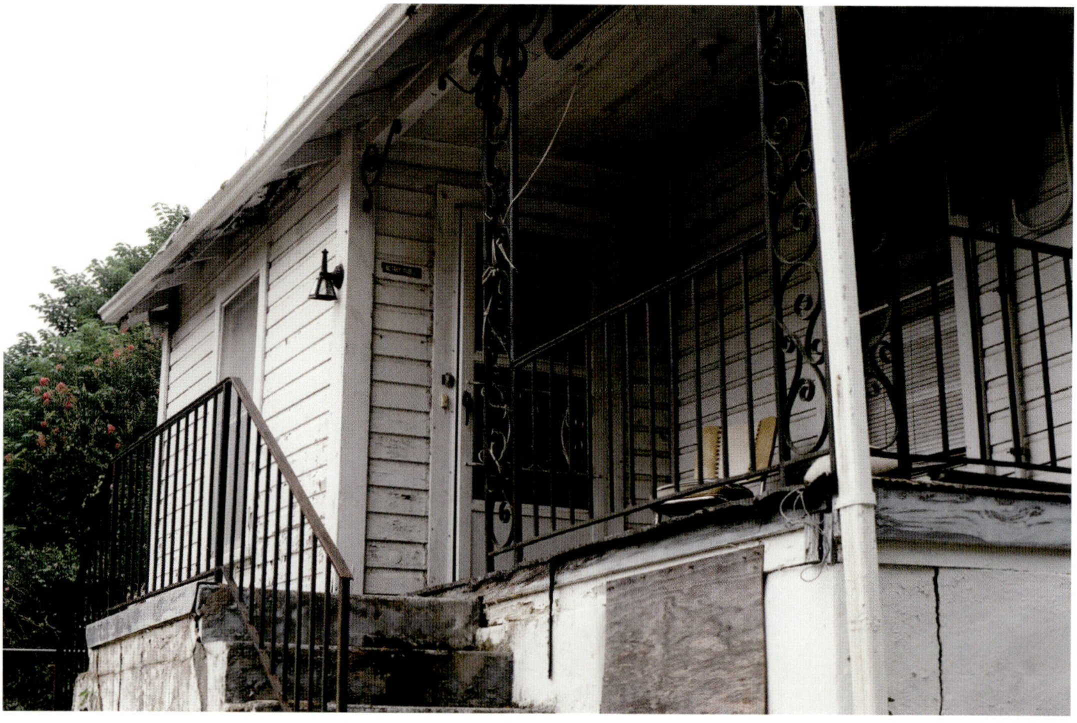

A close up of the house reveals that older furniture is left on the porch, untouched. A sign hangs by the door reading, "Notary Public."

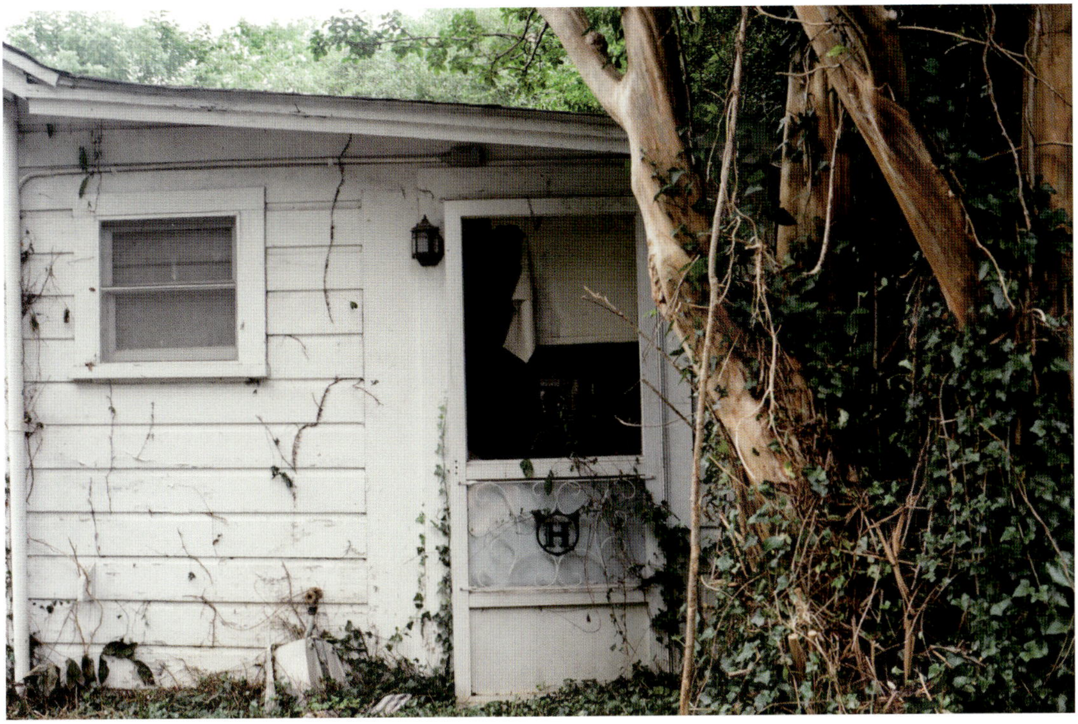

The door is cracked open, the curtain is torn, and vines are growing over the side of the building.

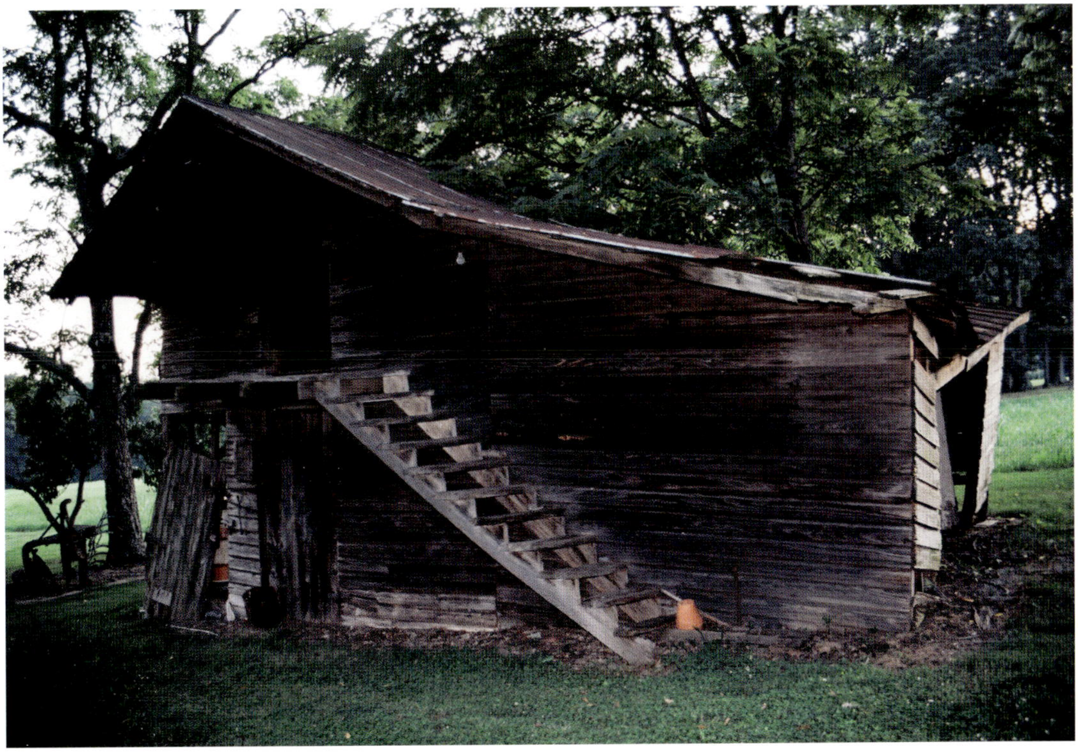

This barn is included in the sale of the house. Its more stable wall faces the road.

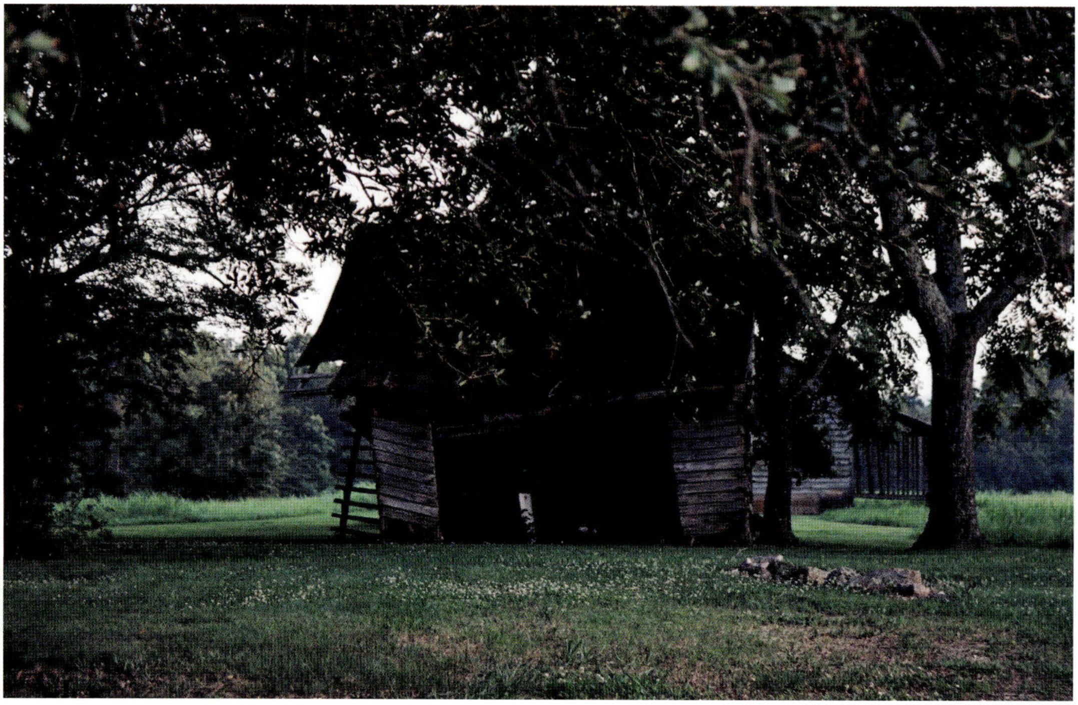

Another view of the barn shows clearly that it is mid-collapse. From this angle the stairs are shown as their true off-center.

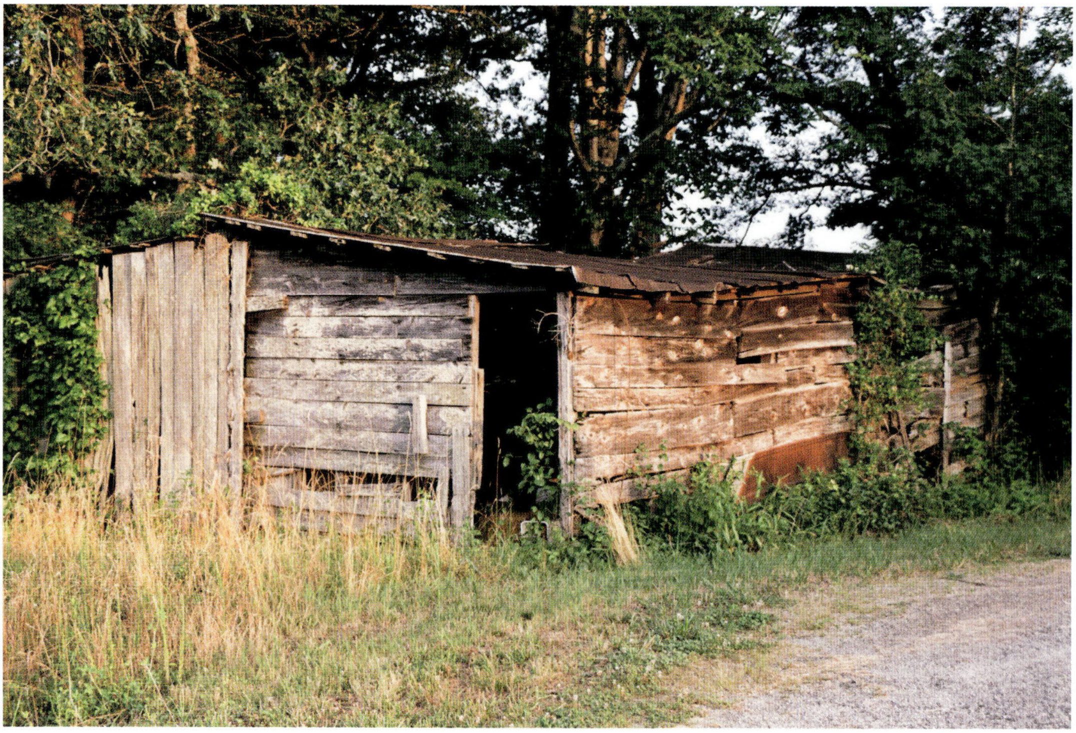

A new view of the shed, with less visible missing boards, making it difficult to discern how fitful the structure is.

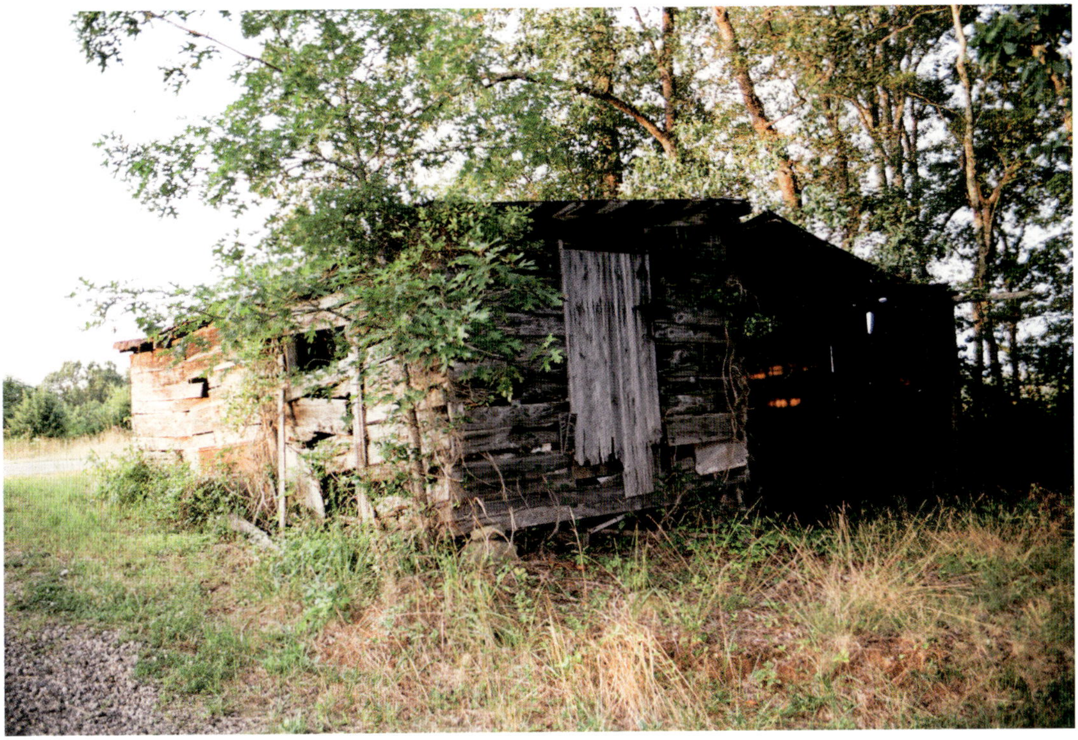

A shed spotted off the side of the road, missing boards and sagging in fits and starts.

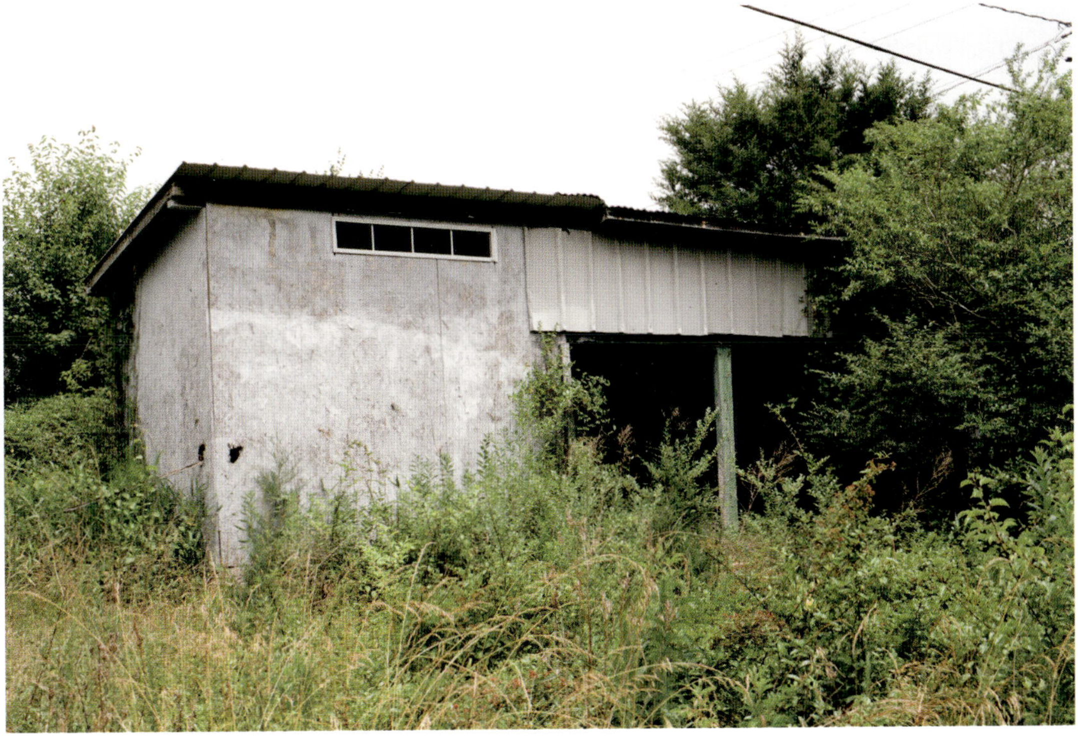

Another hand-built shed with multiple mediums such as tin siding, plywood, and a green wooden pillar.

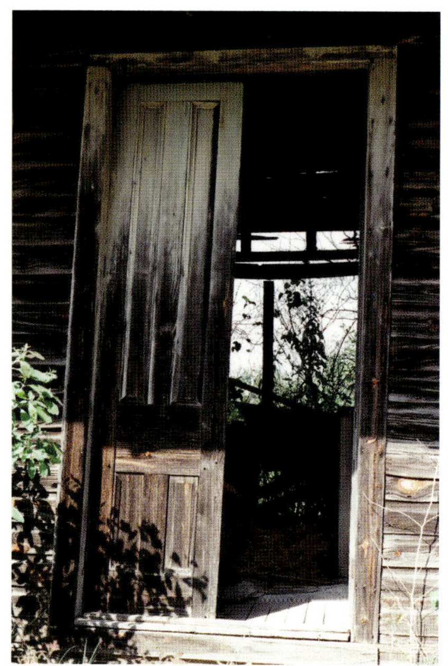

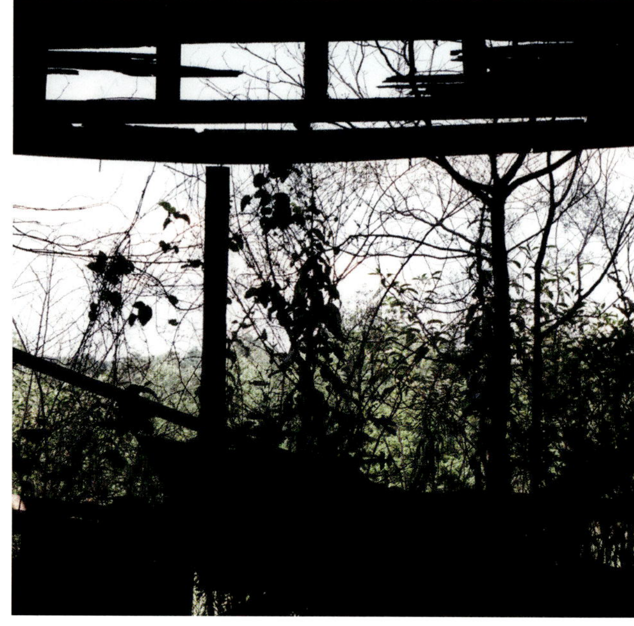

Above left: An uneven structure, with what appears to be a leaning doorway but straight wooden planks at the back.

Above right: The back wall remains standing with few supporting beams. A viewer can easily see straight through to the field and trees beyond.

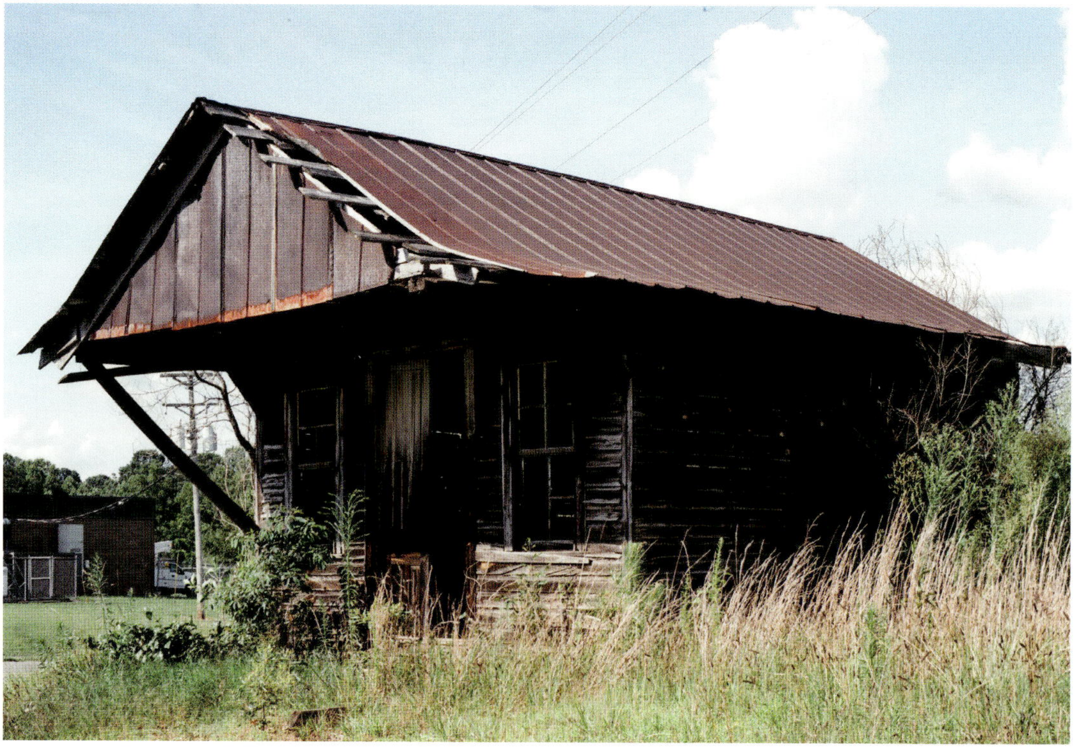

A right-side view of a roadside shed with no surrounding house in sight.

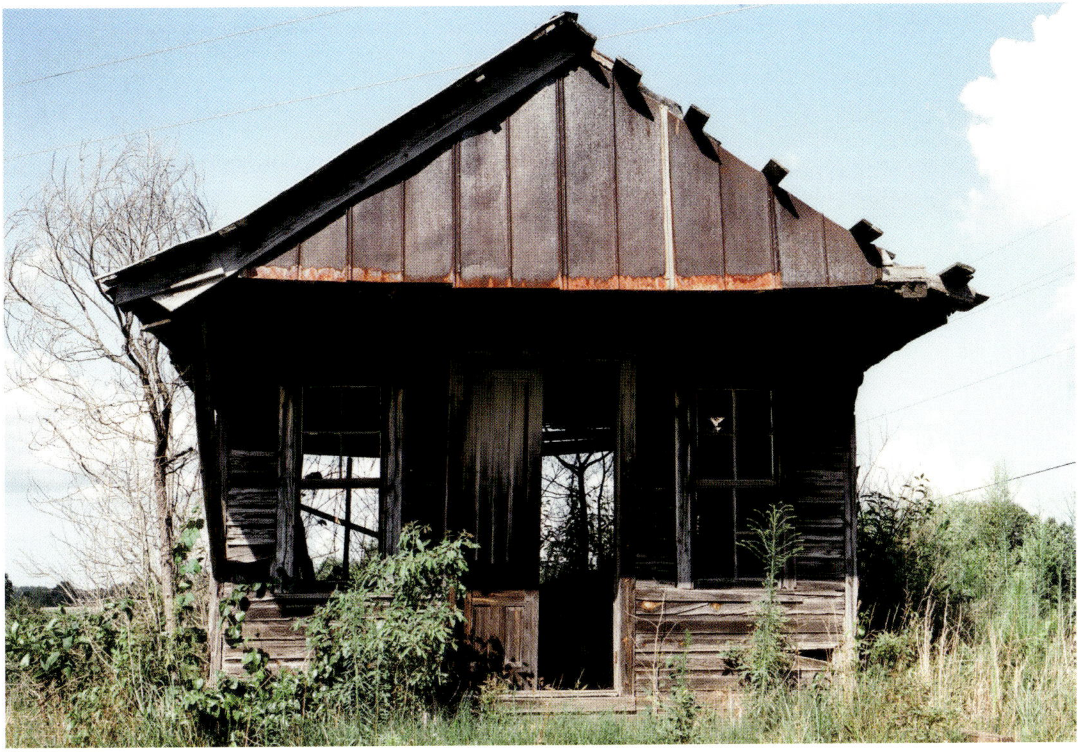

A straight-on view of the roadside shed, showing the missing back wall.

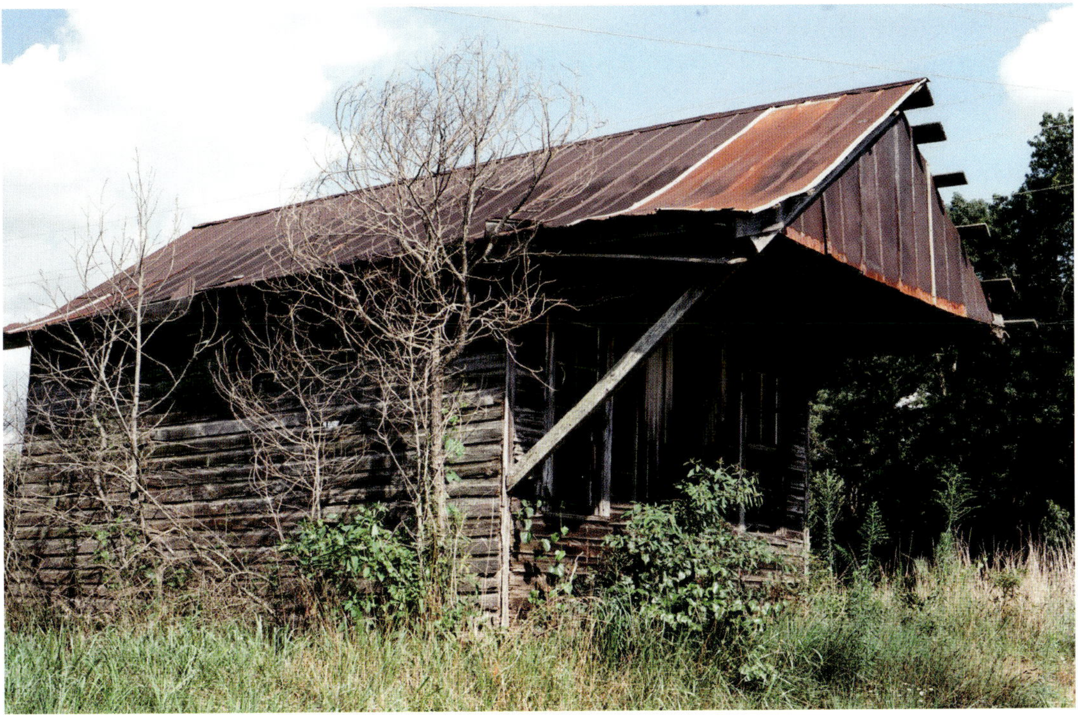

A view of the roadside shed from the left, once again obscuring that a wall is missing.

While not always for the faint of heart, internal spaces allow for a deeper view into the history and present of a structure. Current inhabitants beyond greenery leave their mark in nests, repurposed ceilings and holes in the wall, and any human inhabitants their notes and wrappers. Sometimes I will be tipped off to an interesting set of buildings that are being used for squatting or were used previously, still structurally sound enough to provide more coverage and comfort than a tent or lean-to. This can be off-putting for some, a human element of use beyond when the building was in its prime. These buildings are no longer made for specific consumption: they are open to all nature. A human in need and seeking shelter is no less deserving than the cardinal or the willow extending its branches. All these factors leave a trace of themselves and contribute to the truth of the place: to leave them out is to disrespect that story. Humans, like all other forms of life, leave an indelible mark, and there are many forms that mark can take.

In the end nature moves forward to consume all evidence, sometimes slow and other times swift. Western North Carolina is hospitable to kudzu, and it has no qualms taking advantage of new spaces and moving in to swallow them whole, unless there are other plants or animals capable of slowing its progress. In other areas grasses roam higher and higher to meet swaying tree branches and frame dilapidated wood and crumbling walls. After strong storms it isn't unusual to find sheds and houses buckled by fallen trees, cradling them in the middle of groaning wooden sides. Regardless of the type of gem found off the road, there remains always an element of mystery and beauty that I extend to you with these snapshots of time.

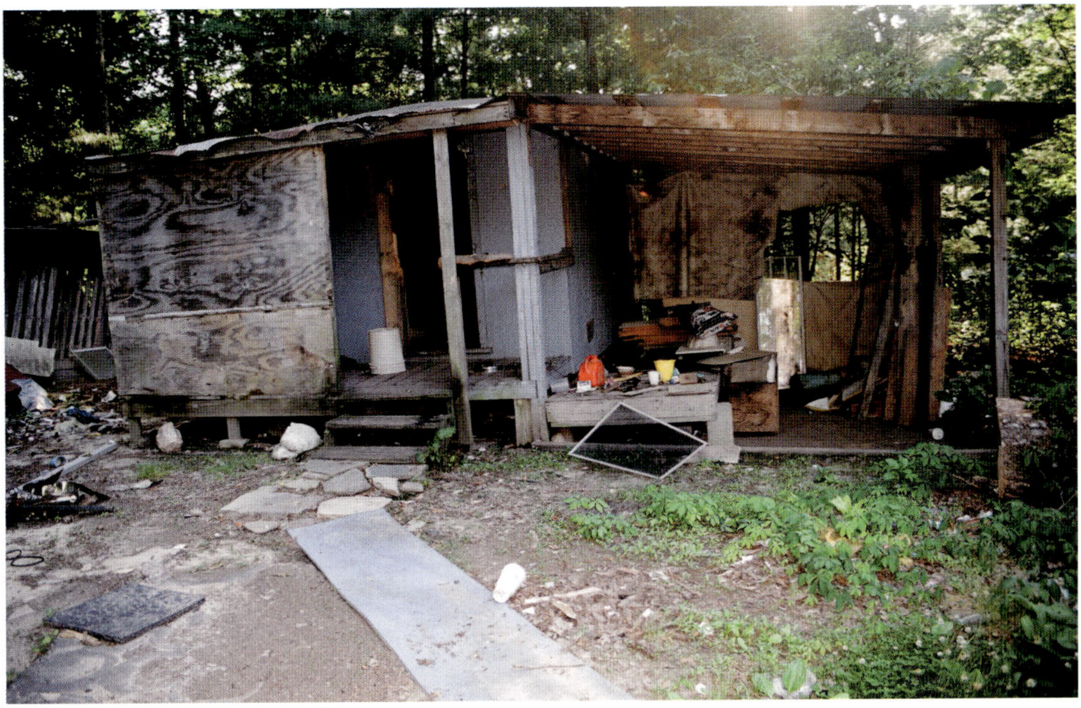

A dilapidated shed is surrounded by trash and forgotten parts to projects.

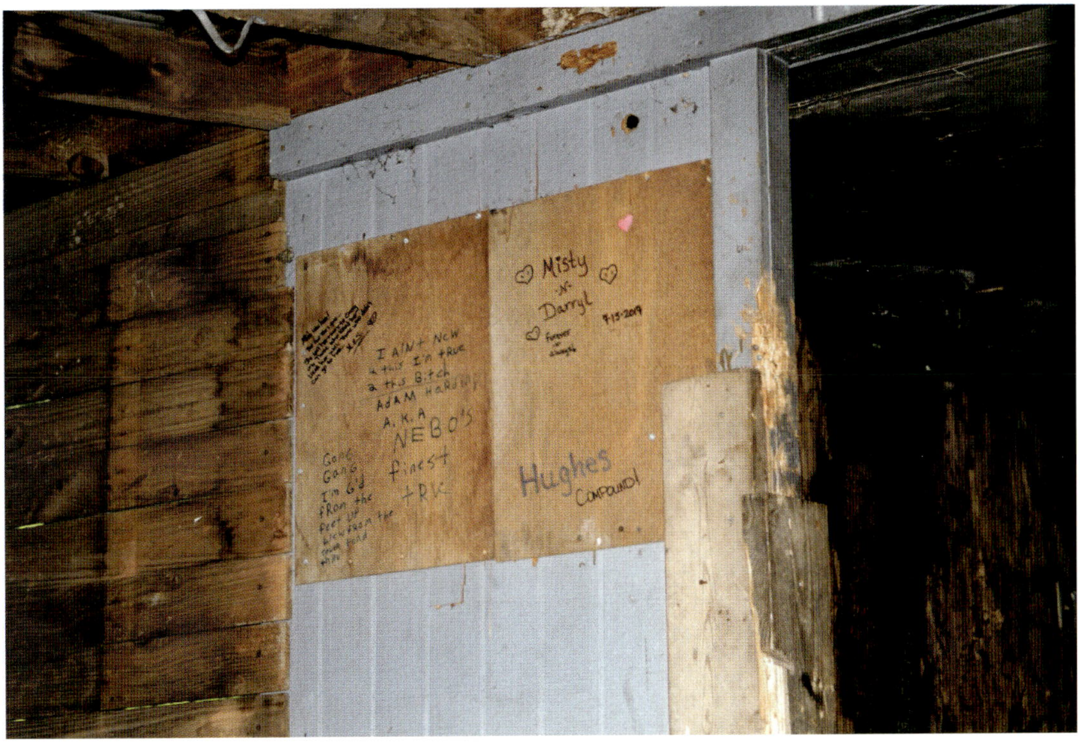

This graffiti marks the entrance to a shed. Just inside, damage can be seen at the ceiling and the wood is visibly mottled.

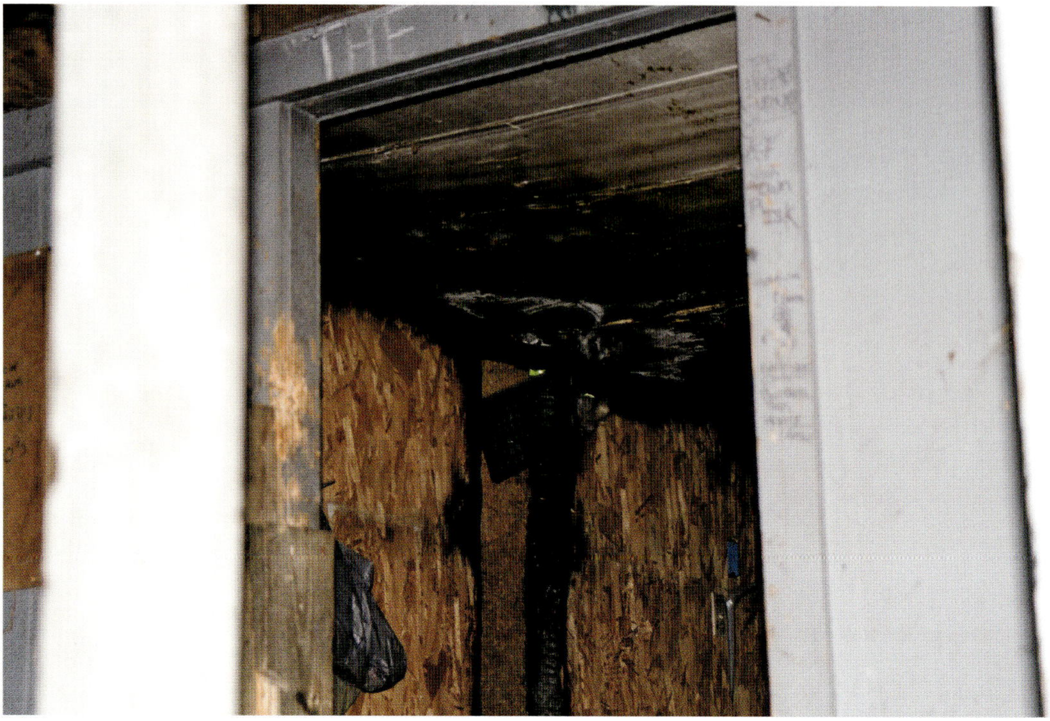

Another view shows more graffiti surrounding the doorway, and the burnt trail of a previous indoor fire that caught on the plywood siding.

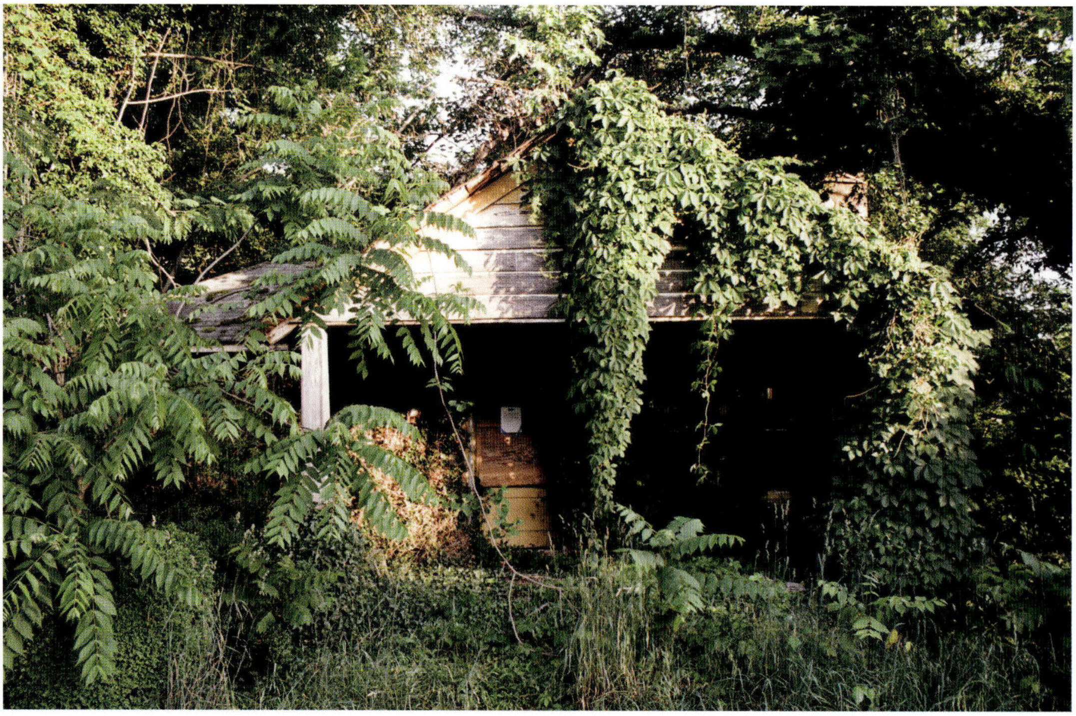

Kudzu has claimed this home, hanging down from the roof and climbing up the outer walls.

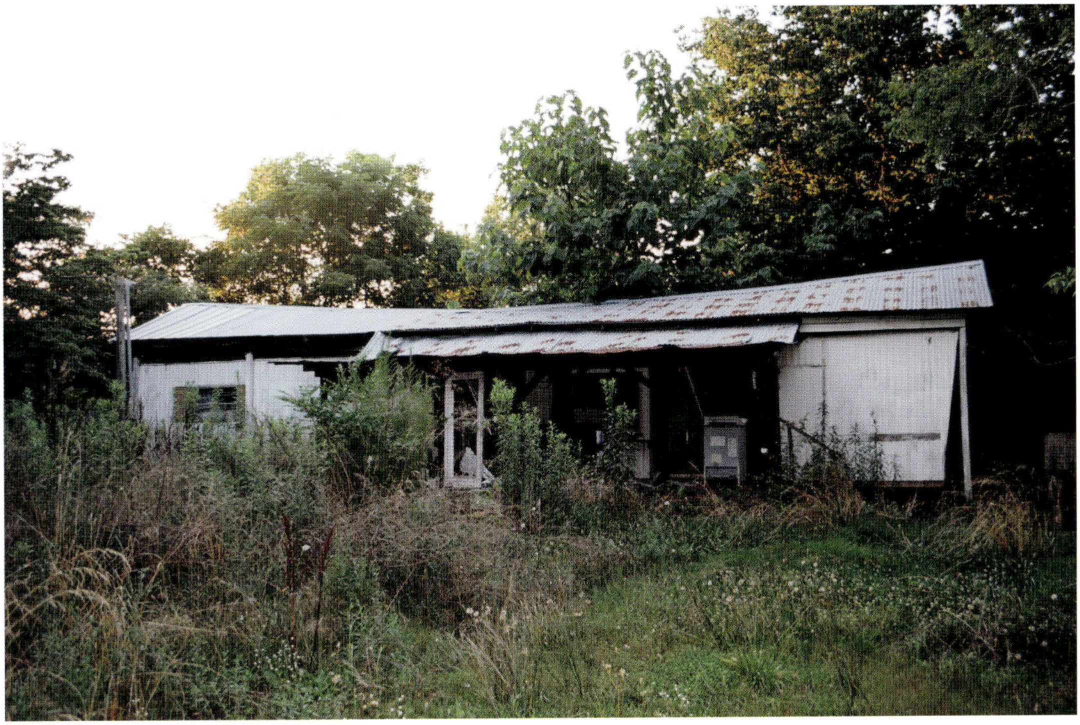

An abandoned trailer is missing its panel siding, allowing the viewer to look inside. This trailer, among others, is hidden off the road.

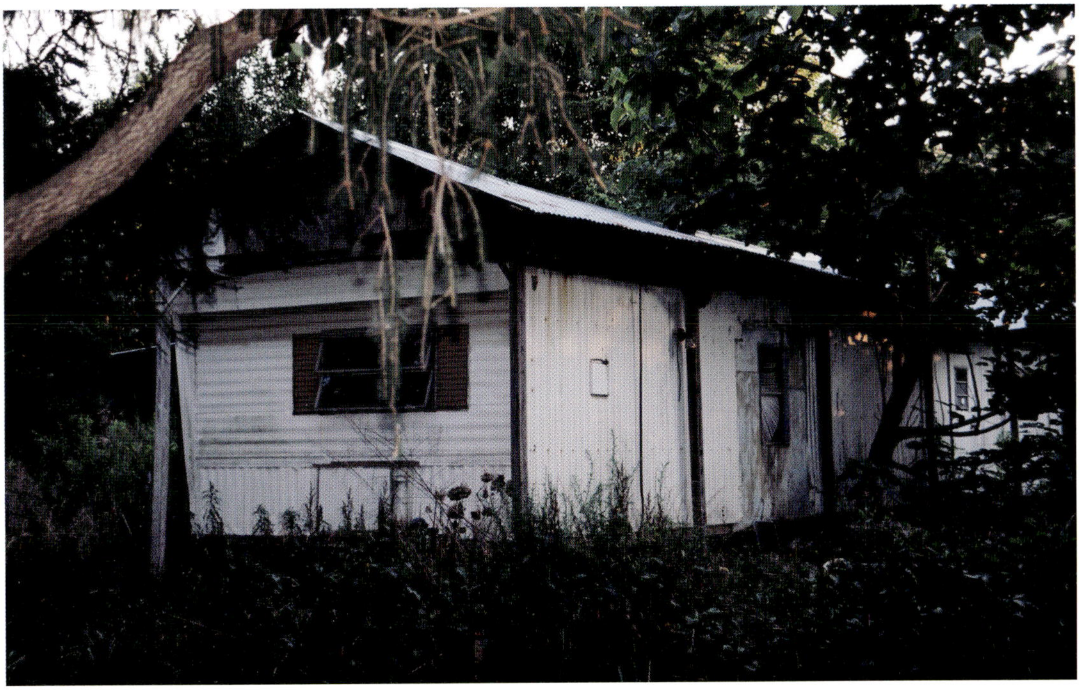

Another trailer, this one is slightly more intact. Its siding bulges in certain areas, and the blinds have been turned sideways.

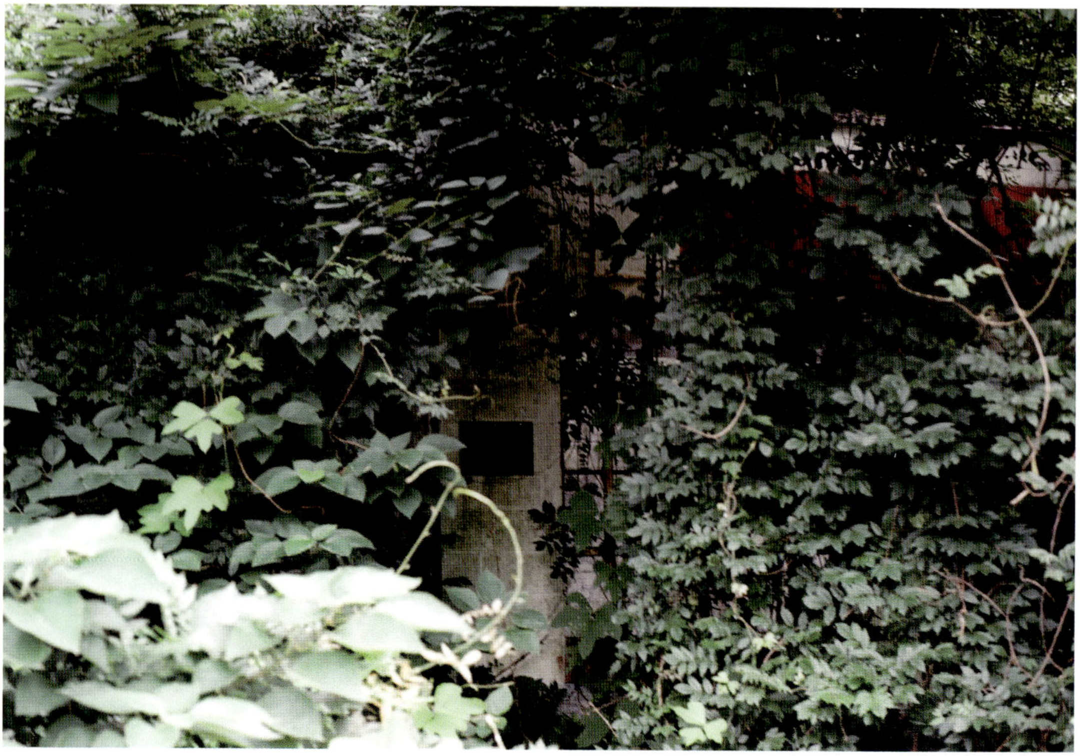

Another home is almost entirely obscured by vines. Only sparse features can be picked out.

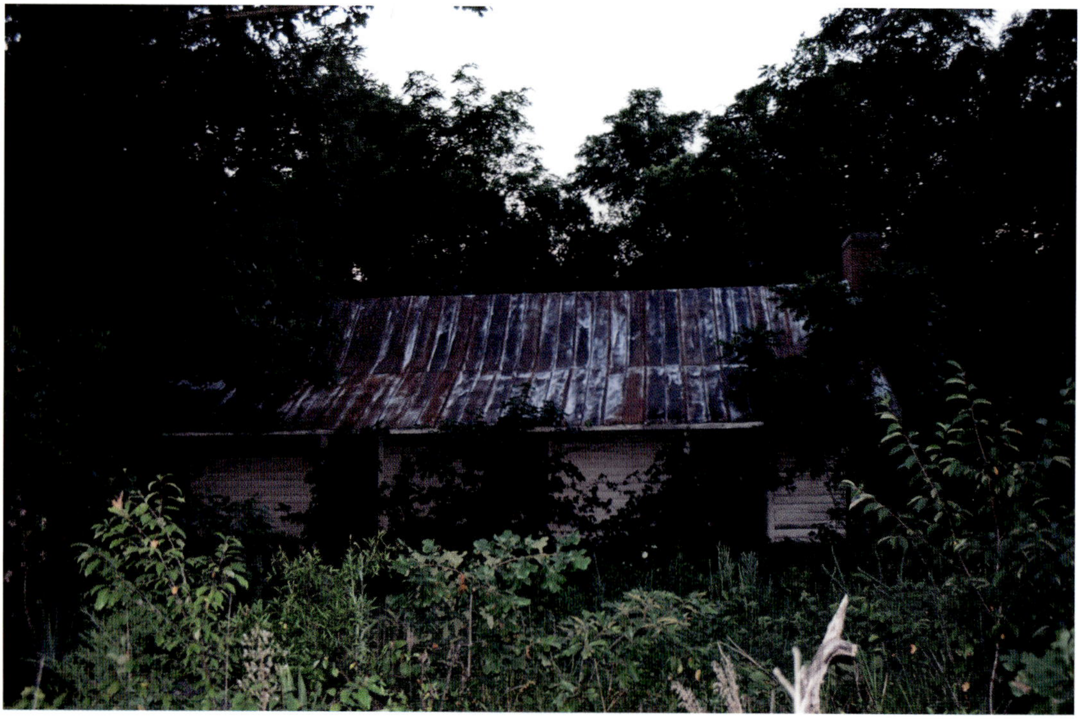

This house is shrouded by small and large trees alike, hidden in underbrush behind a thin line of trees.

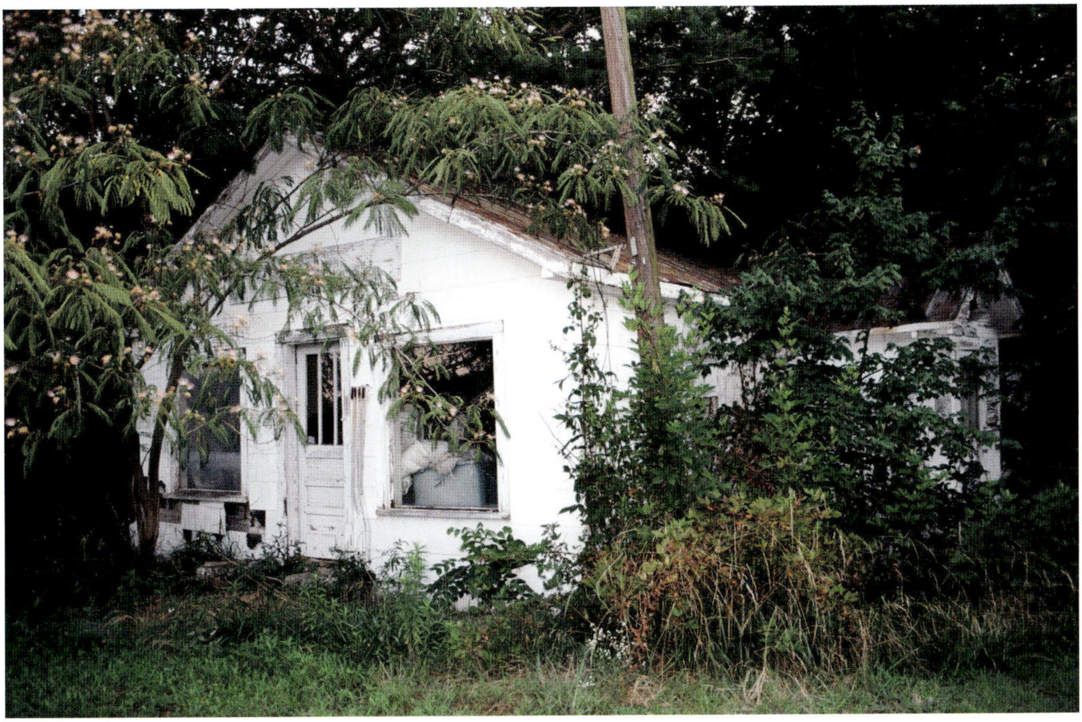

A house full of packed belongings, where wooden sidings have fallen off. The other entrance is inaccessible due to a large bush.

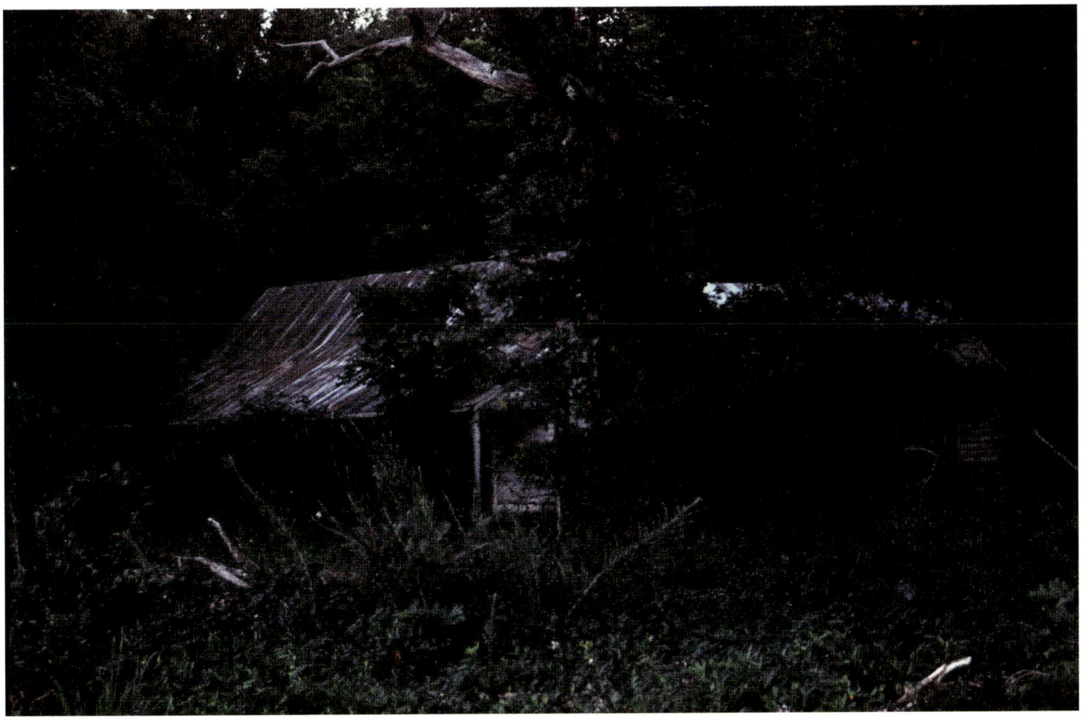

Another view of the house shows the blanketing rich undergrowth and dense trees surrounding it.

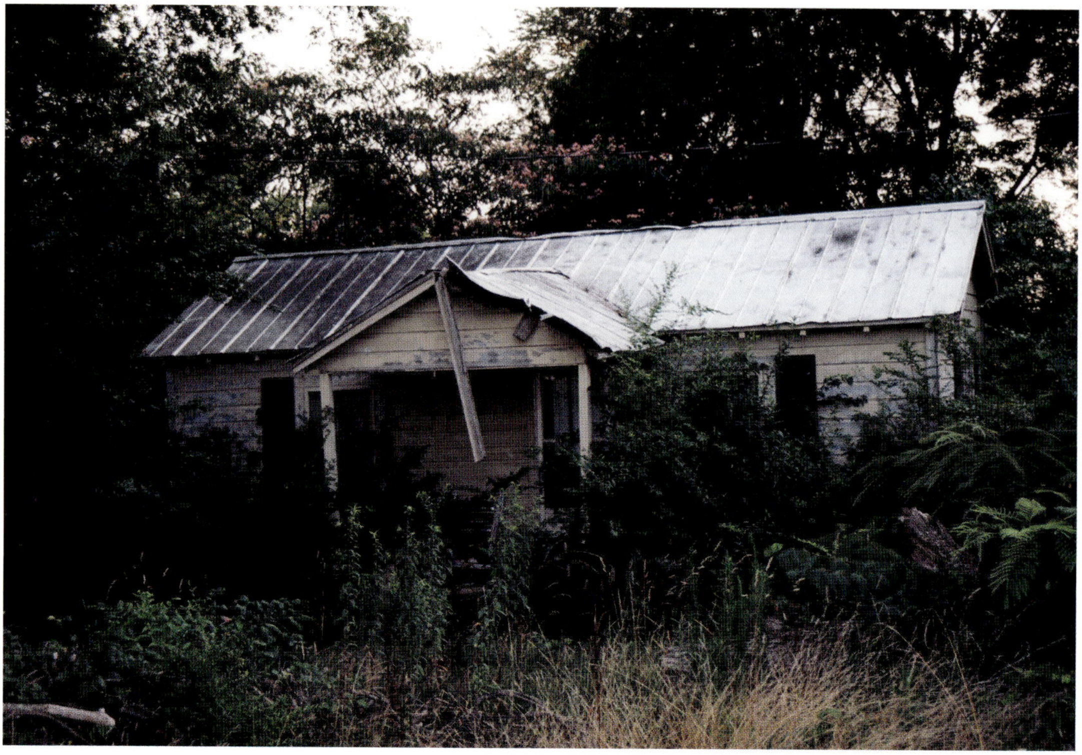

In the same area is another home, this one with a sunken porch and falling tin.

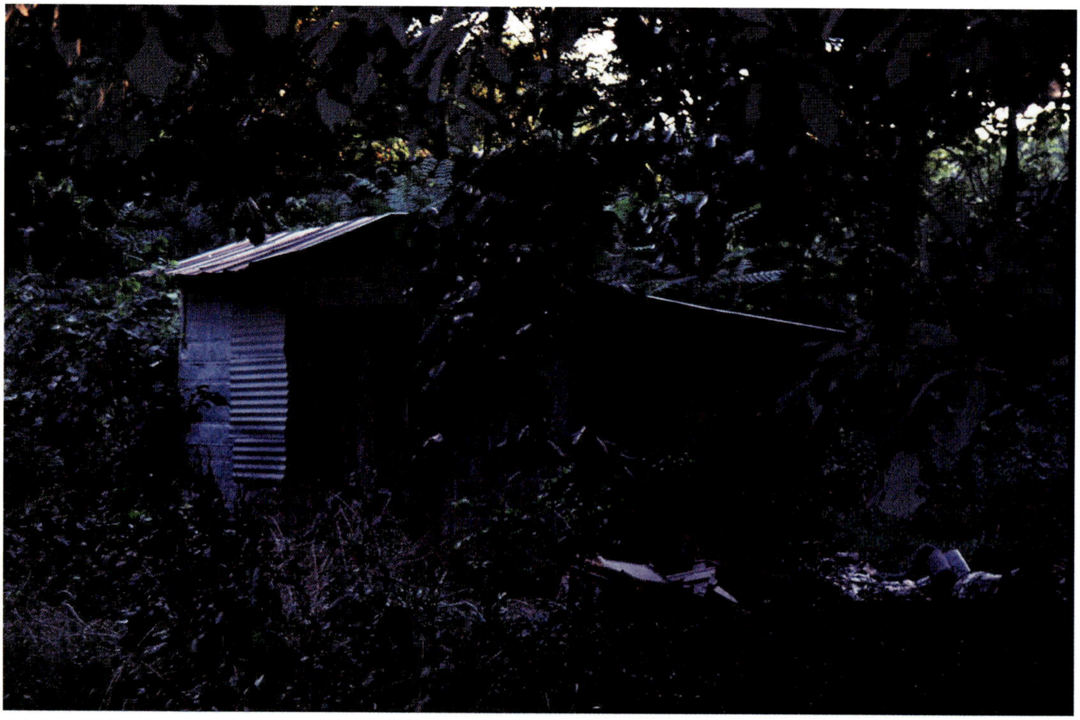

A hand-built shed surrounded by trash and briars lurks in the darkness.

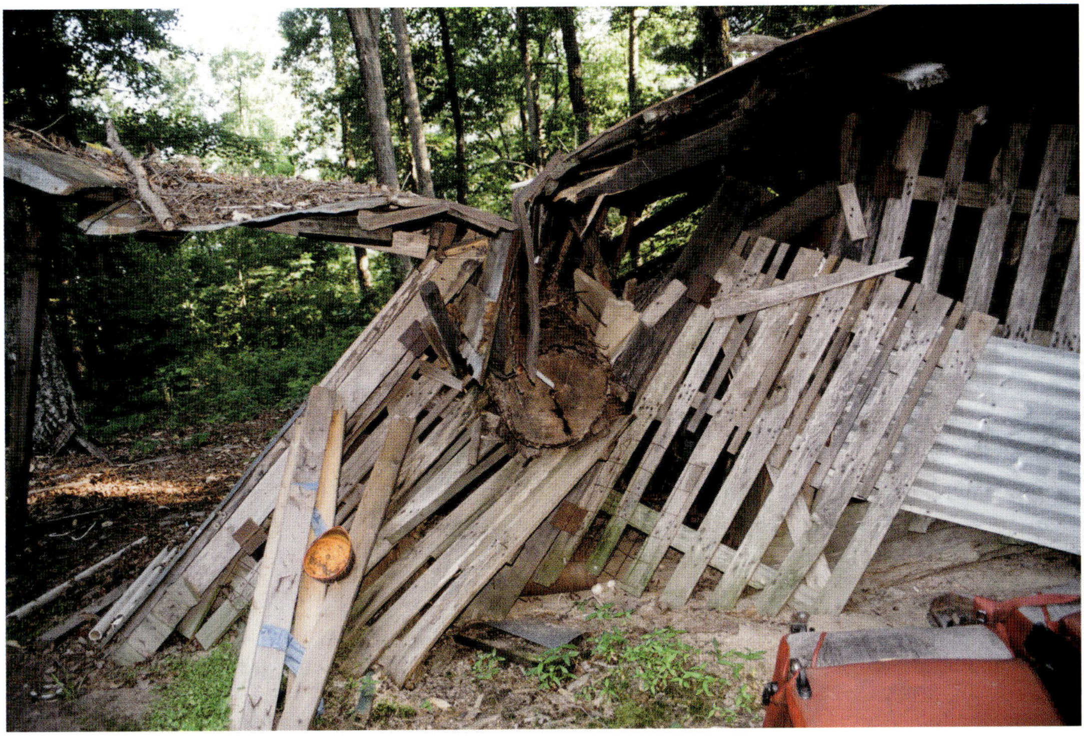

Upon closer inspection this fallen tree is rotting, and other debris can be seen on the roof.

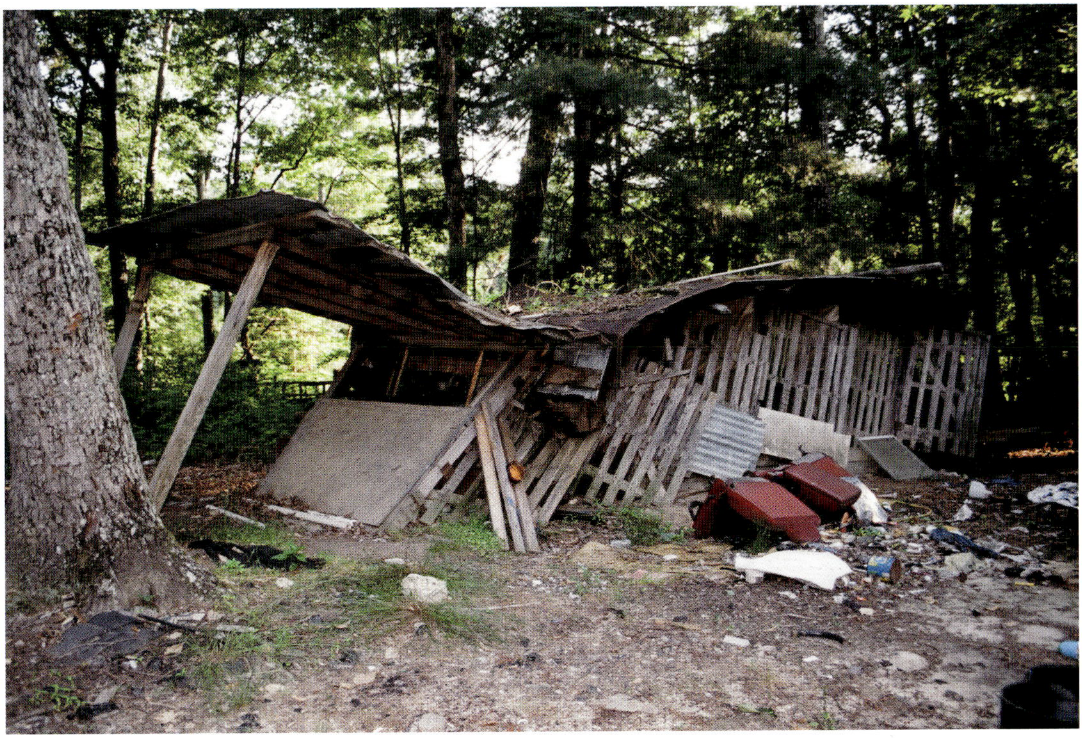

This shed has suffered from a treefall, leaning backwards severely.

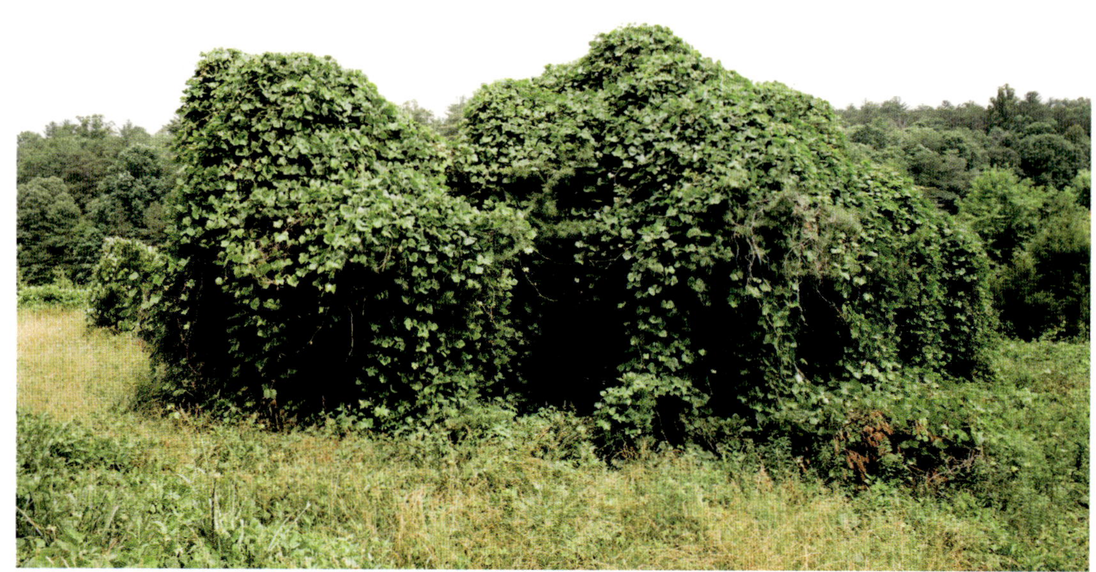

This structure lacks visibility entirely, covered at all points by kudzu.

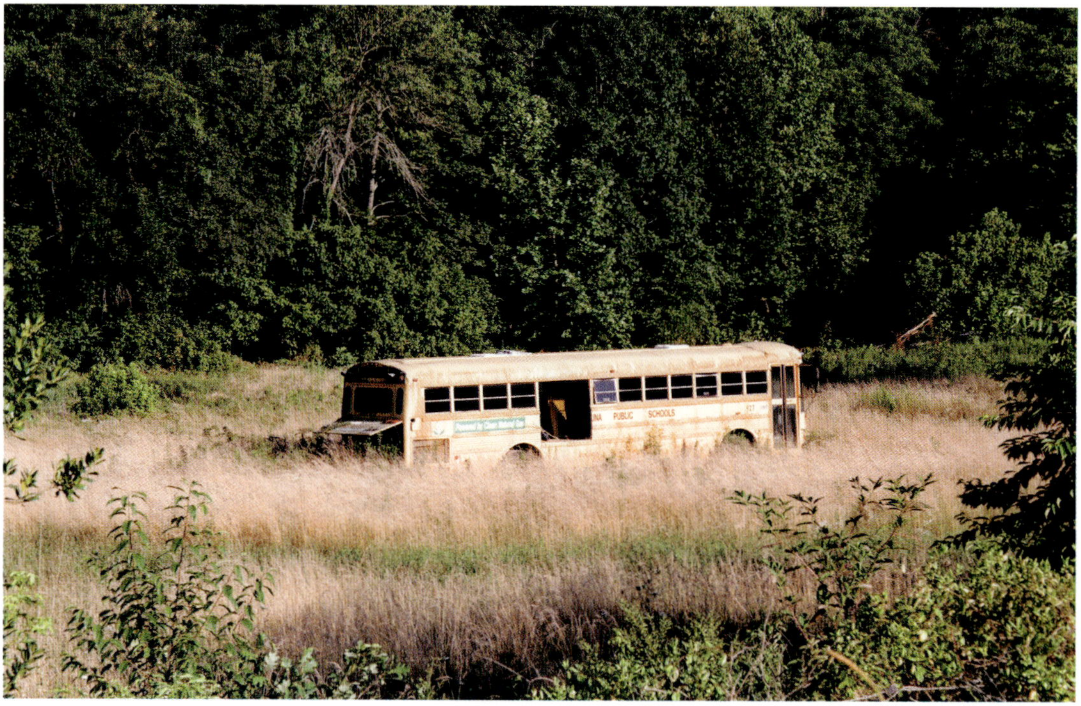

A North Carolina Public Schools bus in a sea of grass, proclaiming it is "Powered by Clean Natural Gas." The back emergency door is open, and the side emergency hatch has been removed.

3

SITE STUDIES

In this chapter I have included smaller sites that I visited which had collections of buildings. Unlike in Roadside Gems, which consists of standalone structures, many of these structures were built together, some even having exact designs. In those instances, you can see a gradient of decay where some parts of the structure are dilapidated in one building but remain preserved in another, and vice versa.

The first in this set of site studies was completed in a location that will not be disclosed in an effort to conserve what remains of the houses and other structures. These houses were first visited by me in high school after a friend told me about them. Back then this group of houses, sheds, and small barn were all standing and not dilapidated beyond some missing doors, broken windows, and soft or collapsed parts of the floor.

When I first began photographing them in 2017, these houses had decayed somewhat from when I was first introduced to them. However, they were still being used for squatting, graffiti, and other "recreation" by locals. More of the floorboards had collapsed, and some walls had started falling. Vines, briars, and other plants had started worming their way through openings in each structure. Even with snow on the ground, the encroaching plants were clearly marking their new territory. The black-and-white photographs of this site were taken earlier, and the houses were much easier to reach due to winter removing a lot of the bushes and underbrush that would have obscured the footpath.

After a bout of tornadoes hit the area, many of these structures were no longer viable for squatting. More walls had fallen, and more of the roof had collapsed or had blown off in the storms. Bushes and grasses became more of an issue and the path to these houses became overgrown with disuse. Once a detour on a designated walking path within a park, now there was no way to know where the path had gone unless you had

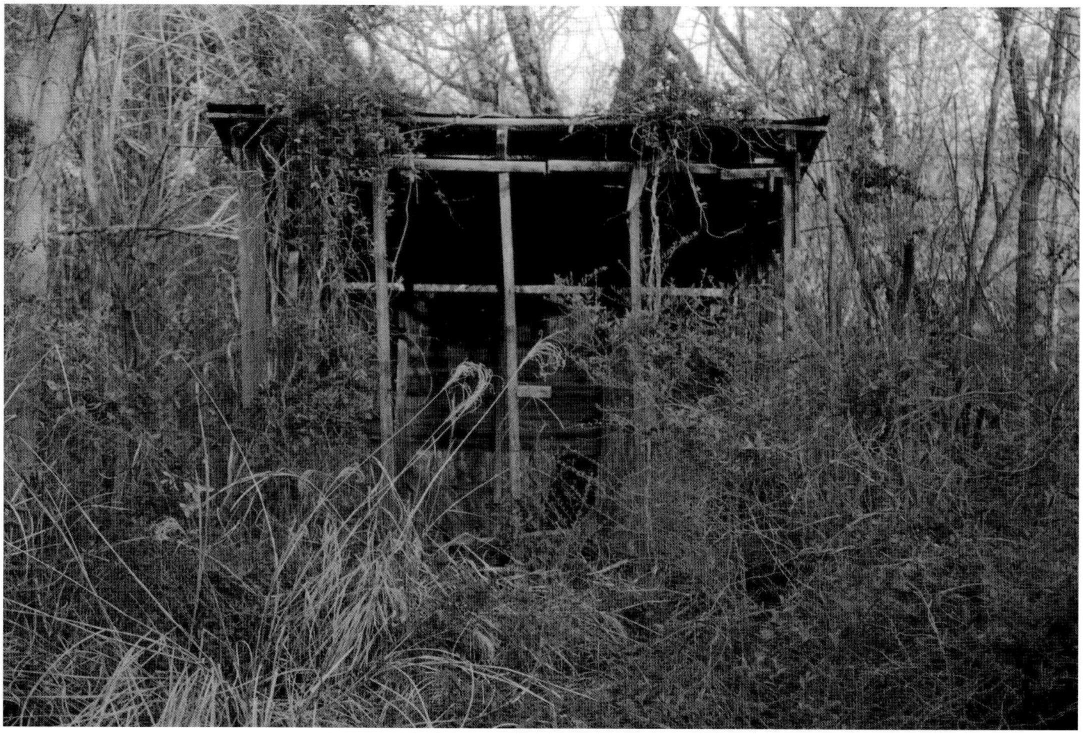

Another shed, further buried in underbrush. This shed has a tin backside.

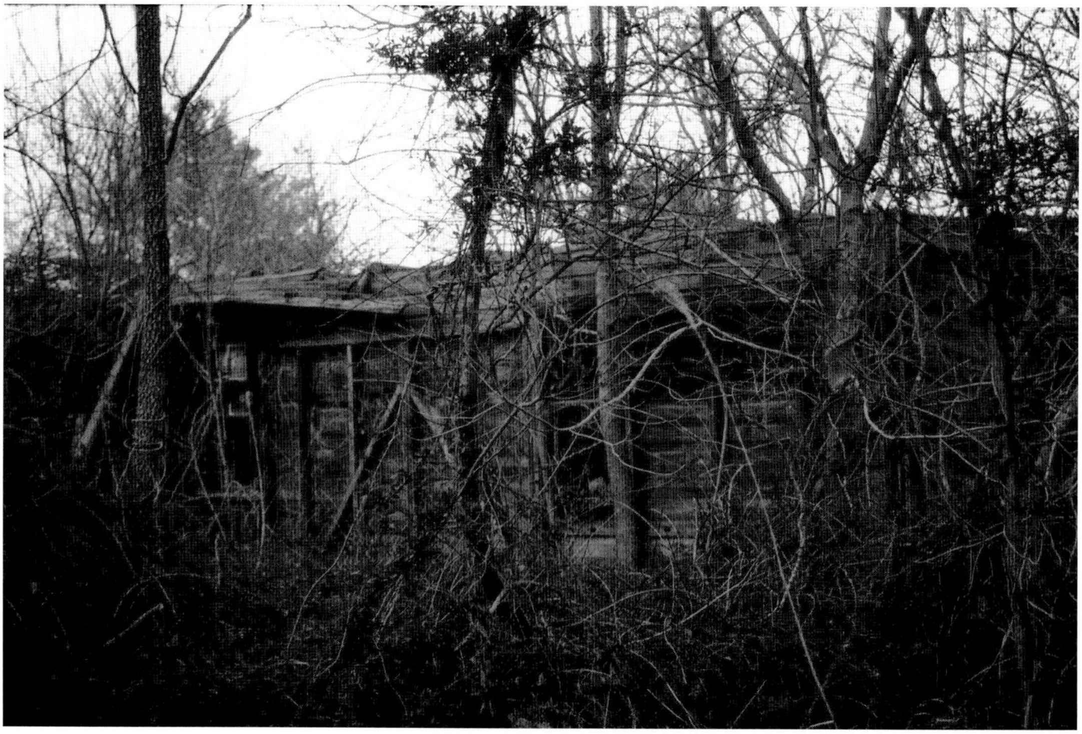

A house torn down to its bare essentials. Trees have grown around and through parts of the structure.

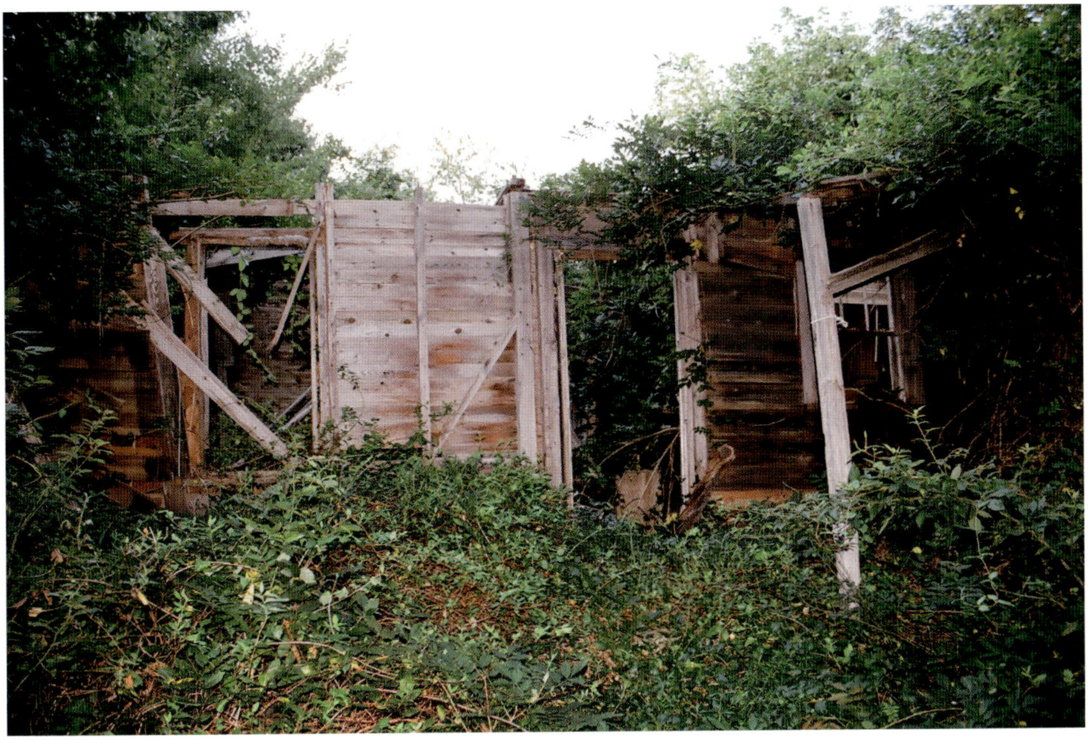

Later, more of the house has collapsed. The front wall, mostly intact, remains.

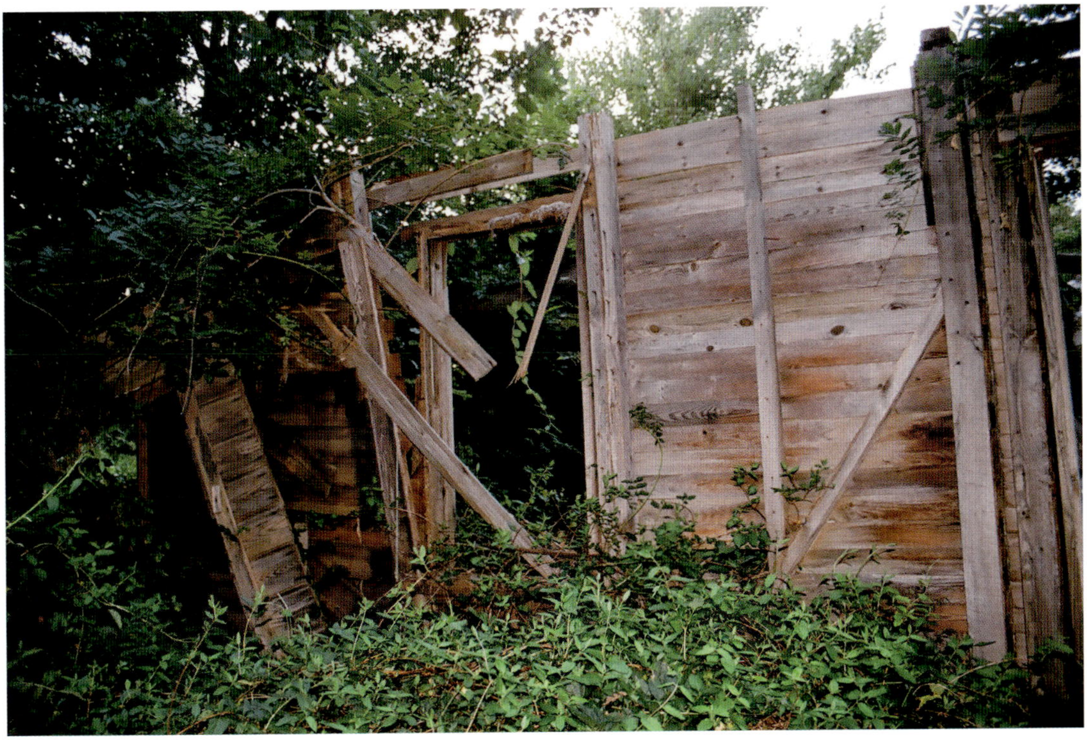

A closer look shows parts of the wall separating from each other. This window frame is torn in two.

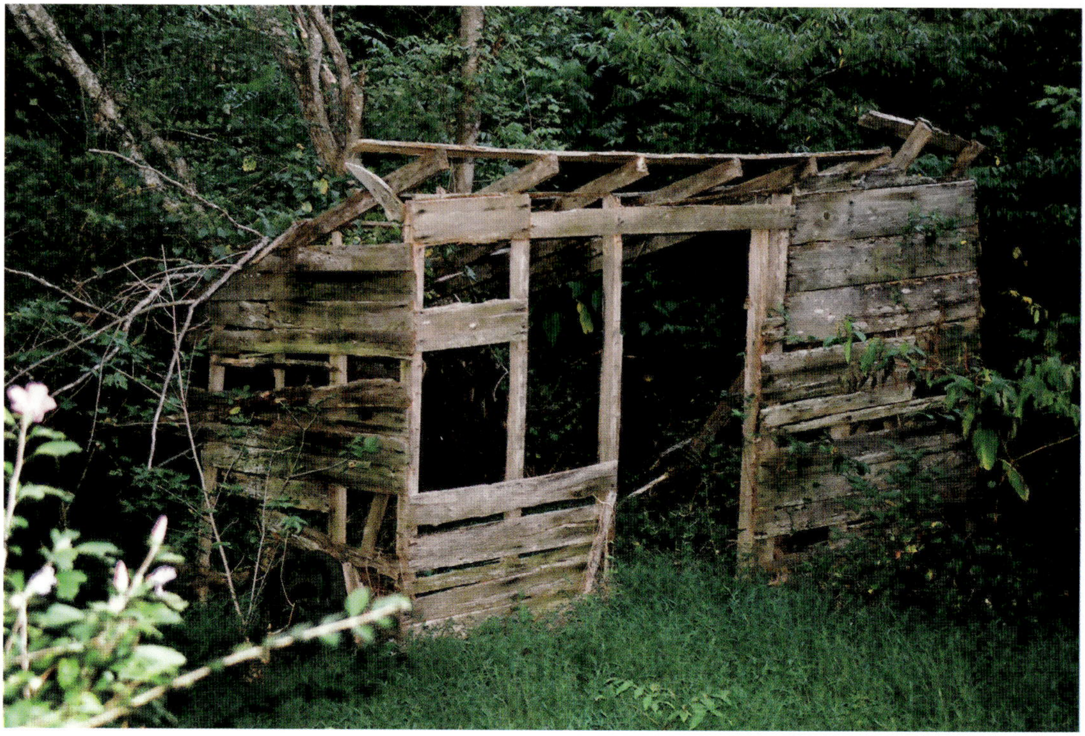

A shed remains standing in the form of an outline.

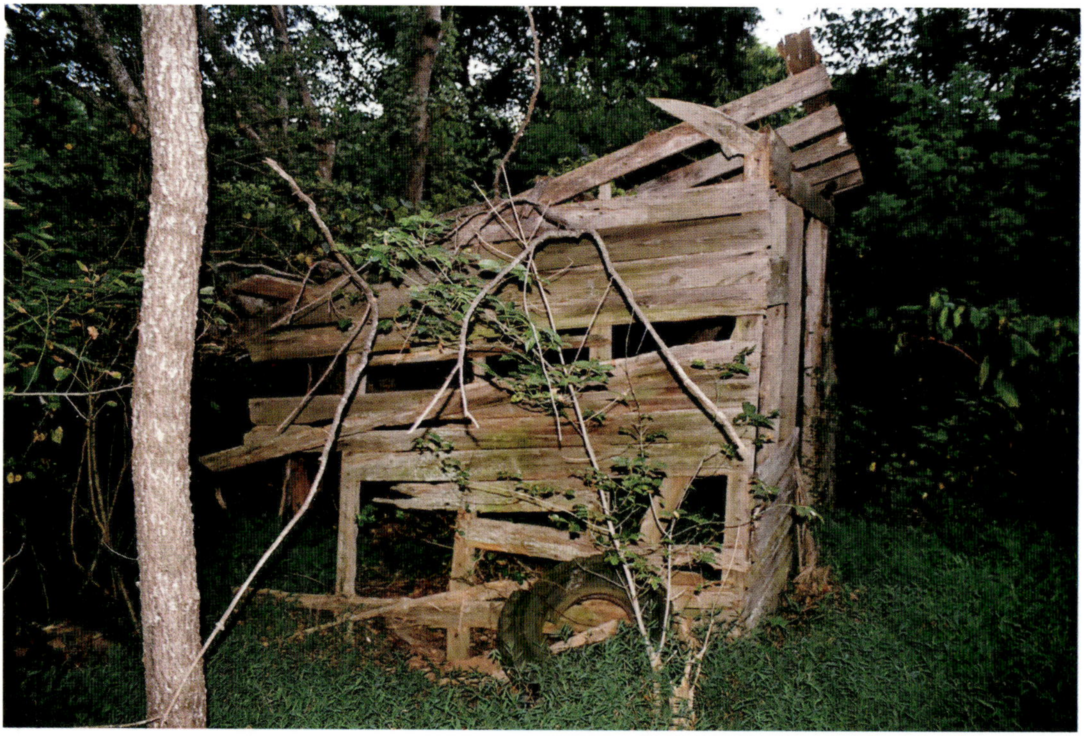

At a closer side view, the missing back wall of the shed can be easily seen.

been previously. In my most recent shooting of the area I had to take several days to cut through underbrush until I could finally clear a path to reach the outskirts of the site. The buildings had been damaged so severely in the storm it was astonishing. Last seen standing sheds were completely gone save for the foundation, some roofs were found lying on the ground, and parts of the walls rendered upside down. One house had now seen two of its walls collapse, the others miraculously still standing.

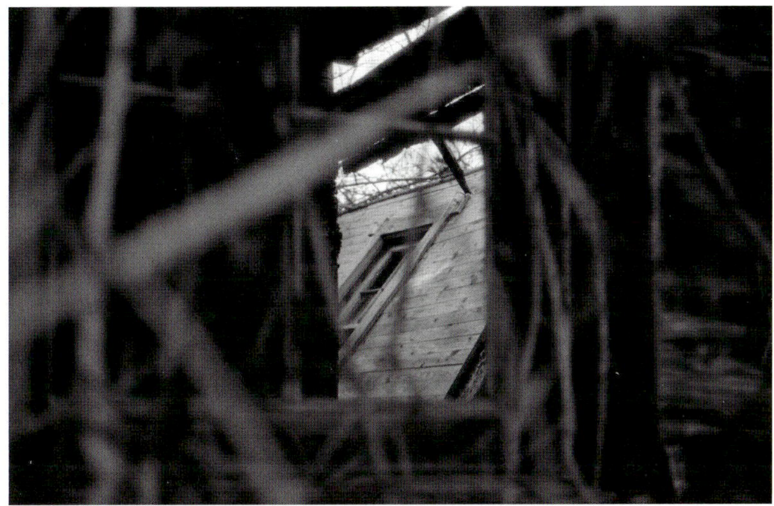

Through a front window frame, a falling back wall can be seen.

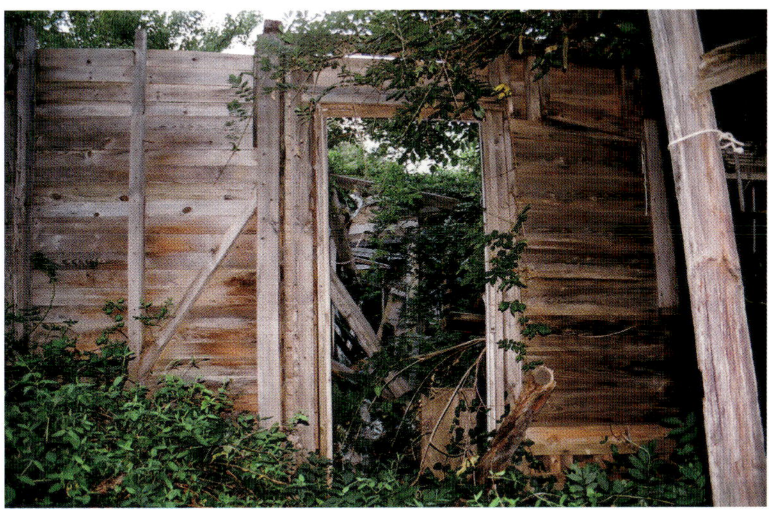

The wall, now fallen, is barely recognizable. Plants have grown through and over the newly collapsed material.

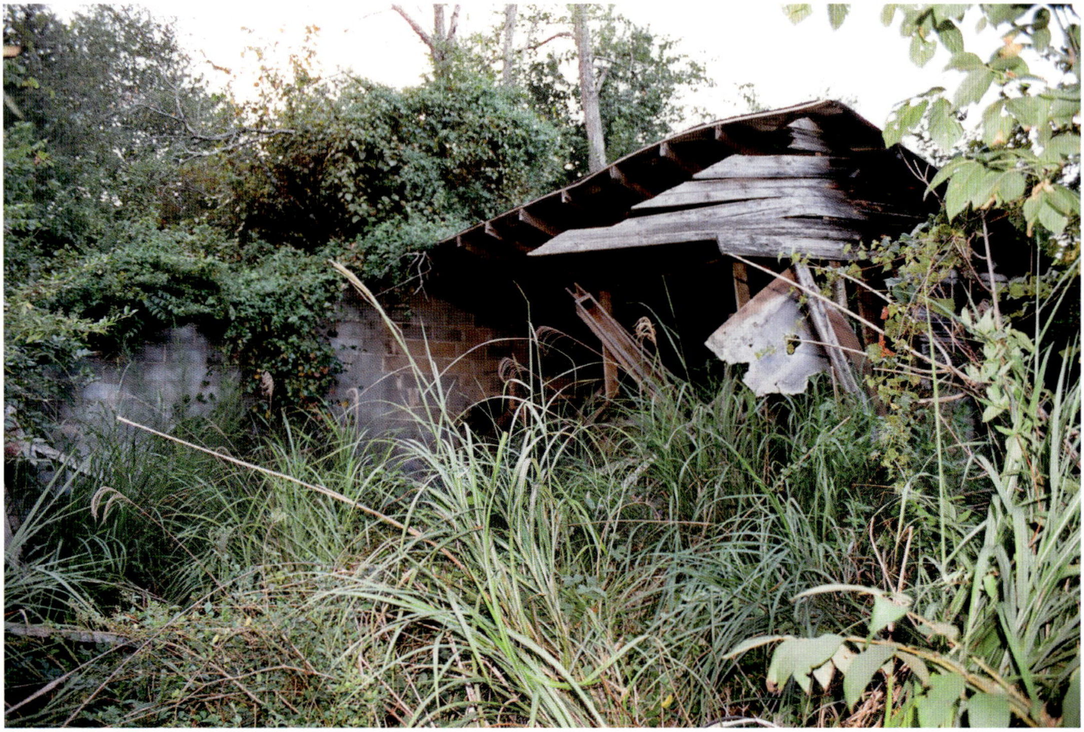

Half of a shed is visible peeking through overgrowth. The other half is nowhere to be found.

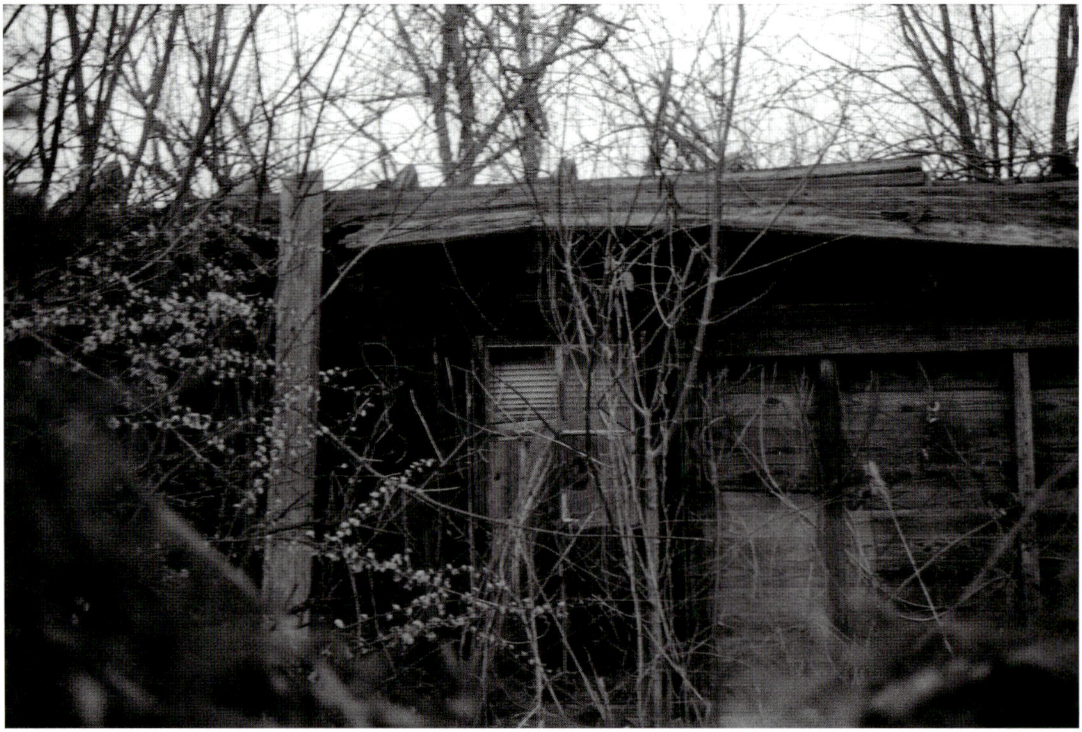

A more complete vision of the house is shown. In the window, blinds can still be seen.

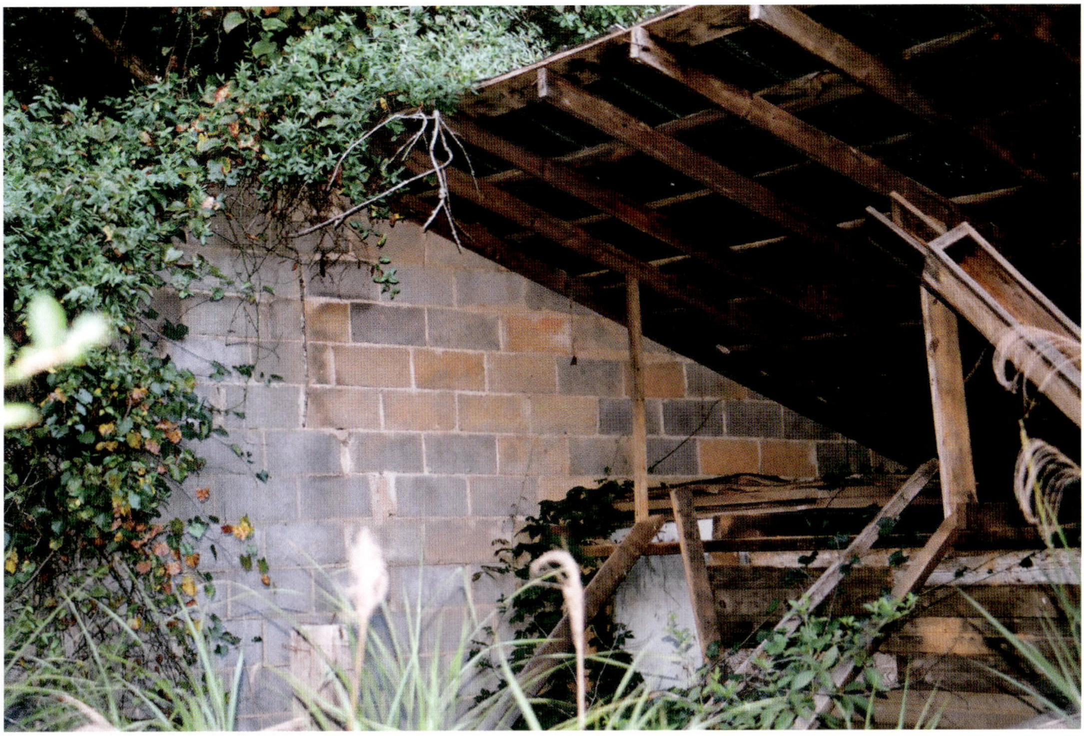

The back wall of a shed is visible, as well as a bundle of unused wood for a never-to-be-finished project.

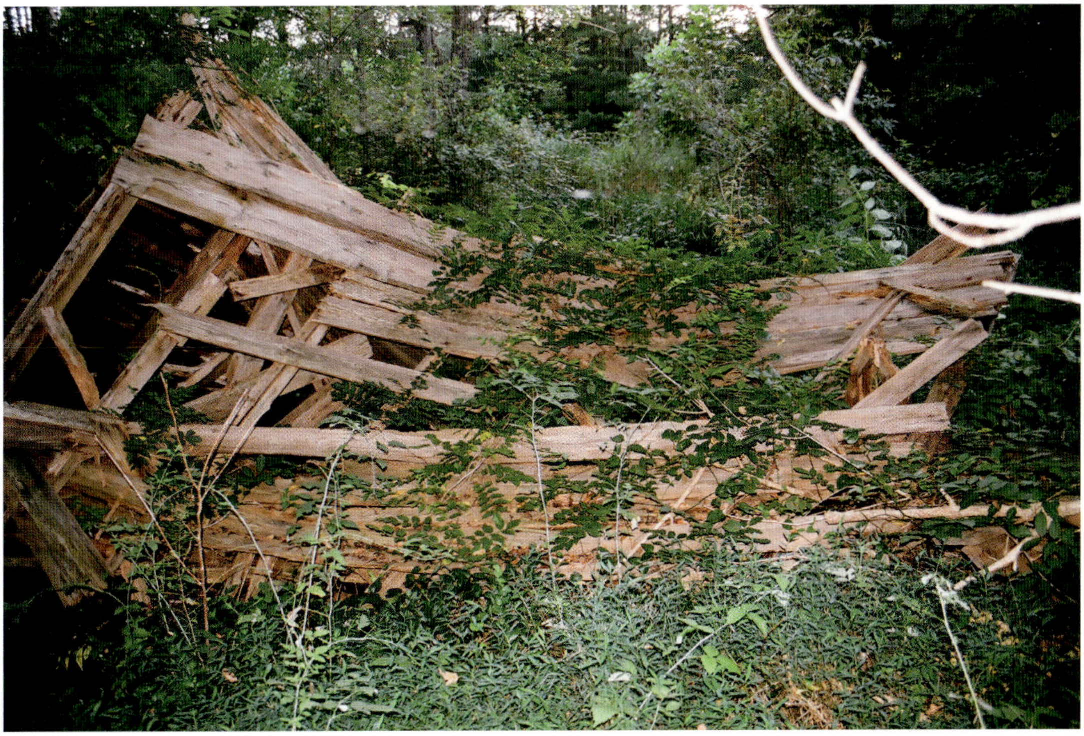

One shed has collapsed entirely on itself.

These homes, with the land surrounding them, were originally sold to the county for expansion of the park into the area containing them. However, due to lack of money or interest, the park did not expand to fully include and utilize this land. While signs pointed to a trail going through the area, it was not well kept, even when in standard use. I cannot recall seeing any official markers, even more informal ones such as paint on trees or plastic tie offs to indicate the trail. Over time this trail became overgrown and was left to its own devices. Even after cutting a path back into existence to reshoot the area, it quickly grew back over, and it is likely many visitors to the park are now unaware such a path ever existed.

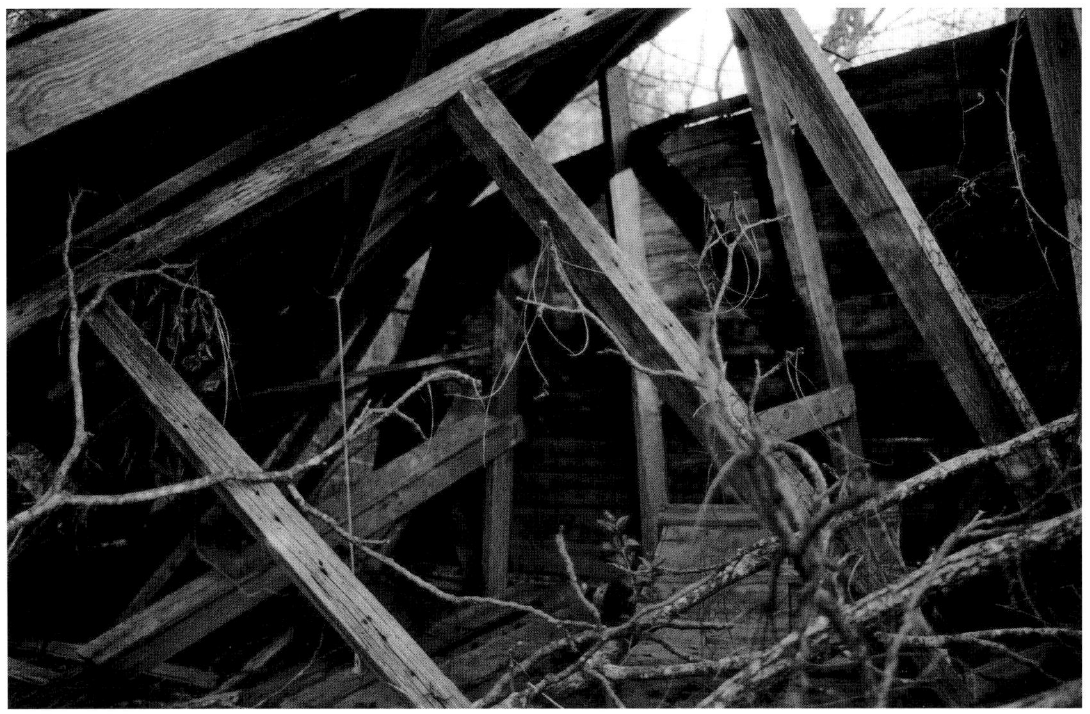

Two walls are twisting together, folding in on the remains of the previous wall.

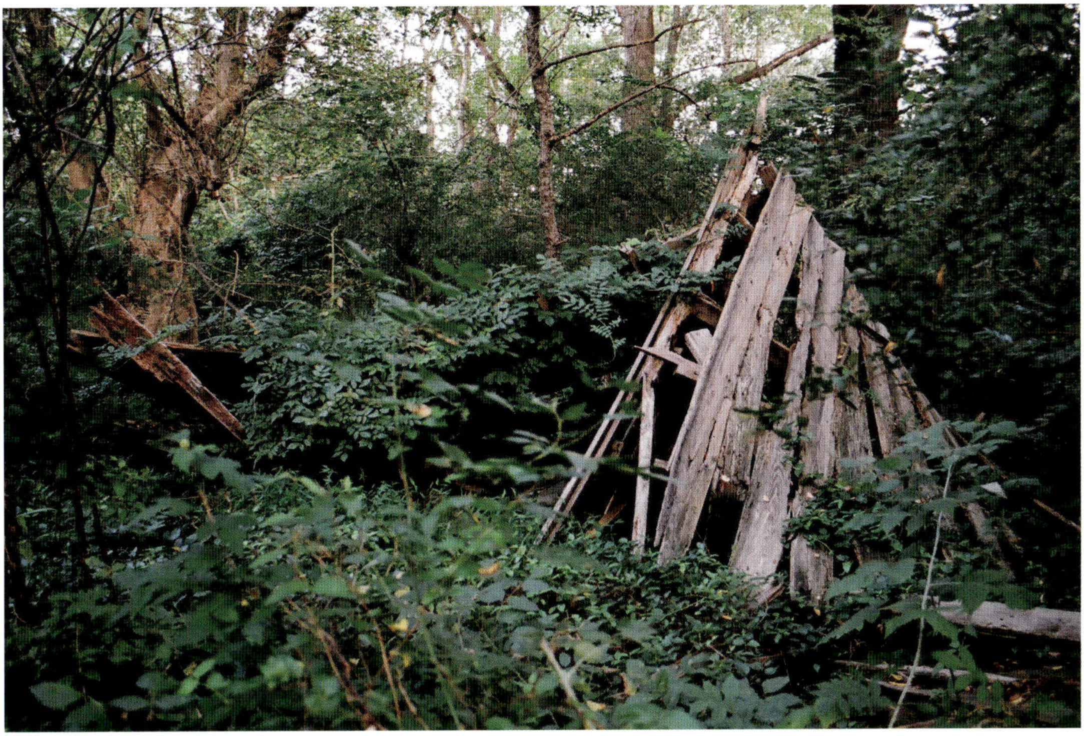

These remains of the previous barn can be witnessed.

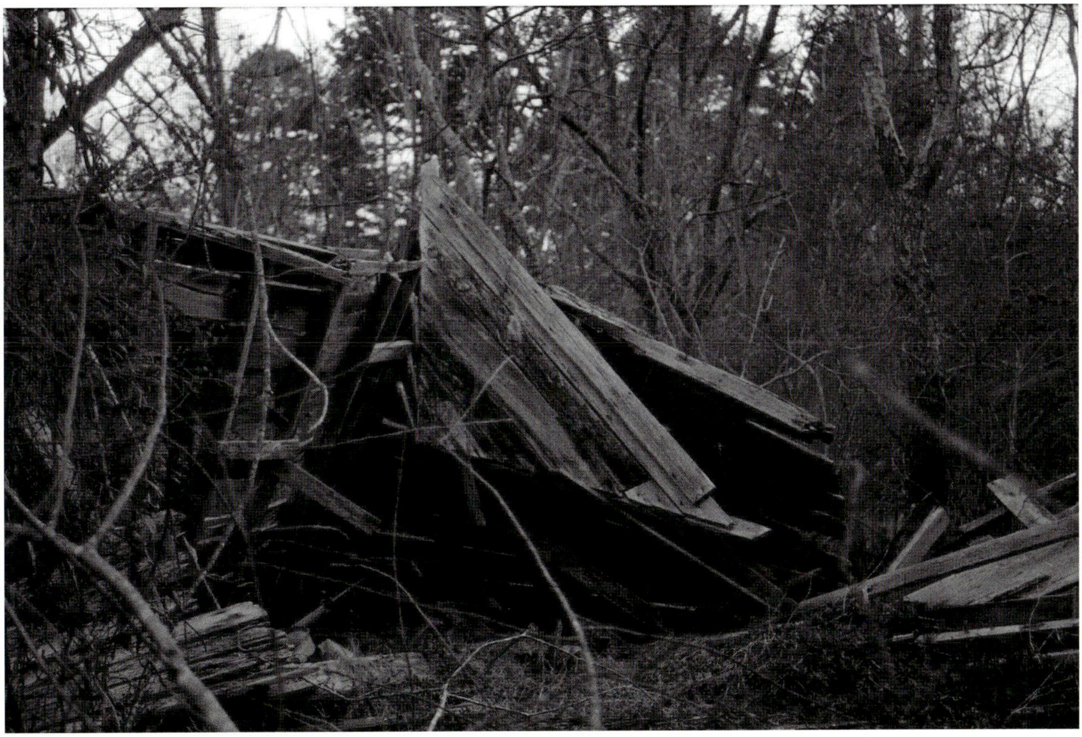

Having fallen entirely, the roof of the barn is inverted.

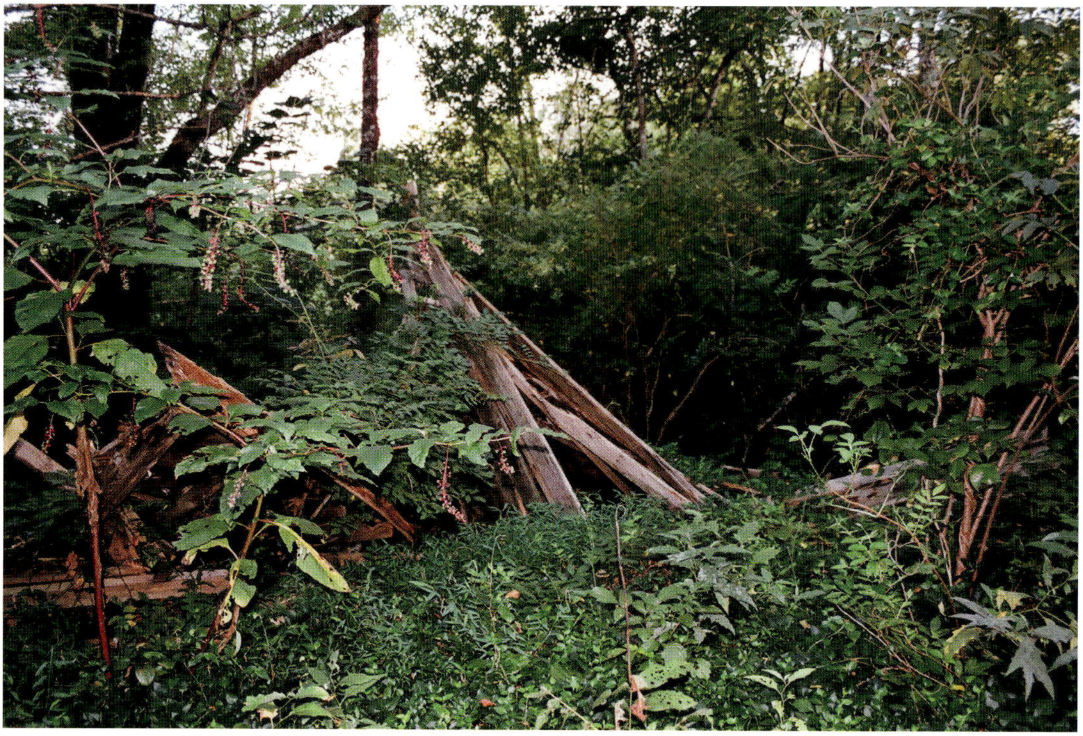

Some parts of the barn have been scattered further, such as these.

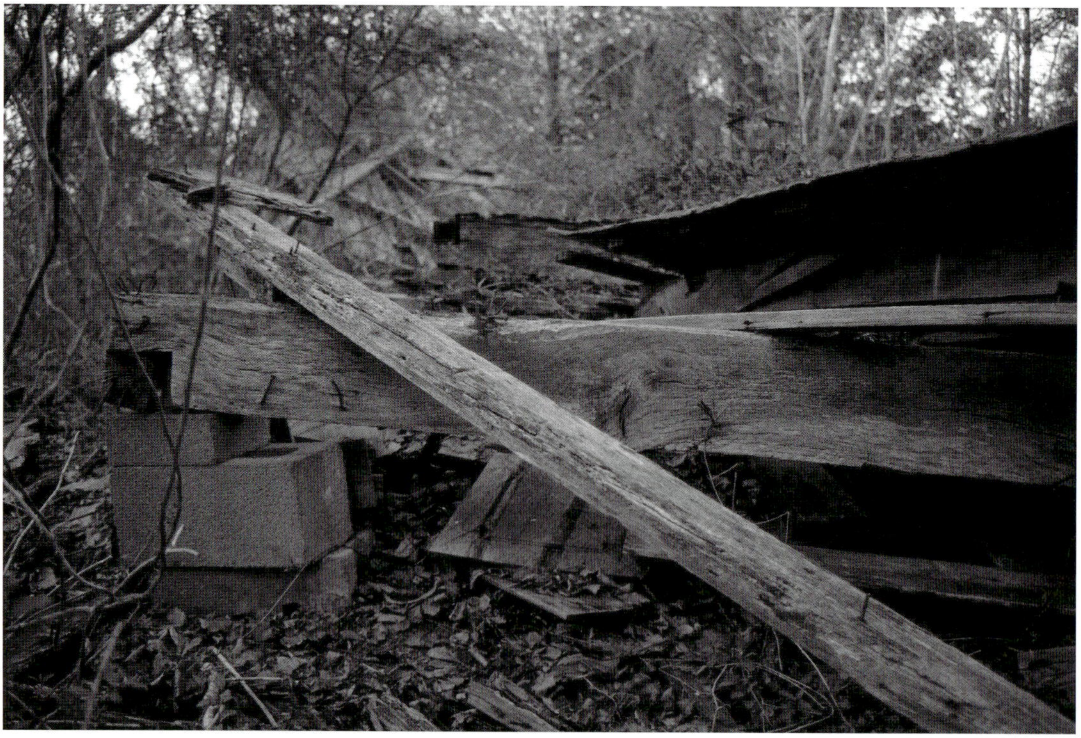

A foundation remains, holding up boards full of untethered nails.

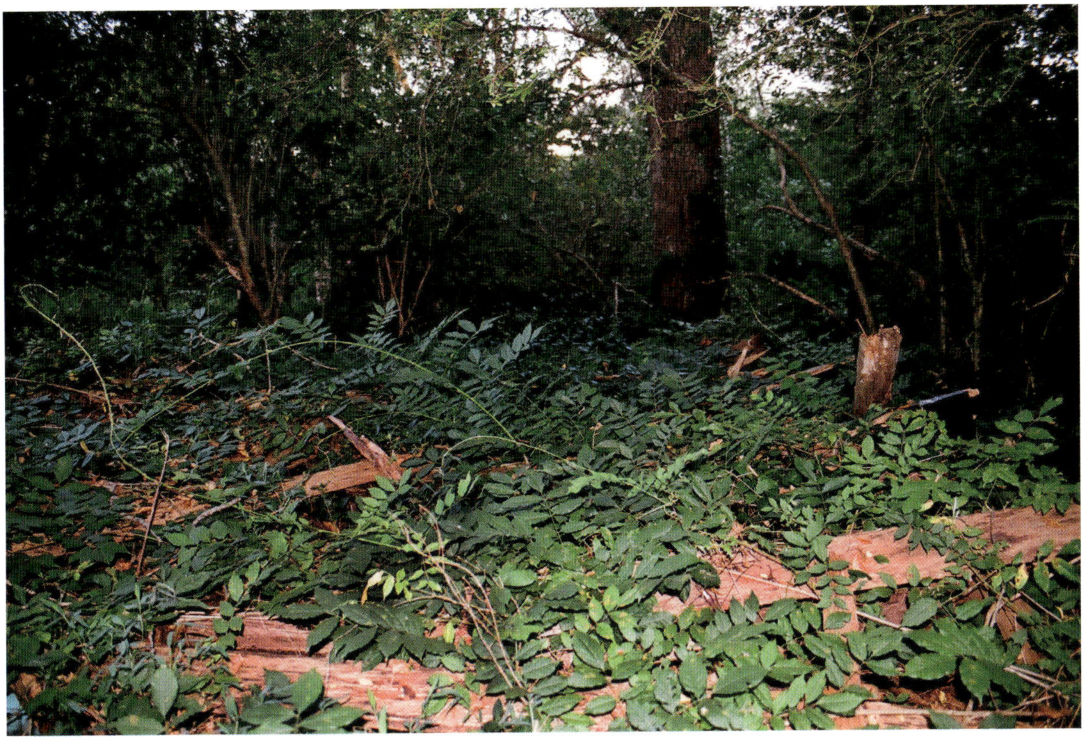

Vines obscure fallen planks, possibly belonging to one of the sheds.

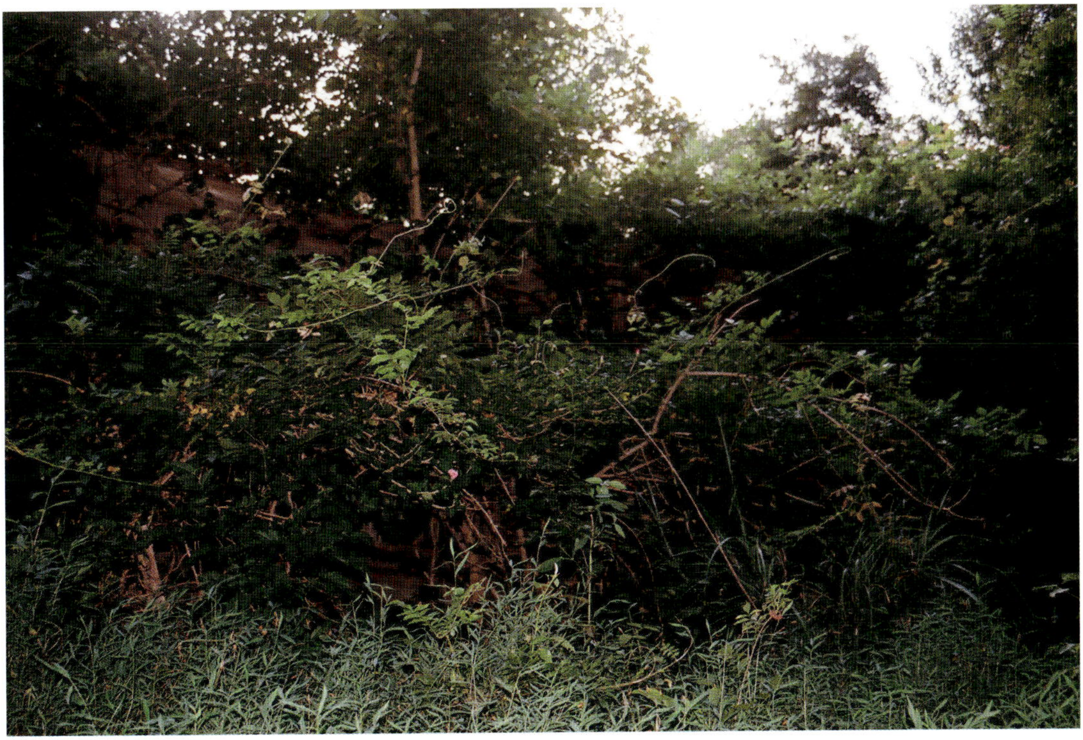

More vines obscure parts of the larger barn.

The next site includes a set of buildings which belong to Broughton Hospital, known previously as the Western North Carolina Insane Asylum. These buildings, listed as staff cottages, originally housed workers for the hospital. They run along the east side of Enola Road in Morganton, North Carolina, found south of I-40. These cottages were built and used in 1920 in a pilot program to not only house growing staff numbers but to treat certain patients within a different environment.[1] The lawn surrounding the houses remains well-manicured, but the cottages themselves are in disrepair and have not been used in some time. In the crawl space of one such cottage lies rusted medical equipment. In this crawl space forgotten walkers, gurneys, and toilet risers were found piled together. Looking underneath another cottage revealed an assortment of tires and forgotten paint cans.

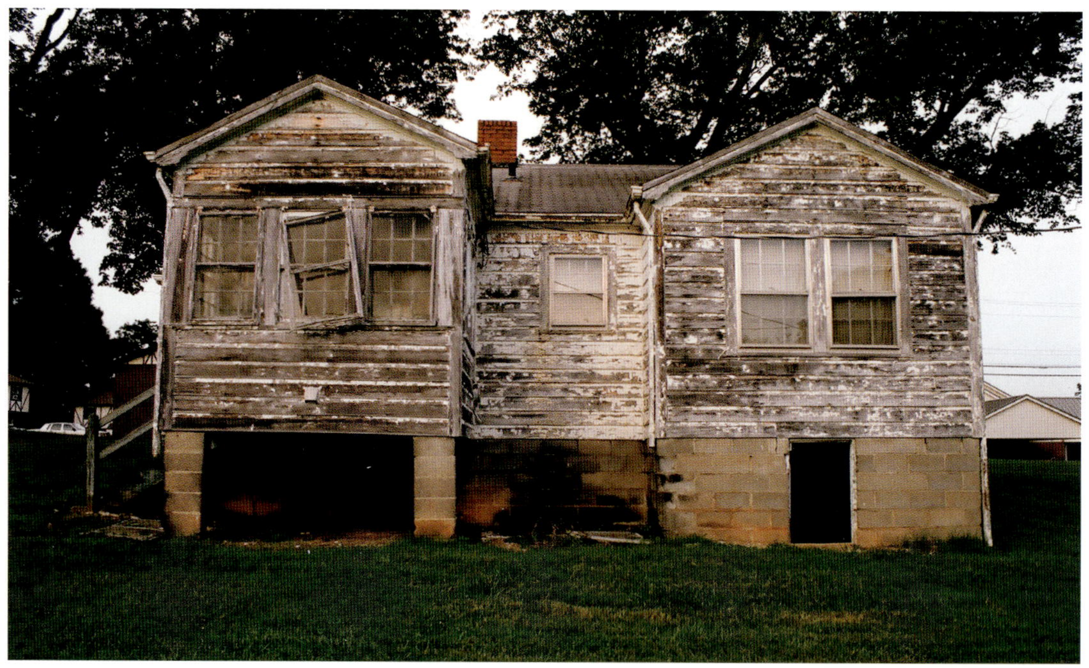

One of several staff cottages, this one is missing its crawl space door and much of its paint while a window frame swings down.

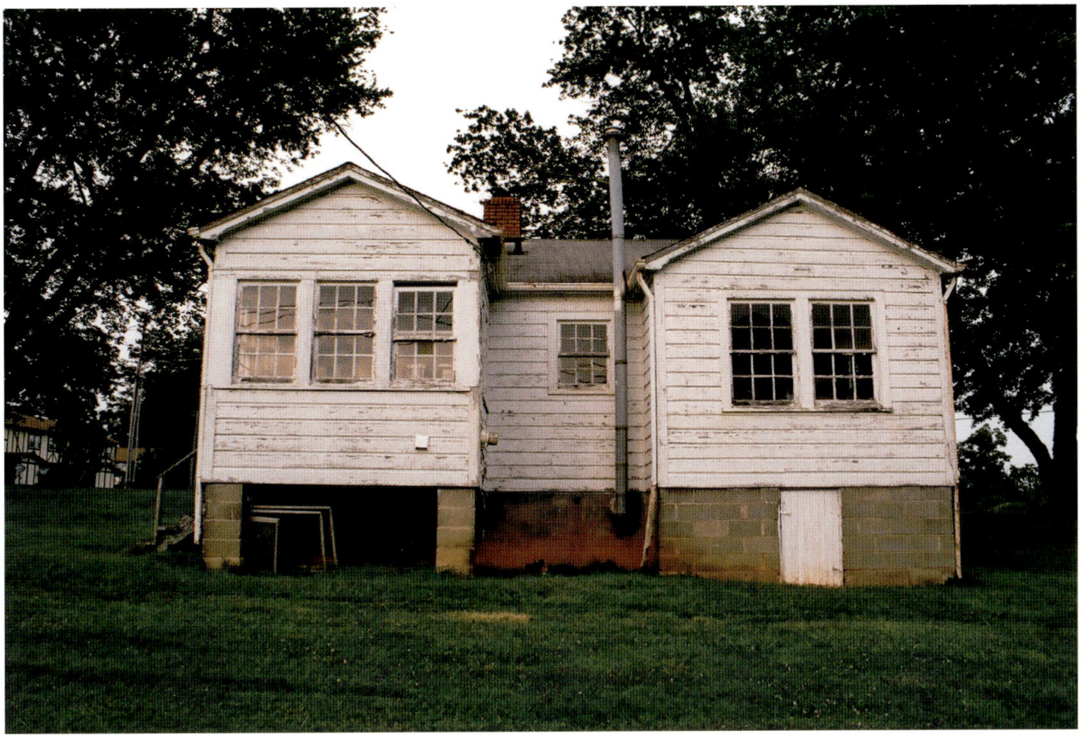

This staff cottage, in contrast, is highly intact.

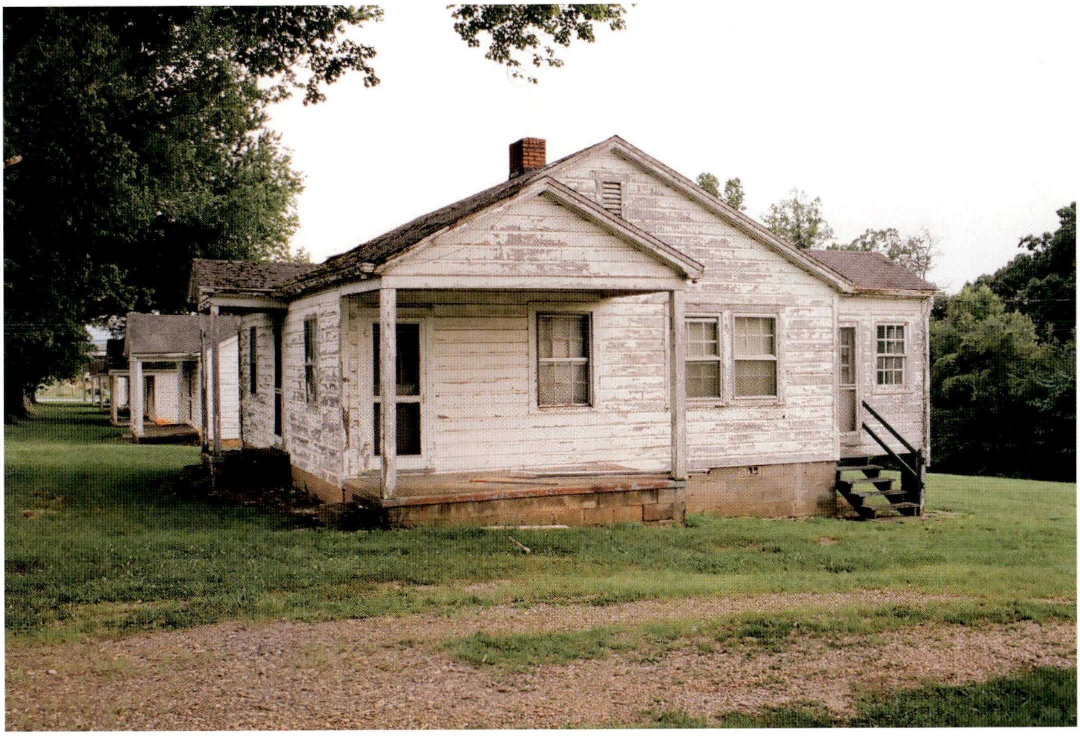

A side view of the staff cottages shows their identical structures and how close they sit together.

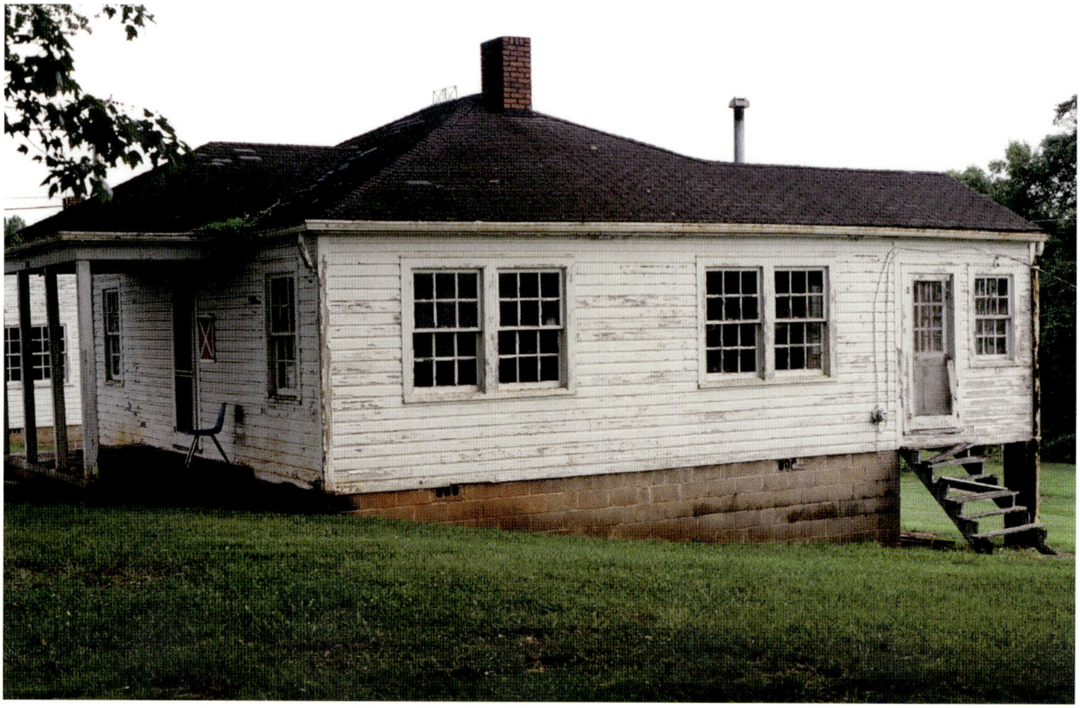

This cottage, marked with a red X, indicates to emergency personnel it is unsafe to enter in the event of an emergency. The stairs on the right have half fallen planks.

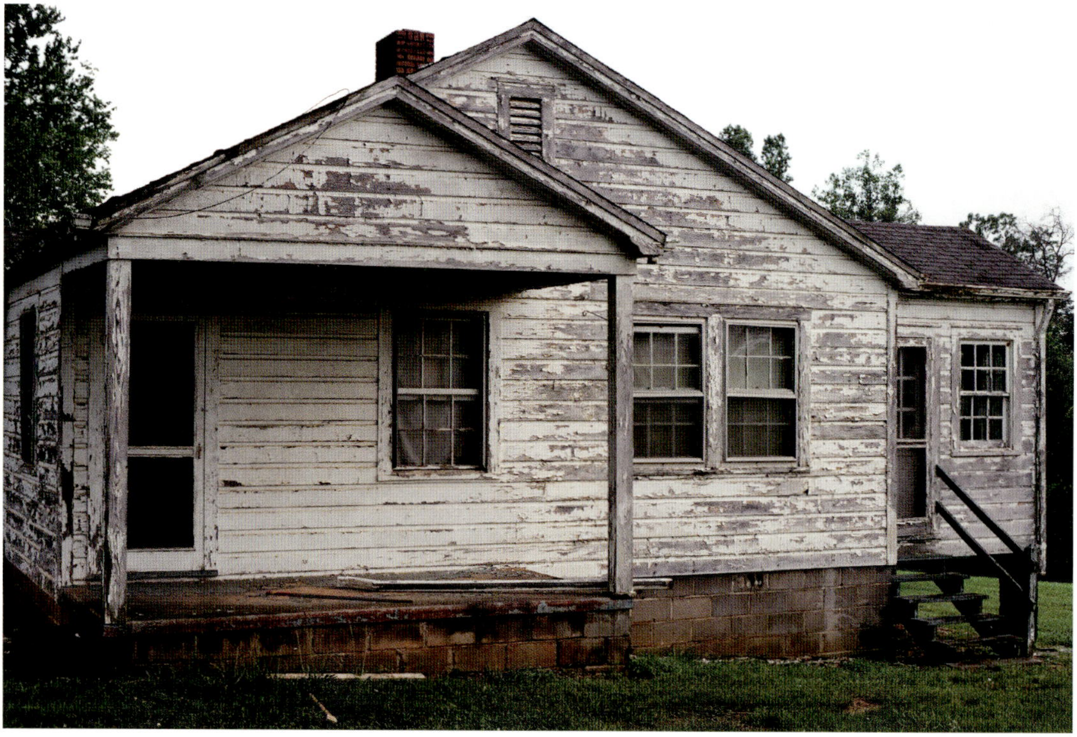

This cottage, despite a mass of peeling paint, maintains intact stairs and a porch holding a fallen gutter.

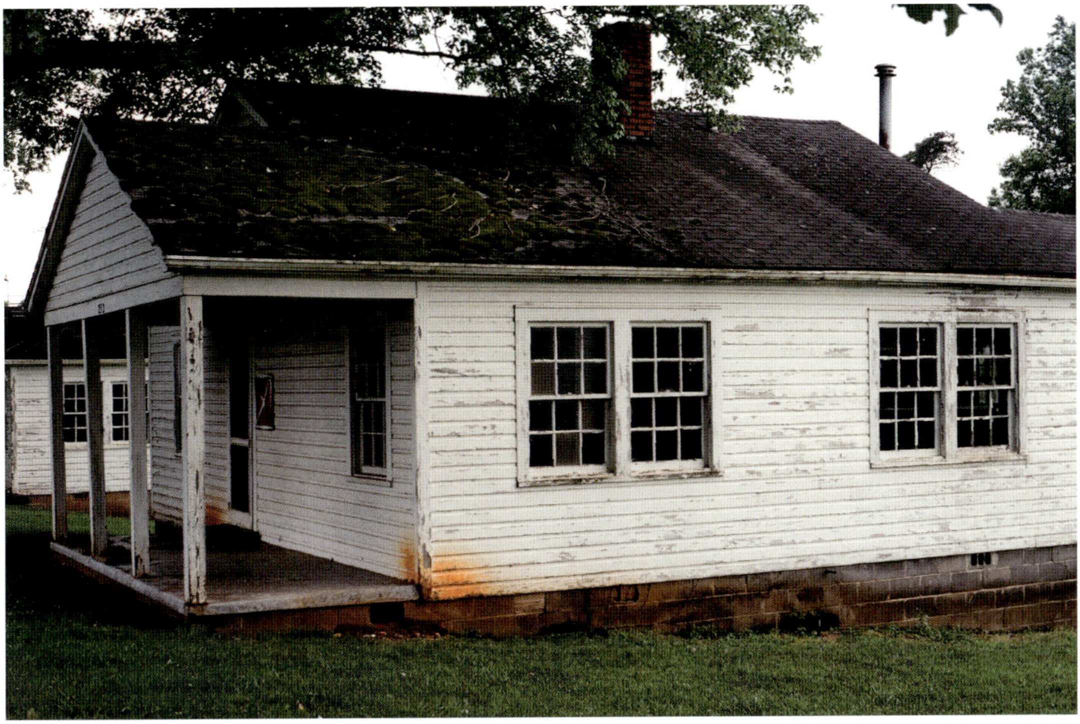

This cottage's roof is covered in dense moss. Yet another cottage marked with a red X, this building is deemed unsafe for entry.

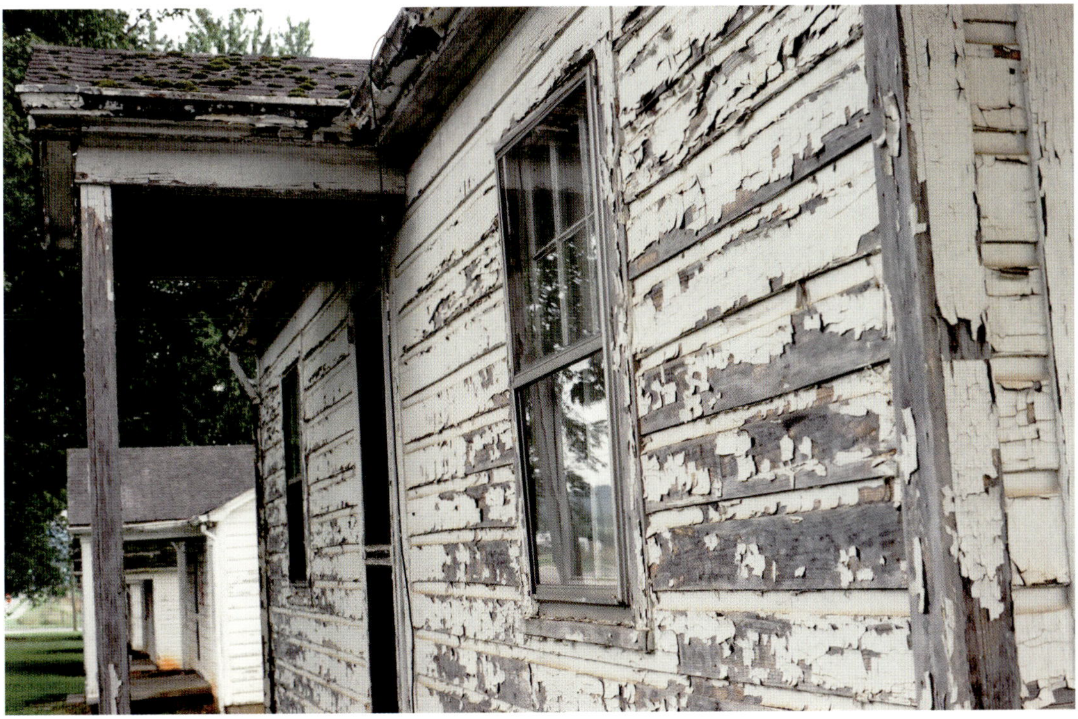

A closer view reveals the discolored wood being unearthed through thick chipping of the paint.

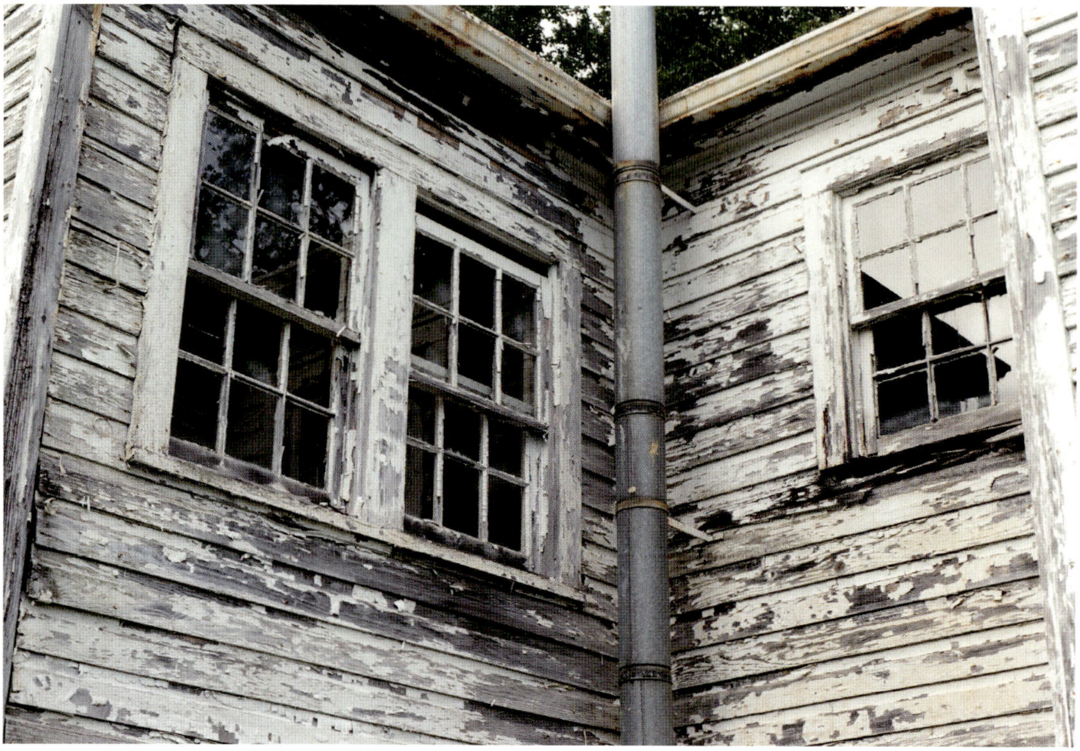

The flue stands strong and unaffected at this cottage; the connecting gutter shows heavy rust.

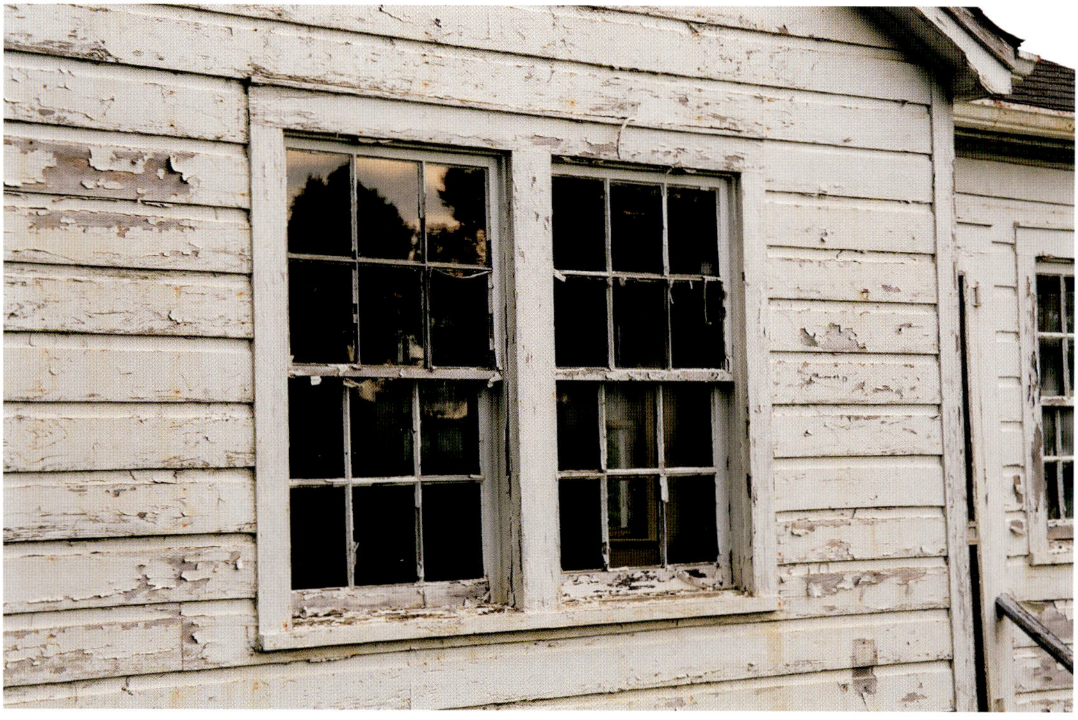

The empty inside of this cottage stares back through the windows.

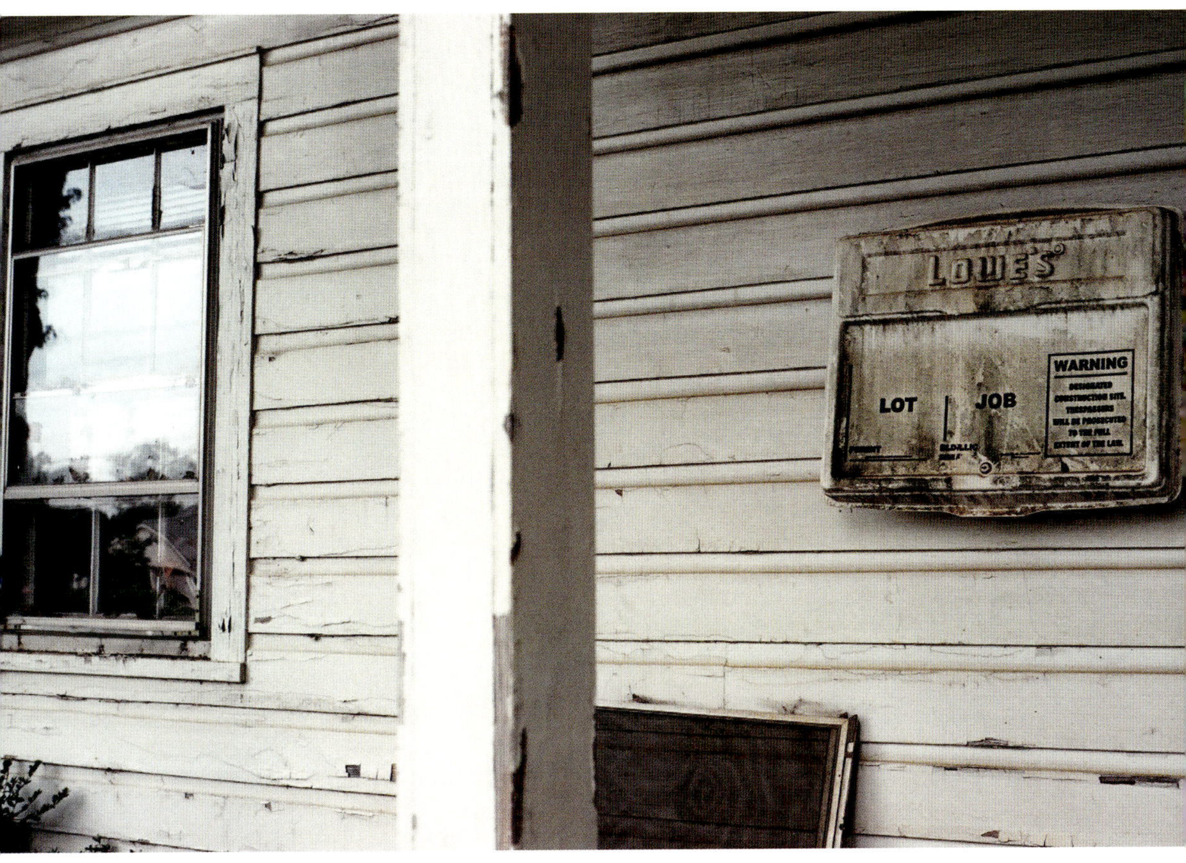

An addition to this cottage shows grime and wear beside a discarded window screen.

Often these cottages had broken or missing staircases and crawl space doors. Paint is seen severely peeling on these buildings, having fallen off in great chunks. Shingles were coming off the roofs of several, and moss can be seen clearly growing on top of the roof of another cottage. While mysterious collections of objects were found in the crawl space of other cottages, one cottage had a gathering of teeming plants making themselves known.

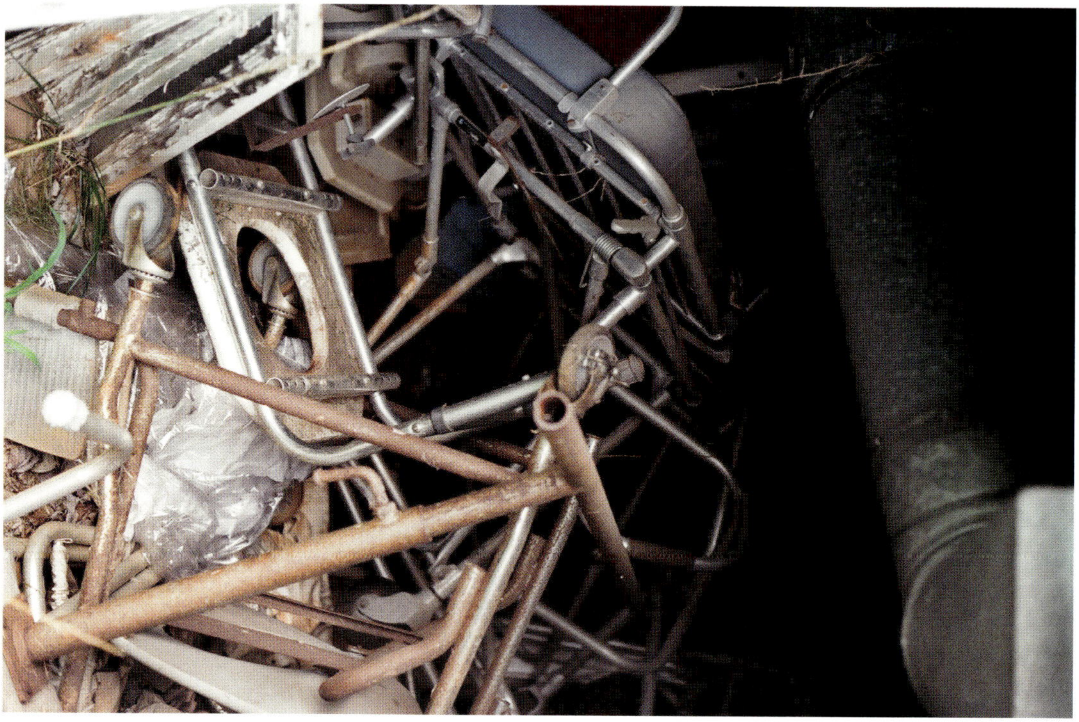

A tangle of metal medical equipment can be seen: a gurney, walkers, seat risers, and more.

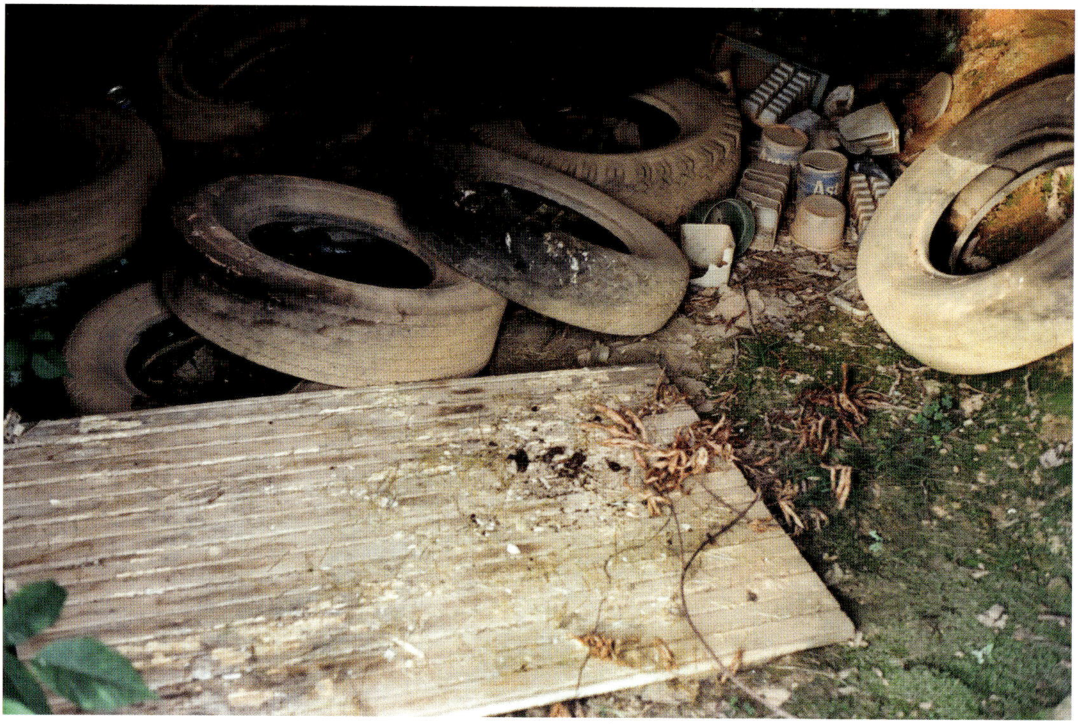

The crawl space door has fallen in or been kicked in. Numerous tires can be seen, as well as paint cans, plastics, and a new growth of grass.

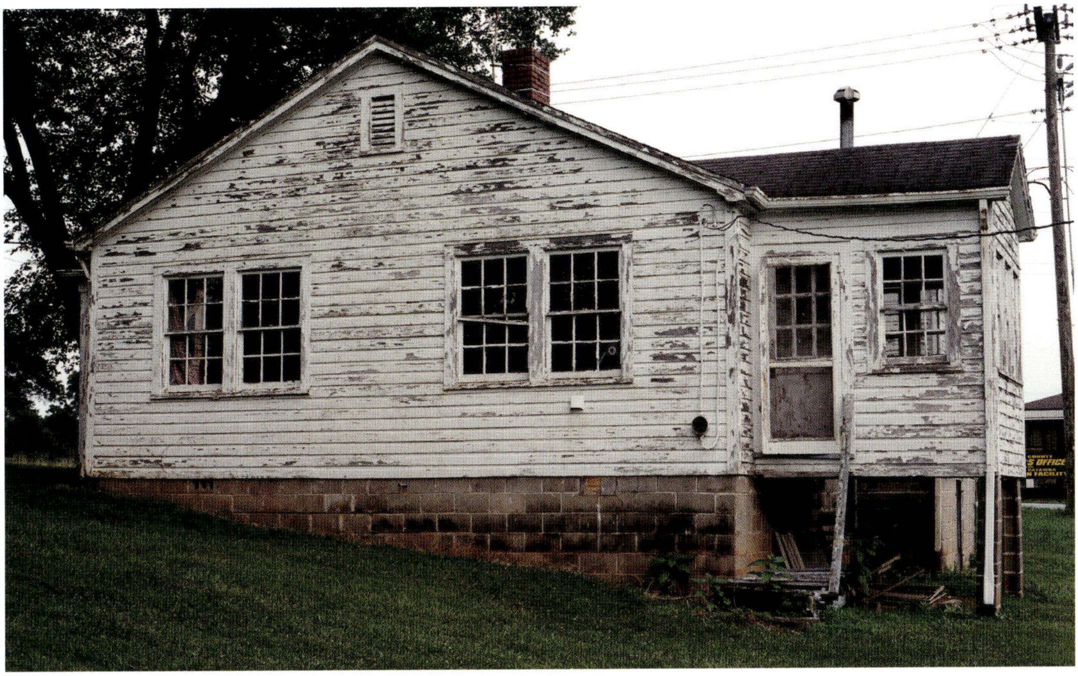

The back stairs to this cottage have fallen but remain attached as one unit.

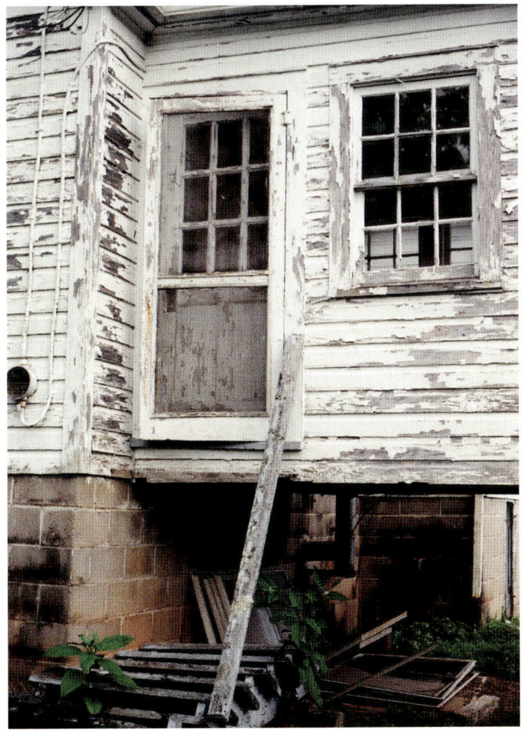

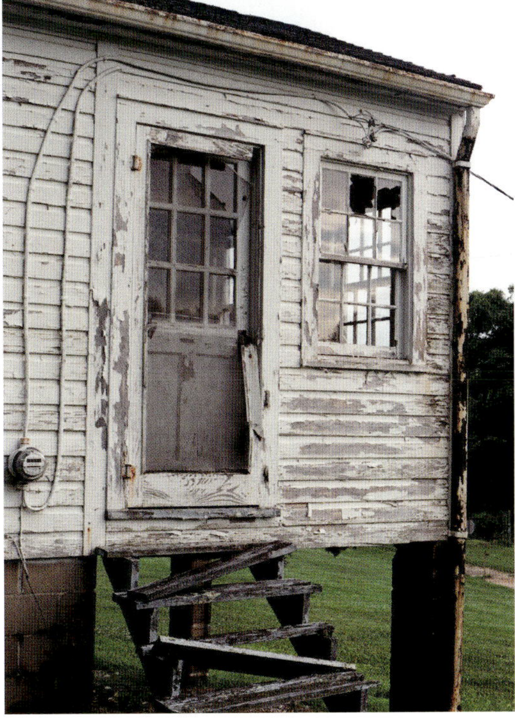

Above left: A closer inspection shows the open screen door and forgotten window screens piled below the house.

Above right: At the half-fallen stairs, the screen door has been broken and ripped, and panes of glass are shattered.

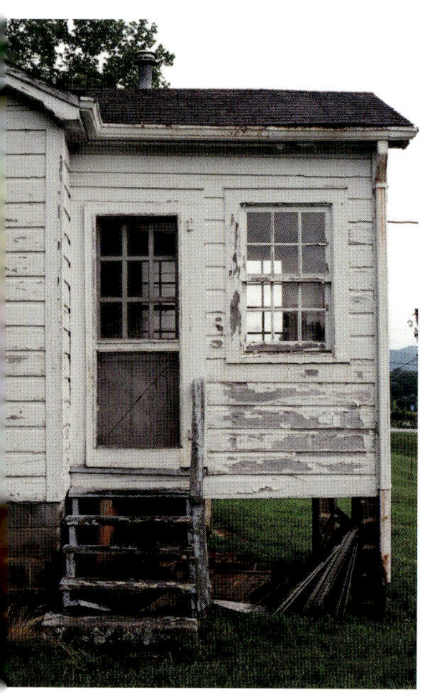

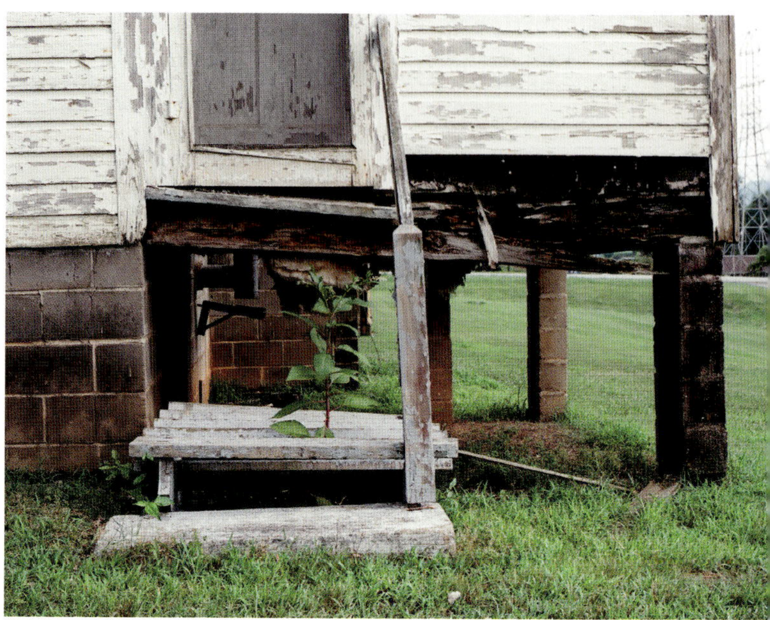

Above left: At yet another cottage there are stacks of window screens below the back stairs, but these back stairs remain standing and a welcoming home to lichen.

Above right: A plant shoots up through a set of stairs, while the floor begins to splint and sink behind it.

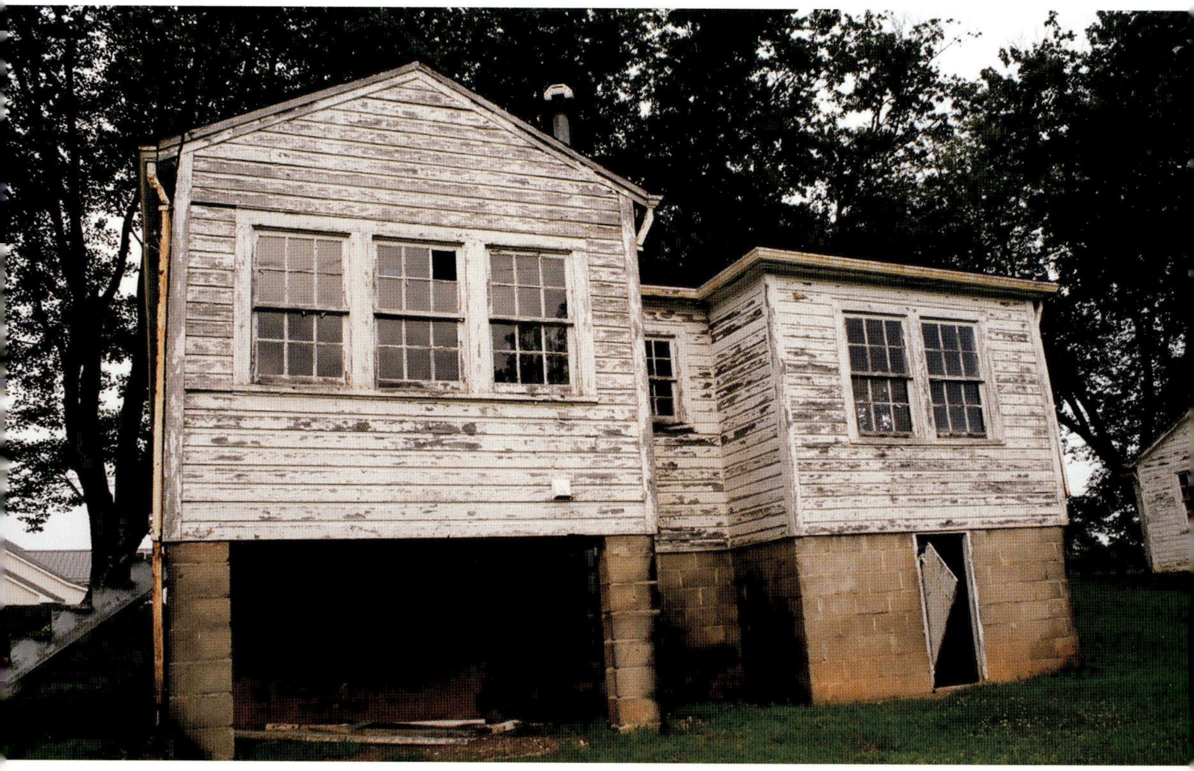

Debris sits underneath this cottage, its crawl space door hanging on the top hinge.

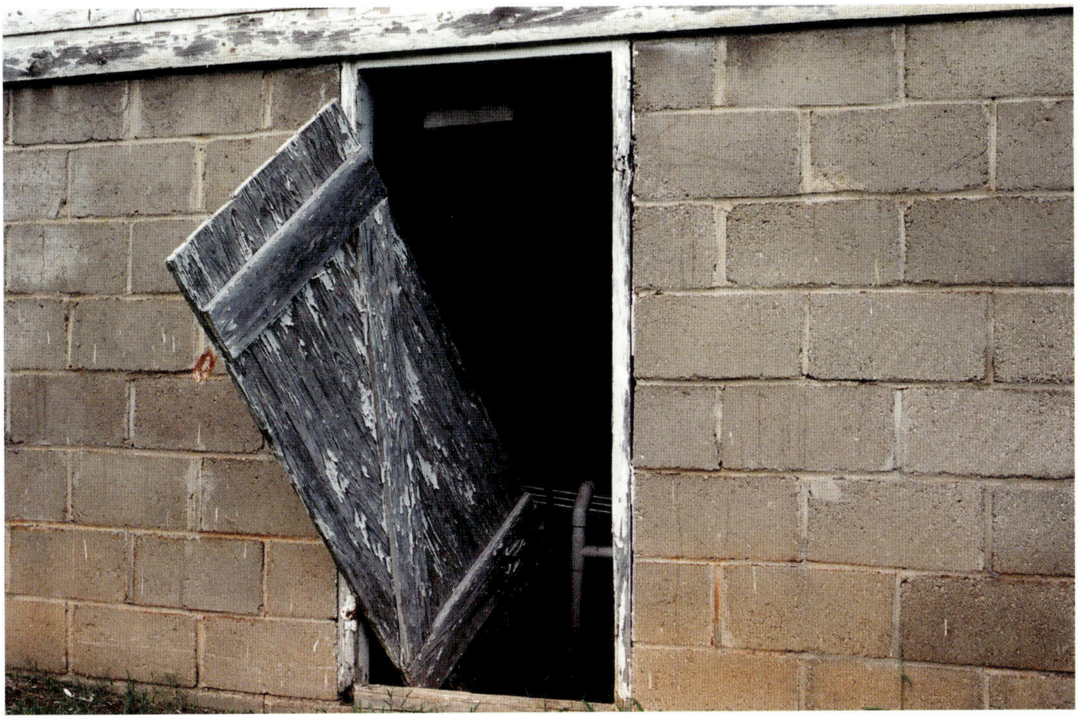

Another view of the crawl space door shows the paint is entirely eaten away on the other side. Through the open space the plumbing of the home is exposed.

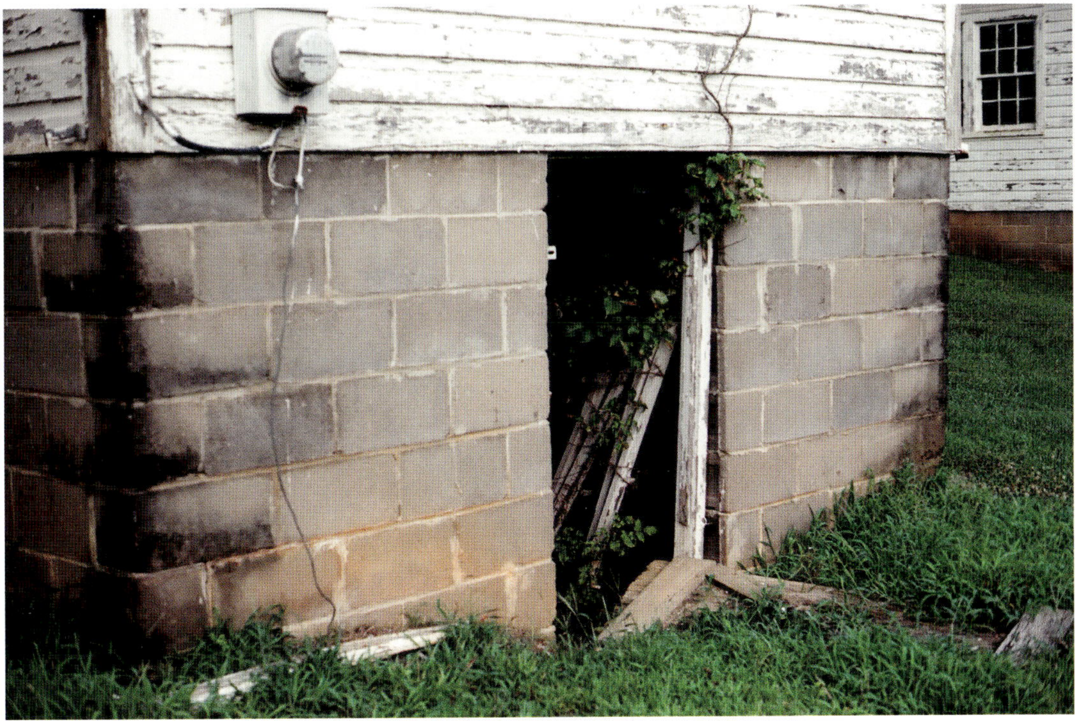

In another crawlspace vines have made themselves at home. The door appears to have split apart after rotting.

While these cottages are no longer in use by the hospital, the hospital remains running to this day, as does the original main building. Created at the heed of Dorothea Dix, this psychiatric hospital is a continuing vestige of Dix's call to mental illness treatment reform. [2] New buildings have been constructed on-site at the hospital grounds, and there are now standard and criminal wings of the hospital.

Neighboring Broughton Hospital is the campus for the North Carolina School for the Deaf, originally built in 1892.[3] While many of the structures remain in use, as the school is still active today, there are buildings on the campus which are no longer functioning components of the school. One of these such buildings is a magnificent house, which stands at the southeast corner of the campus. This house, nested below a tree, appears to cave in towards itself due to a partial collapse of the roof. At the front of the house, the overhang has fallen, and the door has long been boarded up. The chimney from this view is surrounded by the impression of a roof, the lower half that would obscure the majority of the chimney absent. Similar to the roof of some of the Broughton cottages, there is a dense growth of moss on a large swath of the remaining shingles. The paint is heavily worn on this house, missing in more places than it is present. The collapsing roof at the stern of the building is like a cradle, holding dead leaves from the previous season underneath the green overhanging boughs of its companion trees. This house is held in breathtaking contrast by the bright clay filled soil that surrounds it.

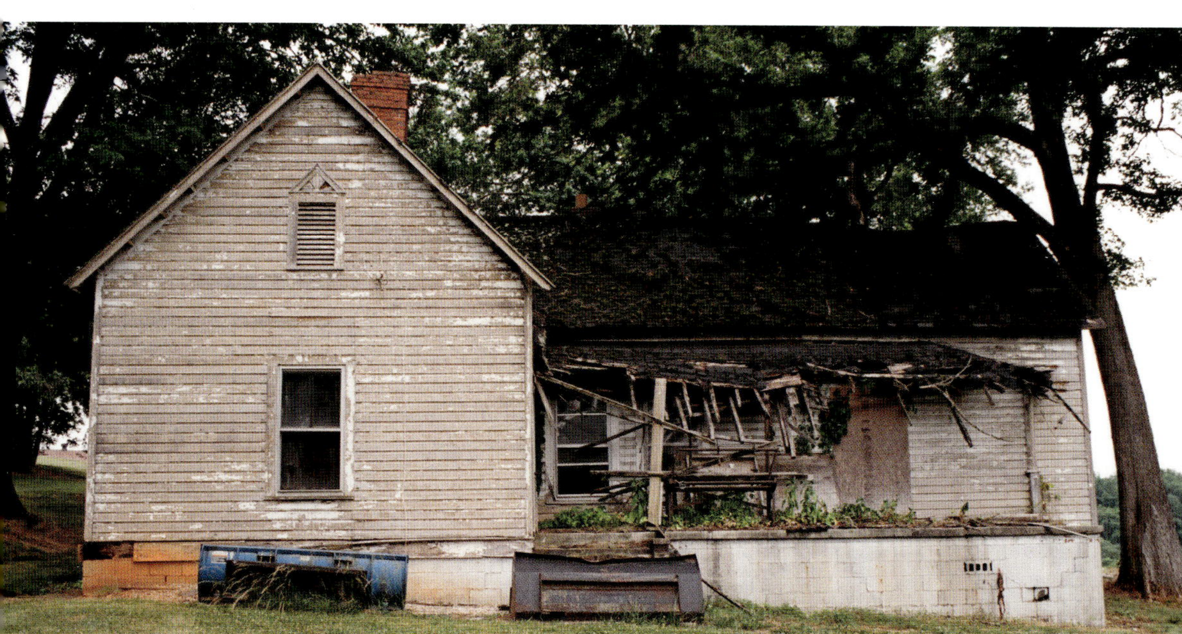

A lone house at the North Carolina School for the Deaf, where the front awning has fallen, and moss grows on the roof.

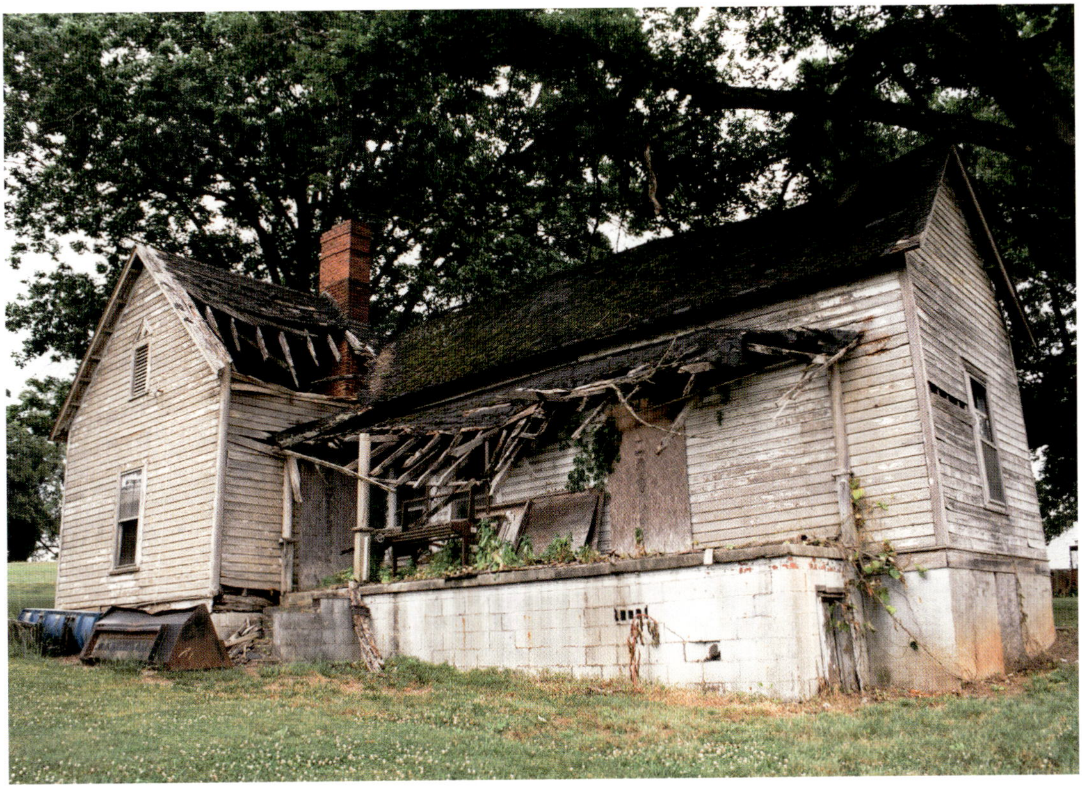

A new perspective shows the front chimney is exposed by another missing piece of roof as we return to the front of the house.

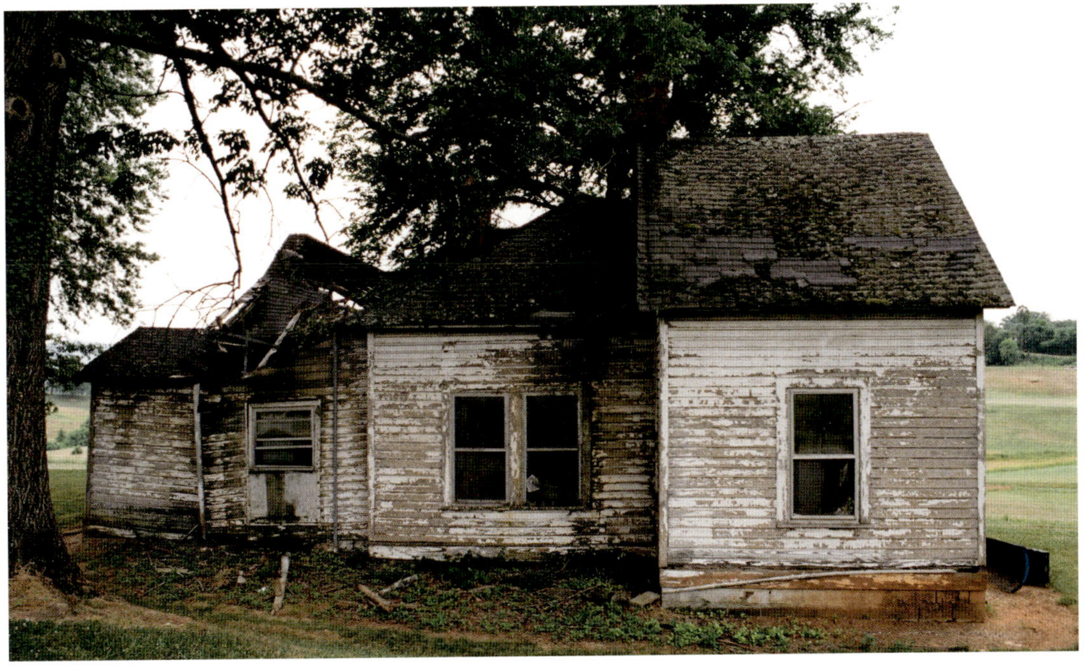

A sharp collapse in the roof can be seen by rounding the corner of the house in a clockwise fashion.

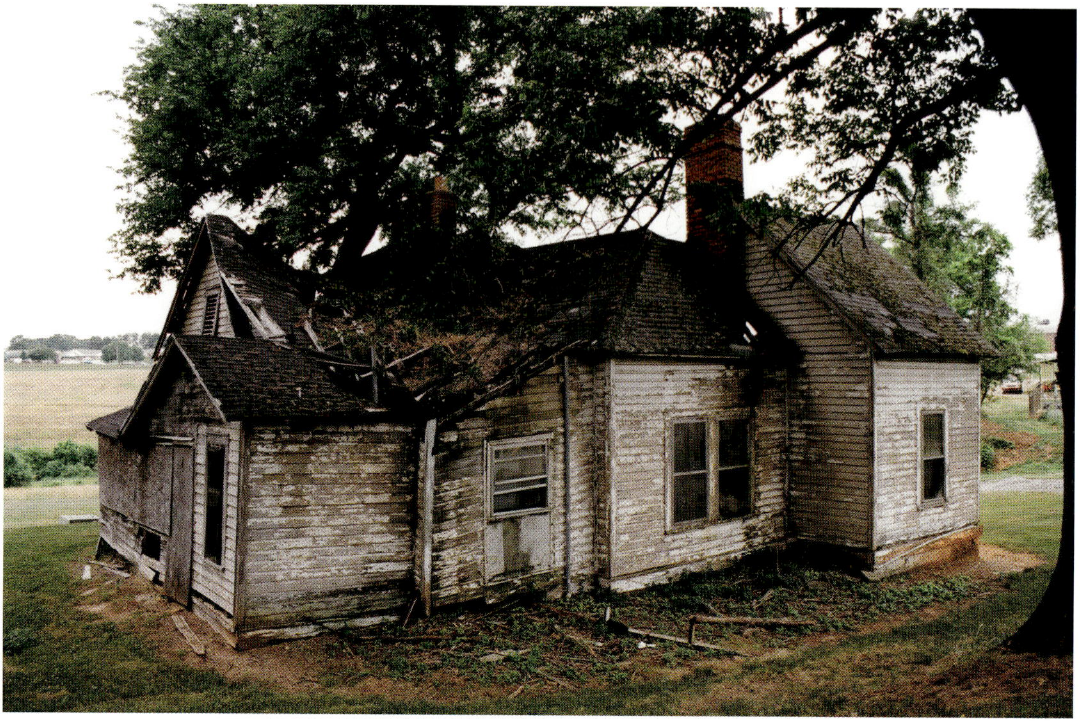

Continuing the walk clockwise, debris is seen in the cradle of the falling roof. The house is leaning in towards this sinking point.

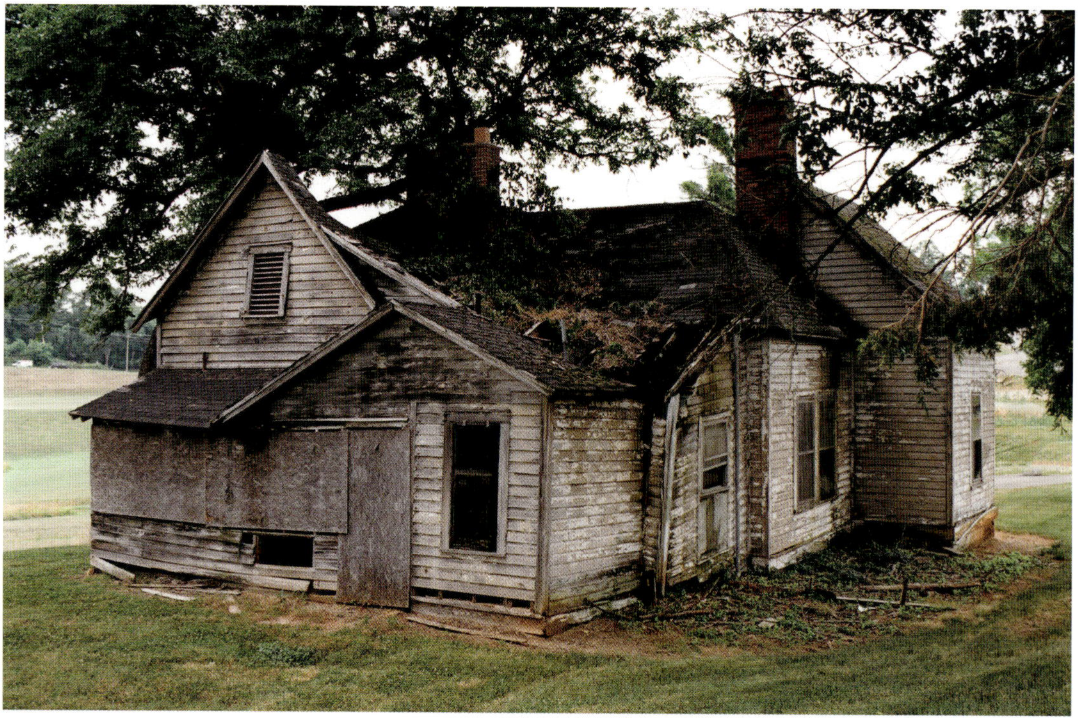

At the back of the building plywood patching is seen, as well as the slouching of the building at its left and right sides.

4

ATTENTION TO DETAIL

Sometimes the truly fascinating aspects of an abandoned structure are not the larger, easily seen features such as a caving roof or the pattern of mottled and chipped paint. Certain structures require closer inspection, whether it be on the original handiwork of the maker, which is now exposed, or the results of intervention after abandonment. At points there are trees that may be seen growing into the side of a house. There are belongings that weren't deemed a concern, left by a previous owner. Some new additions and signs of life from squatters and those passing through deserve attention as well, such as graffiti and decorations old and new.

The ways in which people have designed for their own homes, their pets, and their aesthetics provides a lingering presence. Regardless of the amount of time these owners have been apart from these structures, some aspect of their personality can be gleaned by what remains. The effects of the previous owners do not end when these people move out, pass on, or otherwise leave these places to their own devices. Paint choices, hand built addons, doghouses, and any left items all give clues to the lives lived in these places. Even as these things change somewhat over time, it is very unusual for every facet to be erased quickly by time.

The insides of homes can be just as expressive if not more so than the exterior. Some buildings have been left devoid of furniture, markings, and decor, while others show heavily the presence of those who were there before. Even in those places where the inner house has been scrubbed of human interaction, there lies the animal and natural world as decay and new life takes over. Fallen and rotting doors, crumbling paint, rusted-through nails, and sagging ceilings can indicate a closer approximation of the state of some buildings. While a roof and siding may look incredibly intact, the change from within can tell a more truthful story.

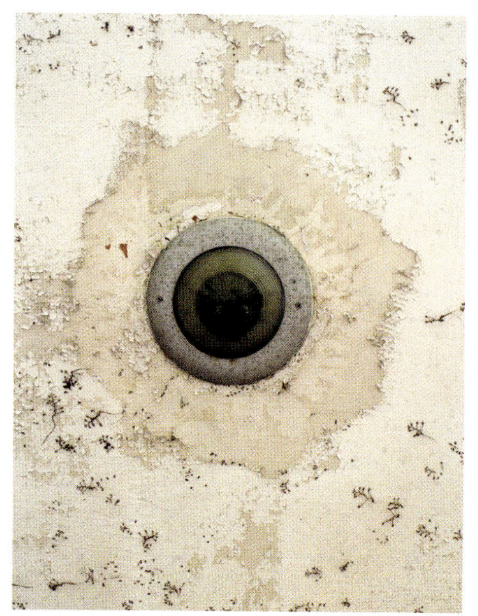

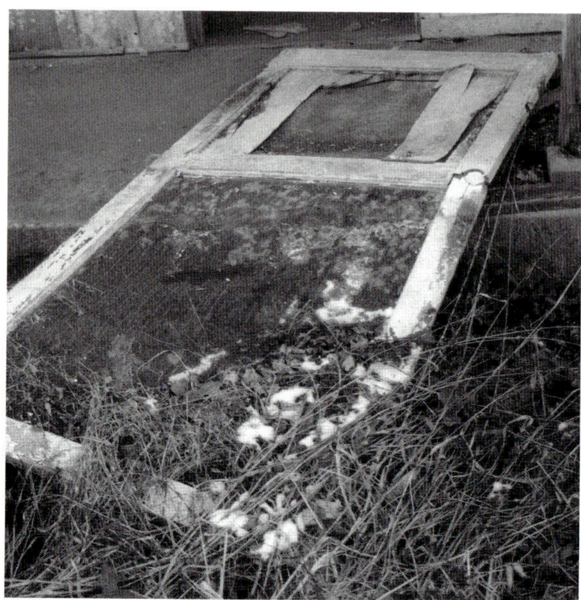

Above left: On the ceiling of the old high school gym entrance, paint peels and life teems.

Above right: A fallen screen door lays on the porch, catching snow.

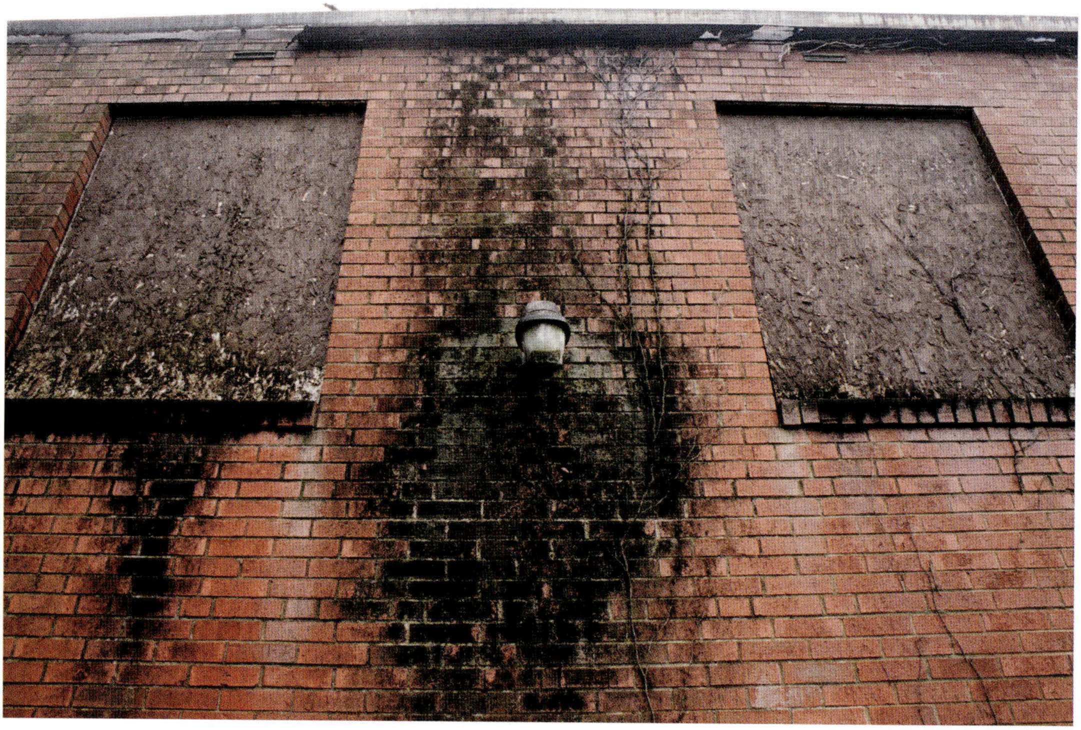

Another building of the high school has plywood in place of windows, where moss and lichen grow around the floodlight.

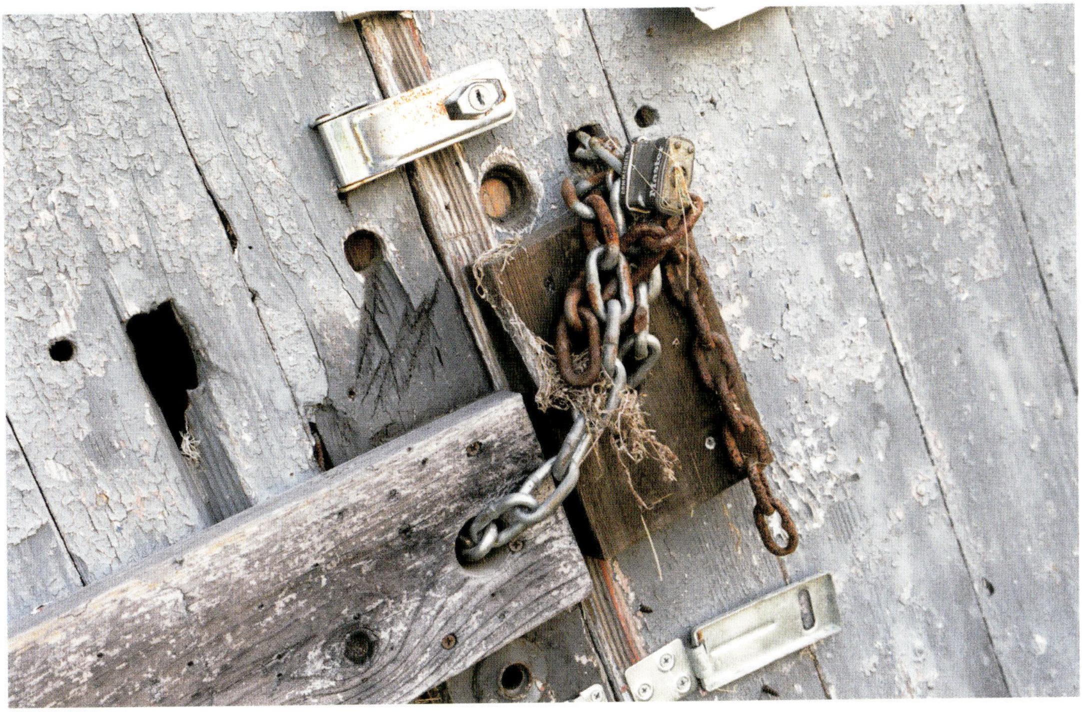

A custom wooden design made for locking a barn door. The chain has been untouched for so long it is rusted through in some places.

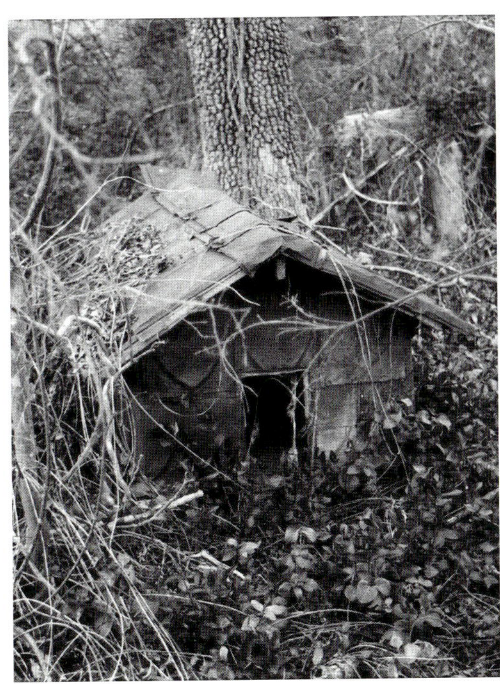

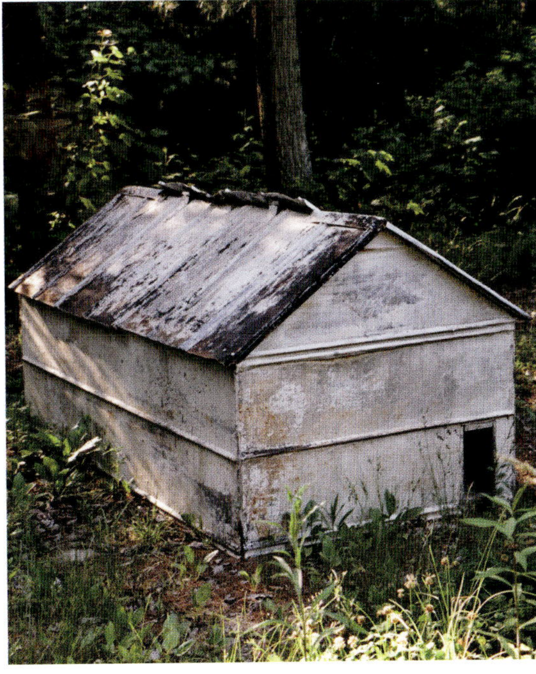

Above left: A doghouse fashioned from shingles remains barely visible thanks to sparse growth in the colder months.

Above right: A white tin doghouse remains standing while the buildings surrounding it have collapsed.

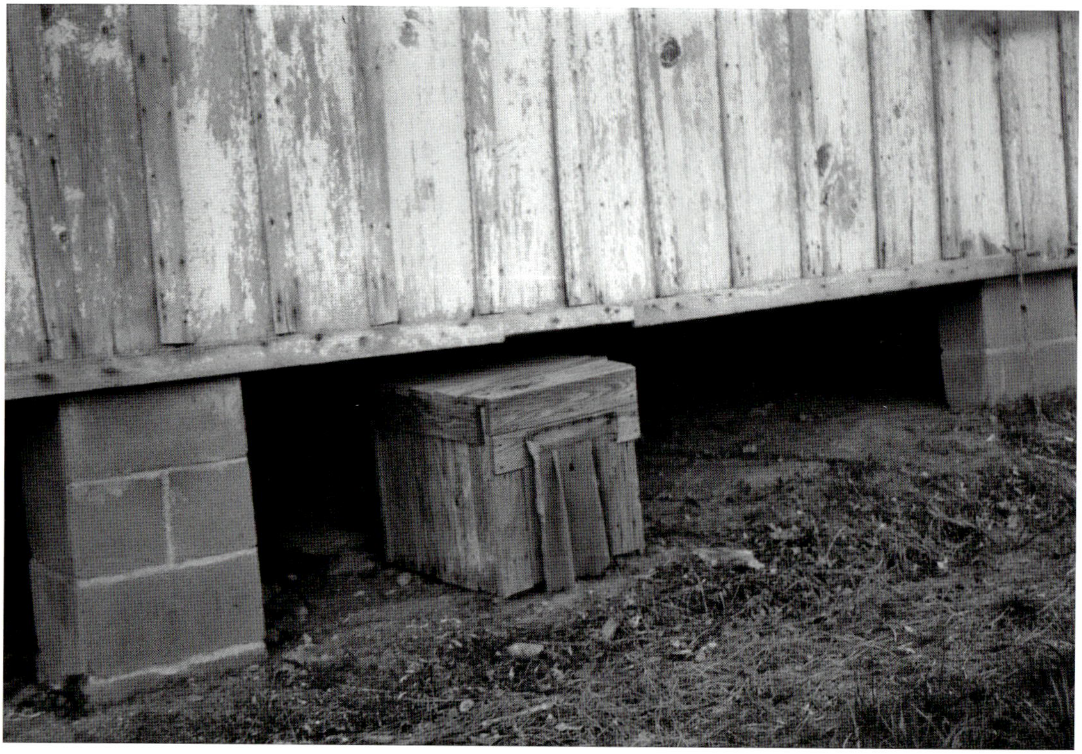

A handmade wooden doghouse with a privacy curtain is nestled under a home.

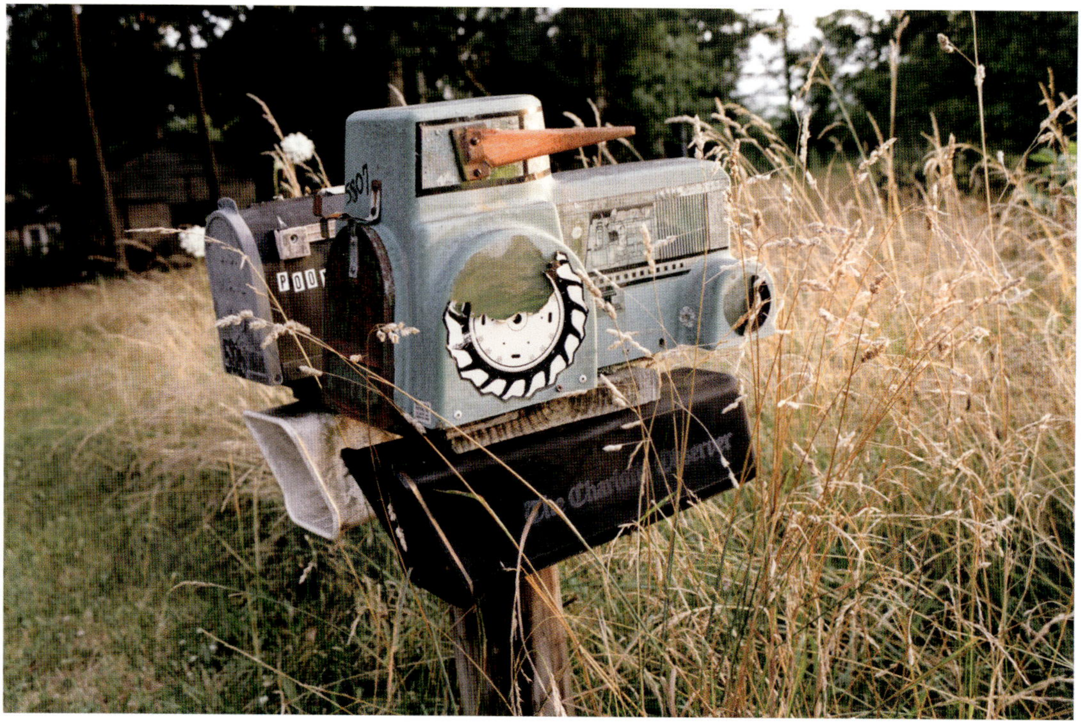

At an abandoned house, a mailbox designed to appear as a tractor has begun rusting and peeling.

Not to be forgotten is the original design of internal fixtures such as the base and ceiling boards, the chimney, and the walls. The remnants of these features can give further clues to the age, skill, and ambitions of the designer, and can also act in beautiful opposition to any additions made later. In considering these places, these images, let us not forget the smallest detail, even the shadow, as it crawls over what remains.

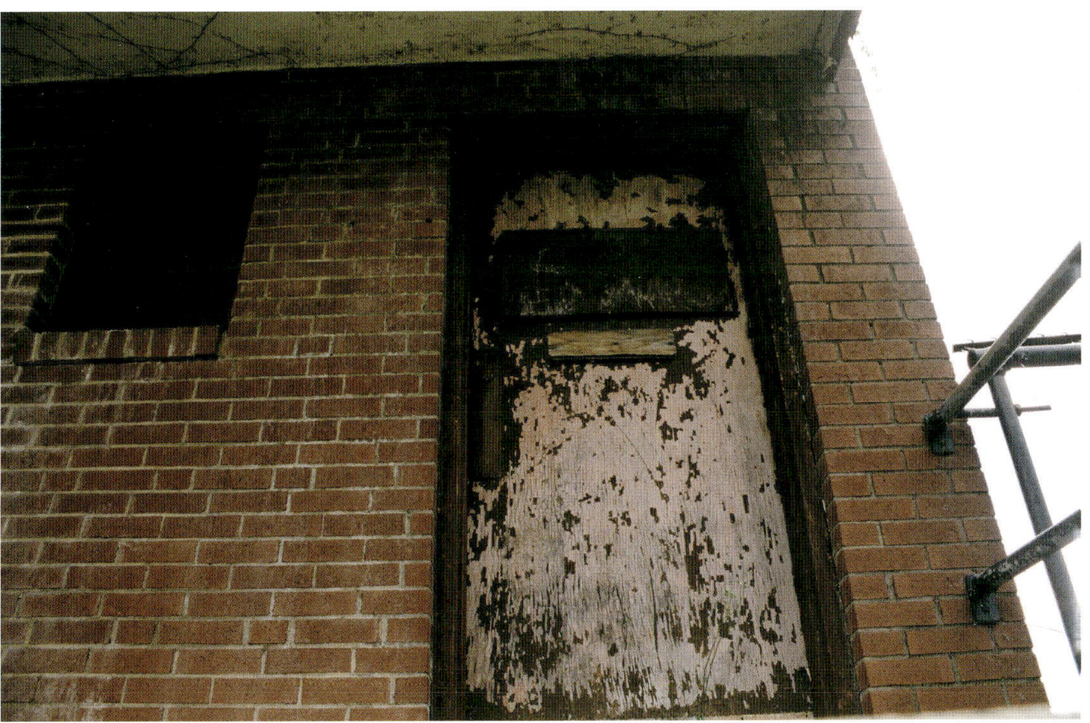

At the high school, an entrance door is mottled with different colored paint and a blank name tag.

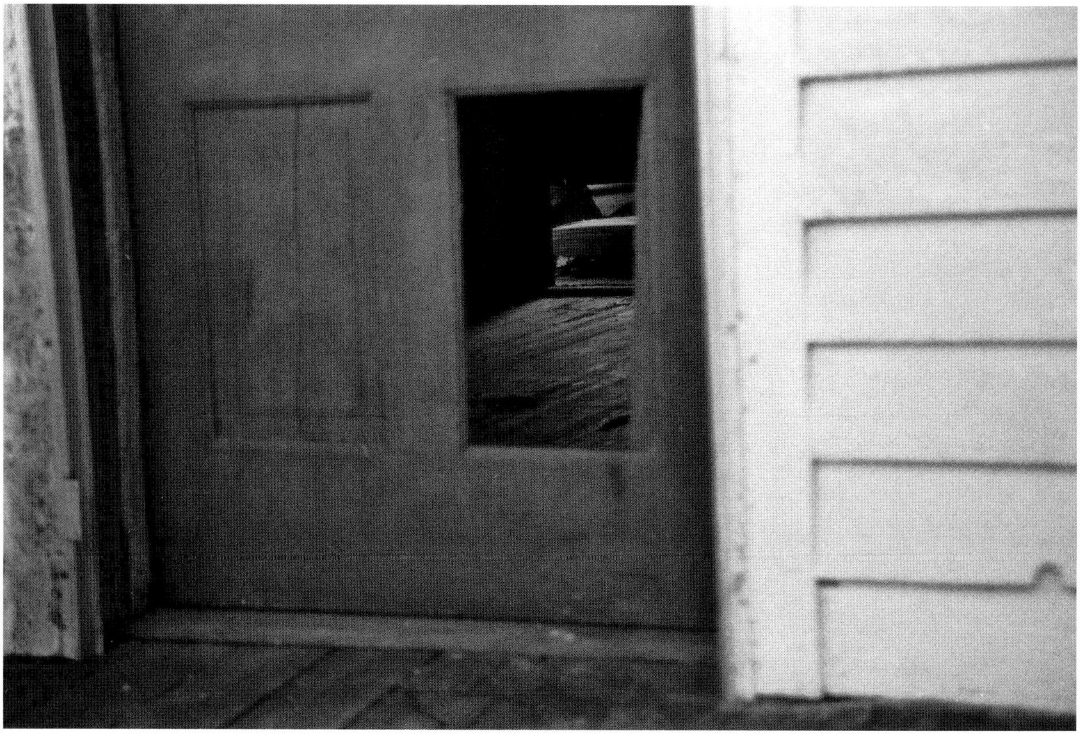

A path inside the mill house can be seen through a hole in the door.

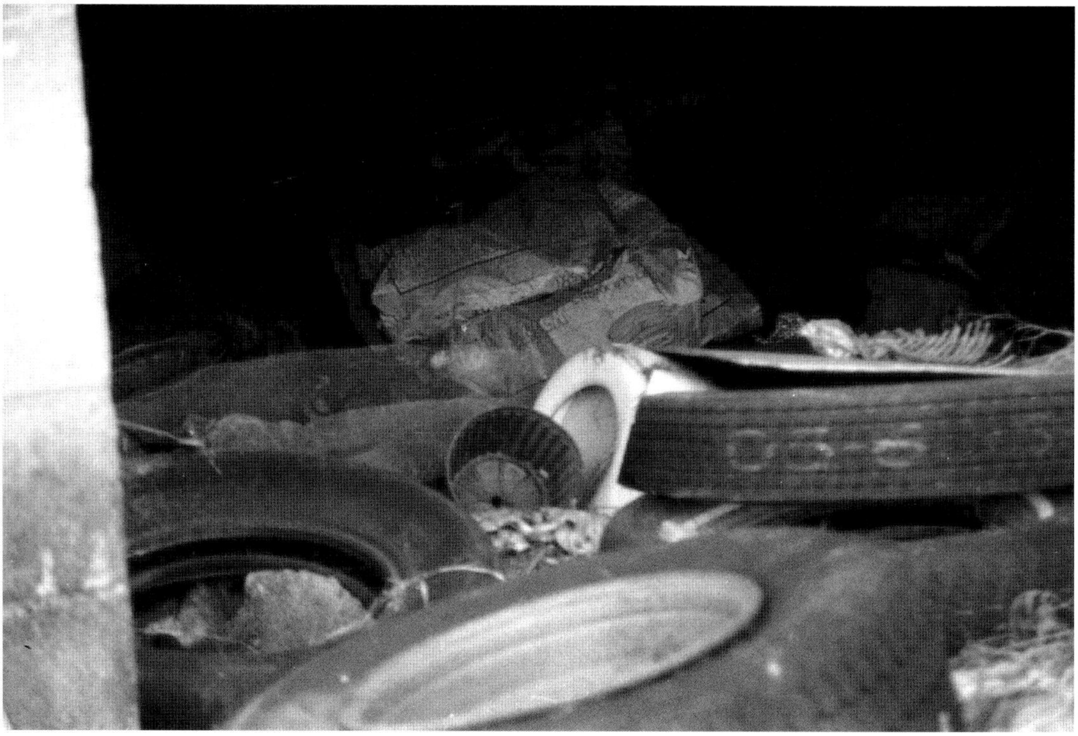

Underneath this mill house, there are assortments of tires, bags, and planters.

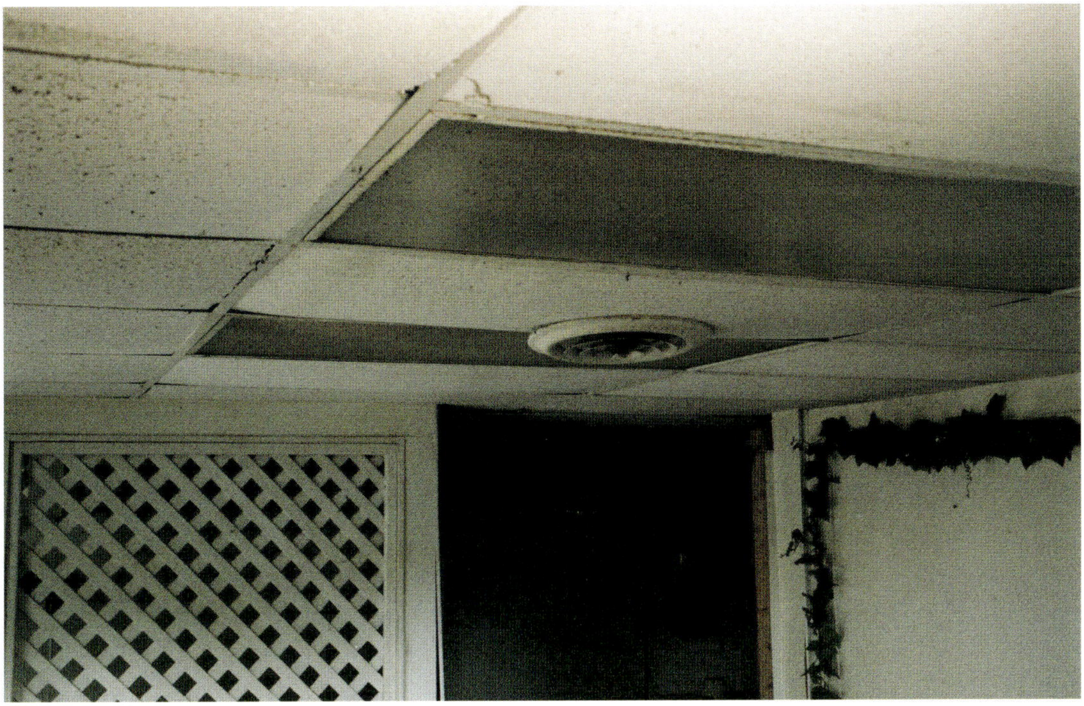

Inside the restaurant a fan hangs low from a ceiling tile, and fake vines wrap around the wall taunting the natural vines found outside.

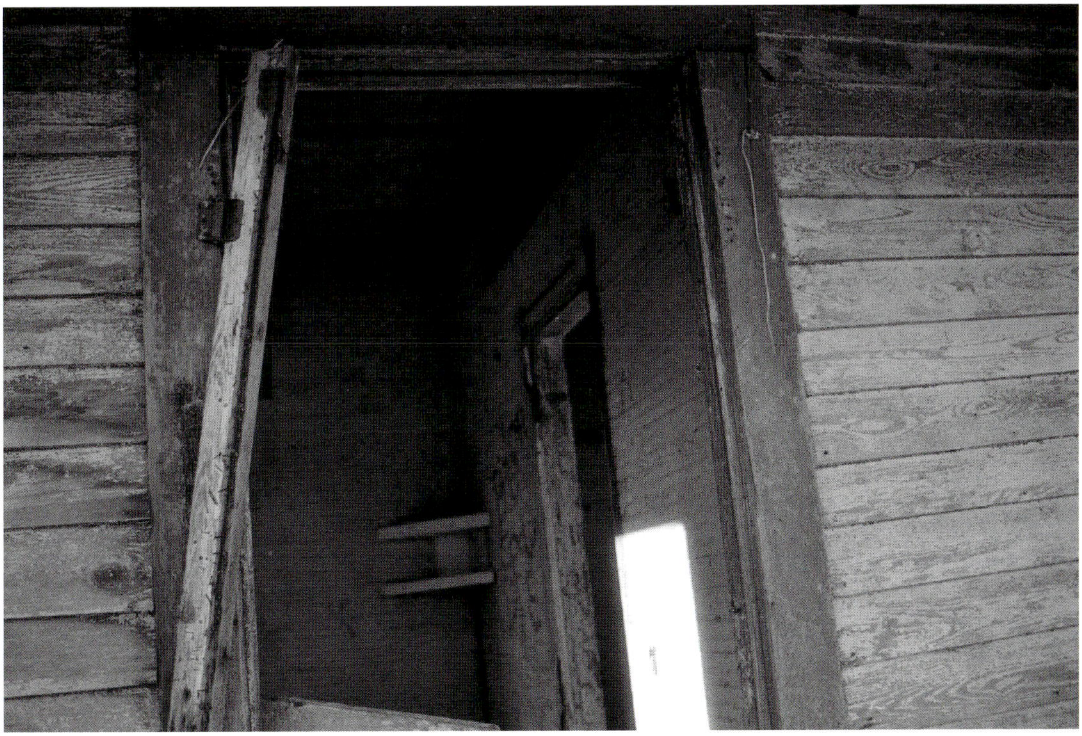

The outer edge of a door is all that remains on the hinge, and beyond the doorway graffiti can be seen.

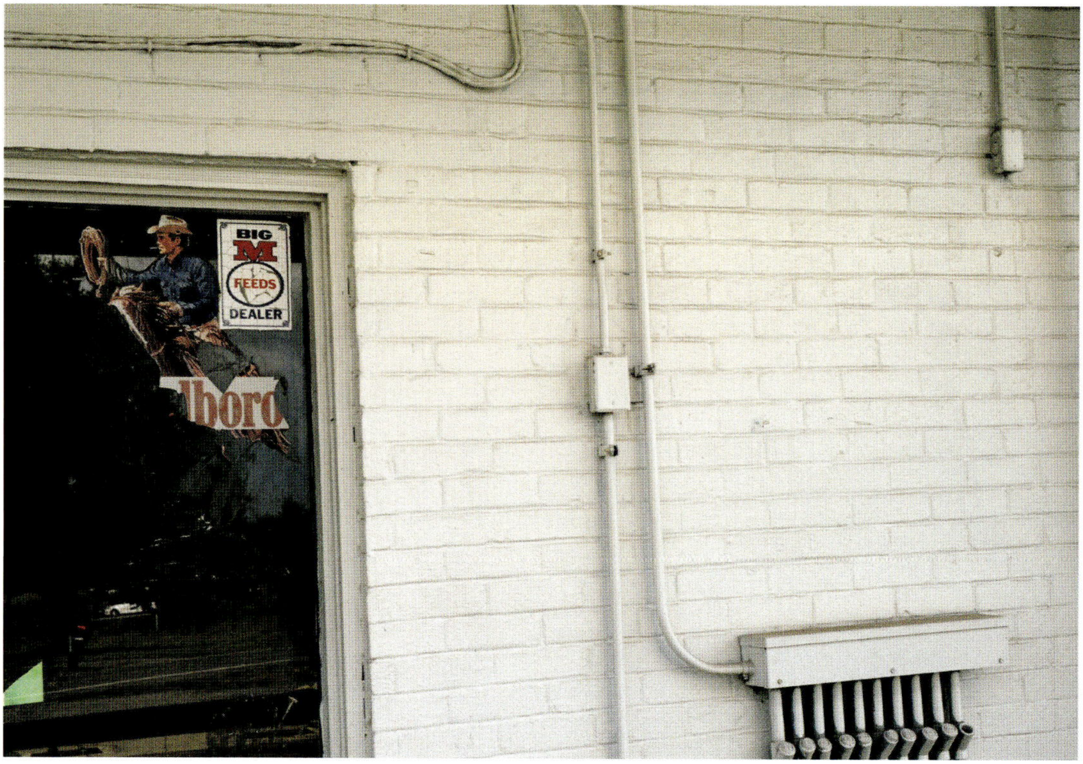

A Marlboro man sits without his horse. Other scrapes and scratches on the glass indicate other stickers joined him previously.

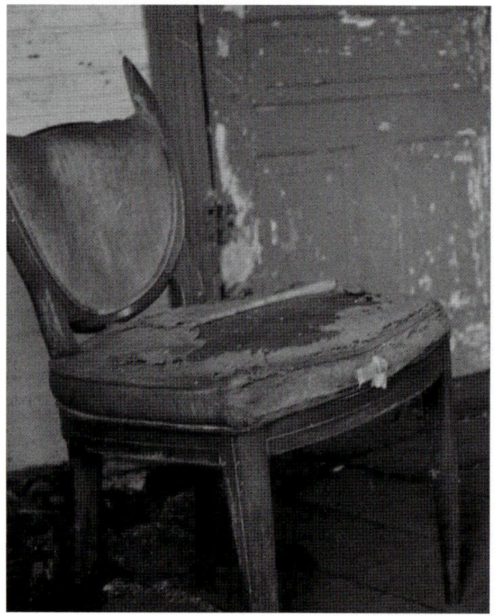

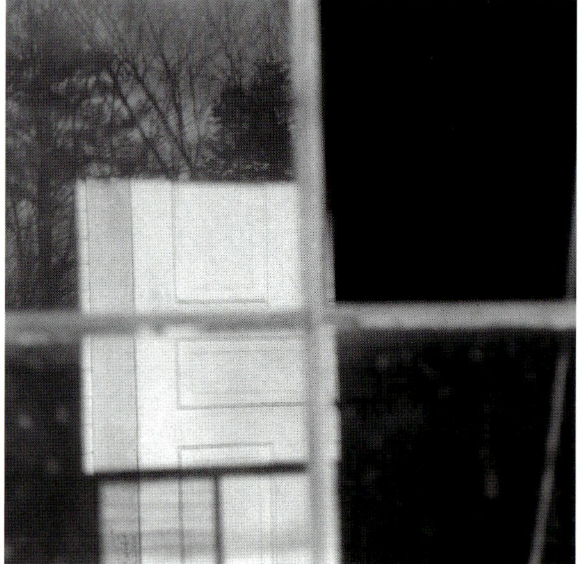

Above left: A torn, and broken chair sits on a buckling floor.

Above right: A forest reflection is displayed on the inner door of the mill house through two of the remaining windowpanes.

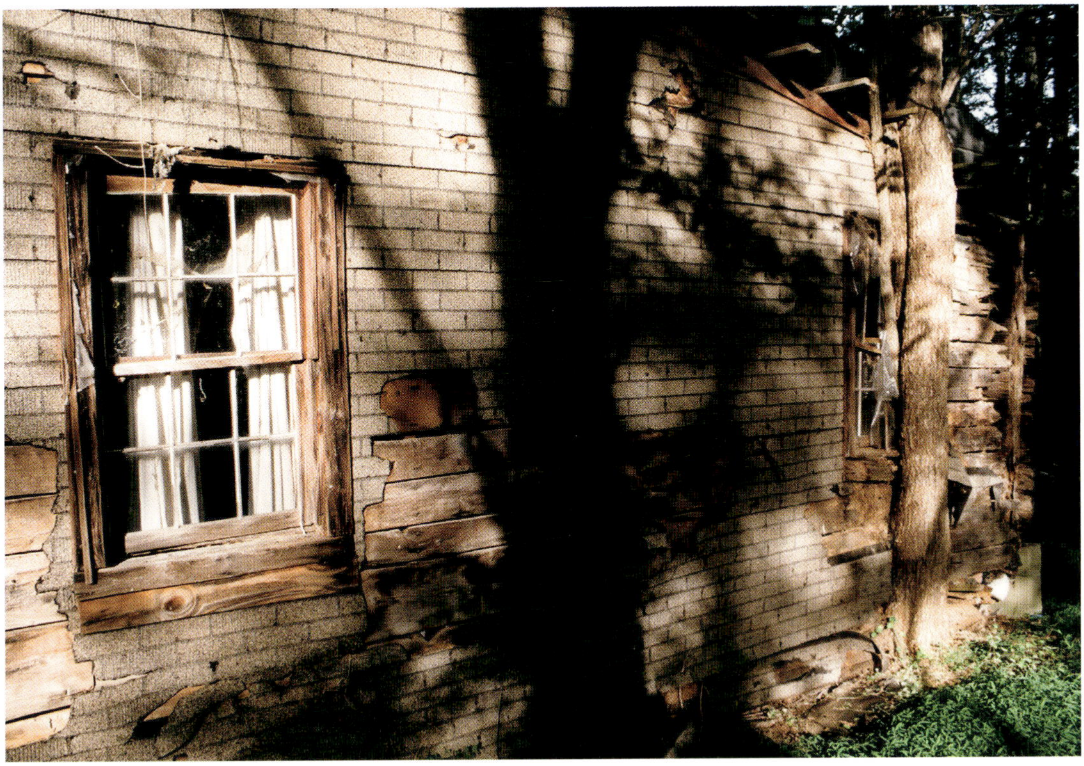

A view of the structure from further away, highlighting how the tree has grown in and around the wall. There are patches of siding missing but curtains still hang inside.

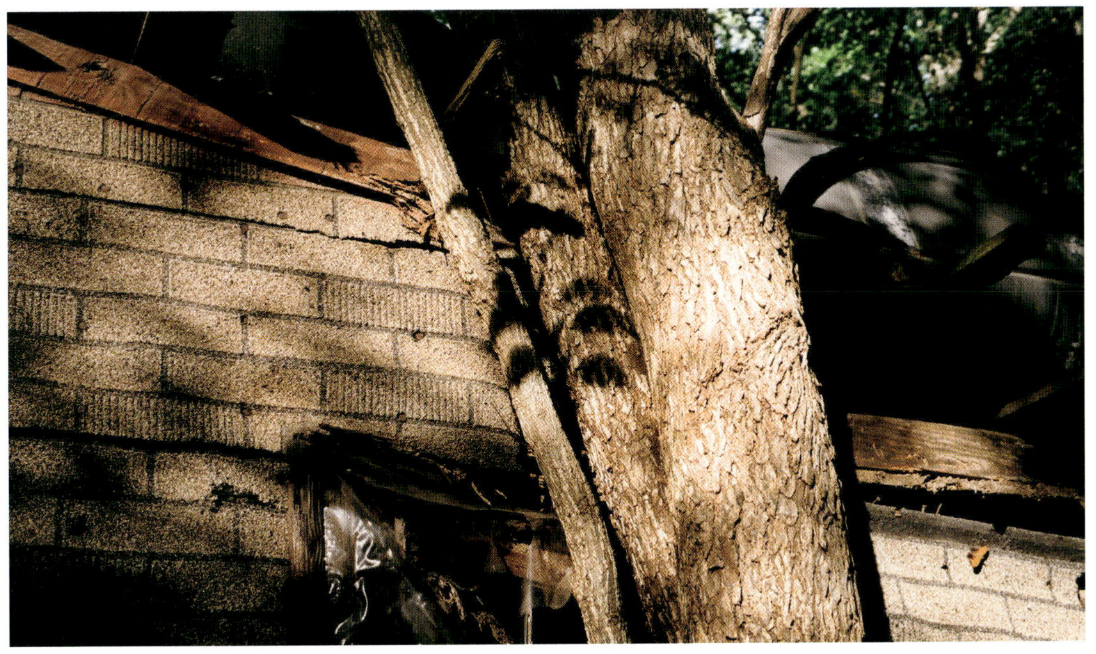

A tree that has partially grown through a structure, damaging it. Shadows from another plant can be seen on the trunk.

ENDNOTES

Henry River Mill Village

1 Carroll, K. "Preserving North Carolina's Last Textile Landscape: The Case for Henry River Mill Village" (master's thesis, Columbia University, 2012), pp. 28-29
2 Kovich, J. "Oral History Interview." By Anna Kovich. Marshall University Special Collections, OH64-37, Huntington, WV. (Marshall University, 1973), pp. 4
3 Carroll, K. "Preserving North Carolina's Last Textile Landscape: The Case for Henry River Mill Village" (master's thesis, Columbia University, 2012), pp. 34
4 Ibid., pp.38
5 Ibid.
6 Kovich, J. "Oral History Interview." By Anna Kovich. Marshall University Special Collections, OH64-37, Huntington, WV. (Marshall University, 1973), pp. 3-4
7 Carroll, K. "Preserving North Carolina's Last Textile Landscape: The Case for Henry River Mill Village" (master's thesis, Columbia University, 2012), pp. 7, 38.
8 Waggoner, M. "District 12 of 'The Hunger Games' is now a historic place." *Associated Press,* June 21, 2019.
9 Ibid.
10 Murphy, Chrissy. "Historic Mill Village frustrated after break in." *The News Herald,* May 17, 2020.
11 Willis, Emily. "Henry River Mill Village renovations move along after busy summer." *Hickory Daily Record,* October 17, 2021.